Chippewa Treaty Rights

The Reserved Rights of Wisconsin's
Chippewa Indians in Historical Perspective

RONALD N. SATZ

*with the assistance of Laura Apfelbeck, Jason Tetzloff,
Anthony Gulig, Timothy Spindler, Tracy Hemmy, and Laura Evert*

Foreword by Rennard Strickland

Transactions Vol. 79, No. 1
Wisconsin Academy of Sciences, Arts and Letters

Transactions is published annually by the Wisconsin Academy of Sciences, Arts and Letters and welcomes articles that explore features of the State of Wisconsin and its people.

Editor
Carl N. Haywood

Managing Editor
Patricia Allen Duyfhuizen

Wisconsin Academy of Sciences, Arts and Letters
1922 University Avenue
Madison, Wisconsin 53705
Telephone (608) 263-1692

Second printing, 1994

ISSN 0084-05.05

For my wife,
Christa,
and
our children,
Ani and Jakob

Contents

Appendices, continued

List of Illustrations and Maps

From the Editor

"I think I have it figured out. I could write about a ten page introduction and you could publish the findings . . . ." Professor Ronald Satz was responding to my previous encouragement, which admittedly bordered on nagging, for an article on the Chippewa treaty controversy. When he proceeded to add that he could have the manuscript completed in two weeks, it appeared that the long sought article would fit nicely in the 1990 volume of *Transactions*. One year, two hundred pages, several maps, and over forty illustrations later, what started as a brief article introducing several documents pertaining to Chippewa treaties of 1837, 1842, and 1854 has developed into the most comprehensive analysis of the Chippewa treaty rights in existence. It includes a comprehensive bibliography, original documents not previously available, new maps, and careful analysis.

Ronald N. Satz is dean of Graduate Studies, director of University Research, director of the Center of Excellence for Faculty and Undergraduate Student Research Collaboration, and professor of American Indian History at the University of Wisconsin-Eau Claire. The author of numerous publications including *American Indian Policy in the Jacksonian Era* and *Tennessee's Indian Peoples,* Dr. Satz has served on the editorial advisory boards of scholarly presses and journals including that of the *American Indian Quarterly.* He has taught courses on various aspects of American Indian history at the University of Maryland, the University of Tennessee at Martin, and at the University of Wisconsin-Eau Claire. In 1989, he taught a statewide University of Wisconsin-Extension Educational Teleconference Network Course on Chippewa Treaty Rights in Historical Perspective. Dr. Satz is among a small number of non-Indians whose biographical sketches are included in Barry T. Klein's *Reference Encyclopedia of the American Indian,* 5th ed. (1990).

Laura Apfelbeck served as a graduate editorial assistant to Dean Satz while a candidate for an M.A. degree in English at the University of Wisconsin-Eau Claire. *Jason Tetzloff, Anthony Gulig,* and *Timothy Spindler* worked as graduate research assistants while candidates for M.A. degrees in history at the University of Wisconsin-Eau Claire. *Tracy Hemmy* and *Laura Evert* worked on this project as undergraduate research assistants in the Center of Excellence for Faculty and Undergraduate Student Research Collaboration at the University of Wisconsin-Eau Claire.

The members of the staff of *Transactions* and the author and his assistants have worked hard to produce this book. It still would not have been possible, however, without the support of the Wisconsin Academy of Sciences, Arts and Letters, and especially its Executive Director, LeRoy Lee, whose encouragement is appreciated by all.

We believe that this book should be read by everyone who seeks to understand the topic. It will shed light on serious issues and do much to abolish ignorance which, as pointed out by Isidore of Seville, "engenders error and nourishes vice." It is in this spirit that we recommend this book to all readers.

Carl N. Haywood

Foreword

Rennard Strickland
*Professor of Law and
Director, American Indian Law and Policy Center
The University of Oklahoma*

> "One barrier that American Indians have long faced . . . is that public understanding of their core issues comes slowly. Special Indian rights are complex and history based, emerging from the deep past . . . . In every instance, the Indian position is fragile because it finally depends on the willingness of opinion leaders in the majority society to learn about the experience of another people . . . . The historical search I suggest is not done out of guilt or romance; it is not a sentimental exercise. Rather, an understanding of a people and their social, legal, and economic experience ought to be reached because it is the essential basis for judging what wise policy ought to be and for assessing how the rule of law ought to operate."
>
> *Charles F. Wilkinson
> Oliver Rundell Lecturer
> The School of Law
> University of Wisconsin-Madison
> April 19, 1990*

Knowing and understanding the rights of American Indians is not an easy task. These are complex and historically based issues emerging not from the whims of contemporary politicians but from the historical obligations of the deep past. Learning about these rights is an historical search, not a sentimental journey. These are questions of law not questions of charity.

Indian law and Indian history are opposite sides of the same coin. One cannot be understood in isolation. Perhaps more than any other field of American jurisprudence, American Indian rights are deeply rooted in ancient ways and historical bargains. The aboriginal inhabitants of the American continents are the original sovereigns. As such, they retain rights that long predate the coming of more recent sovereigns such as our modern national or individual states. The United States Supreme Court has long held that Indian tribes, as sovereigns, hold a unique and significant place in American law with historically rooted rights.

The Wisconsin Academy of Sciences, Arts and Letters performs an important service in making available this work, which is the first product of an ongoing research project on Wisconsin Chippewa treaty rights being conducted by Graduate School Dean and Professor of American Indian History Ronald N. Satz and a group of students at the University of Wisconsin-Eau Claire. This is an important study that shows the significance of historical research in the service of public policy.

Not only does *Chippewa Treaty Rights: The Reserved Rights of Wisconsin's Chippewa Indians in Historical Perspective* provide access to important documents reprinted in the Appendices, but it also helps analyze the historical background of current Wisconsin treaty rights controversies in terms of these documents. In addition, there is a splendid bibliography for those who want to explore the question in even greater depth.

Publication of *Chippewa Treaty Rights* addresses the significant challenge presented by Professor Charles Wilkinson in the Rundell Lectures at the University of Wisconsin-Madison. It does so by providing, in one convenient volume, the materials needed to study and understand the important issue of reserved Indian treaty rights. There is no longer a serious legal question about these Indian rights. The legal status of Chippewa reserved rights is clearly established. As the title of this study suggests, these are rights the tribes continue historically to possess. As the courts have recognized, the treaties did not create Chippewa hunting, fishing, and gathering rights. These rights have always belonged to the Chippewas, who reserved them in their treaties with the United States. Now, thanks to Dean Satz and his students, these documents are available for all citizens who take seriously the task of understanding the historical journey of the people we call the Chippewas.

Every year, for tens of thousands of years, the lakes of northern Wisconsin have slowly shed their winter covering of ice. As spring drives out the bitter cold, the walleye and muskellunge that live in those lakes celebrate this thawing by moving out of the depths and spawning in the clear, gravel-bottomed shallows. For hundreds of years people in boats, using spears, have taken some of those fish back to their families—a satisfying confirmation that another winter has passed. For these native people, the Chippewas, time is cyclical: the seasons pass and return, the fish spawn and then return. For centuries, the people themselves returned each spring to harvest fish—the seasons, the fish, and the people bound together in a continuing cycle dictated by nature.

Illegally prevented by the State of Wisconsin from harvesting their fish for almost 80 years, the cycle has finally returned for the Chippewas; 150-year-old promises made in exchange for land title are once again being kept. After years of enforced absence, the Chippewas again gather when the ice breaks to fish from boats with spears. United States courts have now proclaimed and sustained these ancient rights reserved by the Chippewas.

But the soft, cyclical, pace of nature has been replaced by another, discordant way of measuring time. The peaceful harvest of fish by the Chippewas is threatened by non-Indians who barrage the peaceful fishers with rocks and insults, and who use large motorboats trailing anchors to capsize the boats of the fishers. Because of this, the State of Wisconsin has pressured the Chippewas to give up their ancient rights to fish off their reservations. This pressure has sometimes been applied indirectly, sometimes directly, but always upon the Chippewas. And all because a small group, often acting illegally, creates disturbances in opposition to the Chippewas' federally recognized legal rights.

The Chippewas now prepare for another spring. And just as spring rekindles life, the Chippewas rekindle the hope that their neighbors will come to respect the reality of their sovereignty, their culture, and their rights. A reading of the historical analysis and documents in this book should help all of us understand and appreciate Wisconsin Indian treaty rights. Understanding does not come easily, but it is essential to preservation of the rights of all of us—Indian and non-Indian alike.

Preface and Acknowledgments

The purpose of this book is to present an overview of the history of Chippewa-United States relations leading to the treaties of 1837, 1842, and 1854 and to examine the consequences of those agreements for Chippewa and for non-Indian residents of Wisconsin and for the State of Wisconsin. After the State of Wisconsin denied Chippewas their hunting, fishing, and gathering rights in ceded territory for most of the twentieth century, the Chippewa Indians have recently won court decisions recognizing their reserved treaty rights. Many non-Indian Wisconsinites have been surprised to learn that rights reserved by the Chippewa Indians during nineteenth century treaty negotiations are still valid today. This study examines the course of events leading to the recent court decisions and reviews the white backlash to Chippewa legal victories. Appendices 1 through 6 provide transcriptions of nineteenth-century documents that have shaped the course of Chippewa-American relations, and Appendices 7 through 9 reprint documents issued in 1991 that are shaping the future direction of those relations. It is my hope, as Gary Sandefur of the University of Wisconsin-Madison Native American Studies Program has asserted, that ''if more people in Wisconsin knew the history of Indians in the state, if more people knew how much Indians were forced to give up, and if more people knew about the historical symbolic significance of treaty rights, the misunderstanding over treaty rights and the resentment against Indians would quickly disappear'' (*Capital Times* 1989a).

Chippewa Treaty Rights had its beginnings during the summer of 1989 when Richard Florence and Denise Sweet of the University of Wisconsin-Eau Claire Arts and Sciences Outreach Office suggested that I develop and teach an evening course on Chippewa treaty rights. At the time, I had been engaged in research on Chippewa history for about a year, but it was really a phone call that I received while discussing treaty rights on an interview and call-in radio program for WOJB FM in Hayward a few months earlier that prompted me to agree to offer a course.

A caller had asked if the Chippewa treaties actually contained a provision designating any group of ten or more Indians leaving a reservation together as a war party that could be fired upon by whites in self-defense without criminal penalty. Tensions were running high in northern Wisconsin at the time of the call, and I had already heard several students in Eau Claire ask the same ludicrous question. As a result of the obvious need for accurate information about the Chippewa treaties, I decided to develop a course entitled Chippewa Treaty Rights in Historical Perspective, which I taught during the fall semester over the statewide Educational Teleconference Network (ETN) in cooperation with the University of Wisconsin-Extension Office in Madison. The course attracted considerable attention throughout the state (*Milwaukee Journal* 1989e; *Eau Claire Leader-Telegram* 1989). Larry Peterson, chair of the anti-treaty rights group Protect Americans' Rights and Resources (PARR), announced at a press conference in Park Falls in August that he planned to take the course ''to learn'' (*Park Falls Herald* 1989). For the record, he was *not* among the students who enrolled.

While the course was in progress, Wisconsin Academy of Sciences, Arts and Letters editor Carl Haywood asked me to write an article on the topic for the 1990 edition of *Transactions*. I agreed to do so, but the article eventually became book-length as I responded enthusiastically to Haywood's recommendation that I provide as much information and documentation as possible. I am very grateful to Haywood who, together with retired educator Veda Stone and University of Wisconsin-Eau Claire History Department Chairs Jack Lauber and Thomas Miller, has been a constant source of encouragement during all stages of the preparation of this study. *Transactions'* managing editor, Patricia Allen Duyfhuizen offered many valuable suggestions in the final preparation of the manuscript; her undergraduate intern, Lise Hanson, helped in proofreading.

In undertaking this project, I became indebted to many people. I especially want to acknowledge the contributions of my cheerful, talented, and hardworking student assistants. English graduate student Laura Apfelbeck, editorial assistant in the School of Graduate Studies and Office of University Research, was involved in the project from its inception. She transcribed documents for inclusion in the Appendices, commented on all drafts of the manuscript, and assisted the *Transactions* staff in preparing the final draft for publication. In addition to benefiting from her editorial expertise and attention to detail, everyone involved in the project appreciated Laura's dedication and keen wit. History graduate students Jason Tetzloff, Tony Gulig and Timothy Spindler served as research assistants and transcribed materials for the Appendices. I especially enjoyed their company and conversation on the numerous trips between Eau Claire and the State Historical Society of Wisconsin in Madison. Jason and Tony also commented on early drafts of the manuscript and continued to provide assistance even when they were no longer officially working on the project. Undergraduate assistant Tracy Hemmy transcribed documents for the Appendices and provided assistance with wordprocessing. Undergraduate assistant Laura Evert conducted library research during the final stages of the project and checked the bibliographical citations for accuracy. The team spirit, enthusiasm, and dedication exhibited by these students is greatly appreciated. Students in my undergraduate and graduate Indian history courses at the University of Wisconsin-Eau Claire also contributed to this study by raising questions that led me to investigate various facets of the history of Chippewa reserved treaty rights.

I want to thank University of Oklahoma Law School professor Rennard Strickland, attorney Howard J. Bichler of the Office of Tribal Attorney of the St. Croix Chippewa Indians of Wisconsin, my University of Wisconsin-Eau Claire colleagues education professor Richard St. Germaine and history professor James Oberly, and University of Wisconsin-Stevens Point history professor David Wrone for reading and commenting on early drafts of this work. Helen Hornbeck Tanner, editor of the *Atlas of Great Lakes Indian History,* answered queries regarding nineteenth century Chippewa villages.

Numerous individuals kindly shared resource materials. University of Colorado ethnic studies professor Vine Deloria, Jr. drew my attention to the 1934 Indian Congress at Hayward and provided a photocopy of the proceedings and other relevant information. Biological Services Director Thomas R. Busiahn and Administrative Assistant Leanne Thannum of the Great Lakes Indian Fish and Wildlife Commission (GLIFWC) provided data on Chippewa off-reservation hunting and fishing harvests as did Michael Staggs of the Bureau of Fisheries Management of the Wisconsin Department of Natural Resources and Charles Pils of the Bureau of Wildlife Management of the Wisconsin Department of Natural Resources. Indian educator James La Goo of the Milwaukee Area Technical College provided a photocopy of his collection of newspaper clippings on treaty rights issues. *Eau Claire Leader-Telegram* city editor Doug Mell, *News from Indian Country* editor Paul DeMain, and *Wisconsin State Journal* assistant city editor David Stoeffler in Madison answered several inquiries relative to media coverage of the treaty rights issue and helped me to locate pertinent articles, as did circulation manager Eric Erickson of the *Ashland Daily Press* and GLIFWC public information officer assistant Lynn Spreutels. A note of thanks is also offered to the scholars who shared copies of their unpublished research papers; their papers are listed in the Bibliography.

Andy Kraushaar of the Iconographic Department at the State Historical Society of Wisconsin provided valuable assistance in locating illustrations and providing background information. Realty Specialist Carole Kraft of the Bureau of Indian Affairs, Great Lakes Agency in Ashland, Wisconsin provided information on tribal and allotted lands prepared under the direction of Agency Superintendent Robert R. Jaeger. I am indebted to University of Wisconsin-Eau Claire (UWEC) geography professor Sean Hartnett for producing all the maps for this study. Also at UWEC, Director Charles Brenner and systems programmer Robin Niemeyer of the Office of Academic Computing Services, office automation coordinator Paul Eckardt of the Office of Information Management, and undergraduate business student David Ingle rendered invaluable technical assistance at critical stages in the preparation of the final draft.

Robert M. Kvasnicka and Milton Gustafson of the National Archives and Records Service in Washington, D.C. and Susan Karren of the National Archives—Great Lakes Region in Chicago greatly facilitated my research as did staff members at the State Historical Society of Wisconsin, the Lac Courte Oreilles Ojibwa Community College, the Law Library and the Continuing Education and Outreach Office of the University of Wisconsin-Madison School of Law, the Library of Congress, the McFarlin Library of the University of Tulsa, the UWEC McIntyre Library, the UWEC Media Development Center, the Minnesota Historical Society, the Newberry Library, and the Oklahoma Historical Society. A special note of thanks to UWEC librarian Kathleen Henning for expediting the process of obtaining materials on interlibrary loan and for keeping me informed of all works on American Indians, treaty rights issues, and federal Indian policy that came across her desk.

Funding for the Wisconsin Chippewa Treaty Rights Research Project, which enabled me to gather information for this publication, was provided by the UWEC Center of Excellence for Faculty and Undergraduate Student Research Collaboration and the University of Wisconsin-Eau Claire Foundation, Inc. The project is still in progress, and I encourage readers with knowledge of any pertinent manuscripts or other primary source materials not included in my Bibliography to contact me in care of the School of Graduate Studies and Office of University Research at UWEC.

Finally, I wish to express my deepest thanks and appreciation to my wife Christa and to our daughter Ani and son Jakob for their support, encouragement, and patience. They gently reminded me, as the research for what I said would be a short *article* on Chippewa reserved treaty rights became a project that consumed my evenings, weekends, holidays, and vacations, that they too have certain reserved rights, which they intend to invoke now that this *book* is finished!

Ronald N. Satz
Eau Claire, Wisconsin

Notes to the Reader on Usage

Throughout the text I have used "Indians" rather than "Native Americans" to designate Chippewa or other American natives because, as historian James Axtell has observed, the former term is "simpler, sanctioned by tradition, normatively neutral, and preferred by the vast majority of native peoples themselves, past and present" (Axtell 1986, xi). I have used "Chippewa" to refer to the people of the various Ojibwa-speaking bands and have restricted the use of the term Ojibwa to the language itself except in the captions for illustrations where I have used whichever term appears in the actual title of the work depicted. Following contemporary usage rather than nineteenth-century convention, I refer to the collective members of Chippewa bands as "Chippewas" not "Chippewa."

Since information in parentheses and brackets appears in many of the quotations from original sources, I have used braces { } throughout the book for any information I have supplied. Any italics or underlining used in direct quotations are those found in the original material unless otherwise noted.

Indian names are frequently spelled in a variety of ways in nineteenth century documents and misspelled names of non-Indians and other words also frequently occur in these sources. In order to avoid distracting the reader, I have not used {sic} or corrected misspelled words if the meaning of the words or the identity of the individual is obvious from the context. I have used {sic} only if failure to do so might lead one to suspect a printing error, such as when a letter is missing. Also for the sake of the reader, I have sometimes used modern town, river, and state names, without the awkward prefix "present-day," to locate historical events.

To assist the reader in locating sources cited in the Bibliography, the author's name, the date, and the page numbers of each source appear in parentheses in the text. Information has been deleted only when the portion omitted appears as part of the text immediately preceding the citation or when there is no other work by that author or another author with the same last name listed in the Bibliography. The only exceptions to the use of this format for citations appear in captions to some of the figures because permission to reprint illustrations was usually contingent upon the inclusion of specific information.

Where I refer to a document that can be found in the Appendices, the Appendix number will appear in italics after the usual parenthetical bibliographic citation. Frame numbers are provided instead of page numbers for items on microfilm. Any information I have added to a document in the Appendices is included in braces { } to set it off from parenthetical or bracketed comments by the author of the document.

Finally, I want to emphasize that the use of normatively loaded words such as "barbarism," "civilized," and "savage" that appear in the text should not be viewed as my characterizations but as those of the United States officials or other American citizens about whom I am writing.

1　Early Chippewa-U. S. Relations

The Chippewa (also known as the Ojibwa or Anishinabe) Indians of present-day Wisconsin are the descendants of a northern Algonquian people who lived in an extensive area, mainly north of Lakes Superior and Huron. These people began migrating across the Great Lakes region long before Europeans arrived (Ritzenthaler 1978, 743). Early settlements at Sault Ste. Marie, L'Abre Croche, Mackinac, L'Anse, Green Bay, and Fond du Lac preceded the establishment of other villages in what are today the states of Michigan, Wisconsin, and Minnesota as European trade penetrated into the Great Lakes region and drew the Indians from the backwoods and upriver areas to the points of trade (Keller 1978, 2; James 1954, 19; Mason 1988, 94).

By the early decades of the nineteenth century, according to anthropologist Harold Hickerson, more than three thousand Chippewas occupied seven large autonomous village centers extending from Red Lake in present-day Minnesota on the northwest to Lac du Flambeau in Wisconsin on the east. Three of these centers—those at Red Lake, Leech Lake, and Sandy Lake—were in Minnesota while the Snake River and Yellow River settlements were on branches of St. Croix River in the Minnesota-Wisconsin border region. Another two centers were in Wisconsin at Lac Courte Oreilles and Lac du Flambeau. In addition to the seven village centers, about one thousand Chippewas lived in numerous smaller villages, each with a population of only one hundred to one-hundred fifty people, located near one or another of the larger settlements (Hickerson 1962, 12-13).

Hickerson's population estimates may be on the conservative side. Nineteenth-century Indian agent and pioneer ethnologist Henry Rowe Schoolcraft reported there were more than seventy-three hundred Chippewas living along the southern shores of Lake Superior and the sources of the Mississippi River in the mid-1820s (1828, 98). The dearth of reliable population statistics for Indian communities in early nineteenth-century America is a perplexing problem, but there appears to be agreement among scholars that the bulk of the Chippewa population at the time of European penetration into North America was in Canada and that this population pattern has continued into the twentieth century. The Chippewa country in the United States and Canada encompasses an expanse of land from the eastern end of Lake Ontario westward to the vicinity of Lake Winnepeg in Manitoba and the Turtle Mountains of North Dakota, a range greater than that of any other Indian people in North America (Ritzenthaler 1978, 743; Tanner 1976, 1-4).

Like all Indian peoples in North America, the Chippewas lived close to nature. Their traditional lifestyle involved a seminomadic existence in heavily forested regions through which the Indians traveled, depending on the season, by canoe on the numerous lakes and rivers or by toboggans and snowshoes. Primarily hunters and trappers, this forest people also fished the streams (*Fig. 1*), gathered wild rice in the rivers (*Fig. 2*), and tapped trees to make maple sugar (*Fig. 3*); their lives

Fig. 1. *Indians Spearing Fish in Winter.* A drawing by Seth Eastman, from Francis S. Drake, ed., *The Indian Tribes of the United States,* Vol. 1 (1884). Courtesy of the State Historical Society of Wisconsin. WHi(w6)13551

revolved around these differing subsistence activities according to the changing seasons. Hunting and fishing were such esteemed occupations that a Chippewa boy's first success in each was publicly acknowledged. Chippewa religious beliefs emphasized the existence of spirits in both animate and inanimate objects and guided the Indians in their use of resources (McKenney and Hall {1838}, 99; Ritzenthaler 1978, 746-47; Danziger 1979, 9-14; State Historical Museum 1990-91; Johnston 1990, 66; Vecsey 1983, 10-11, 59-63).

As Europeans ventured into the upper Great Lakes region in the seventeenth century, they introduced such goods as guns, ammunition, metal traps and kettles, and manufactured blankets—simplifying the lives of the Chippewas but also making them increasingly dependent on the traders who supplied these goods. Rapidly, Chippewa culture shifted from the stone-bone-wood-pottery materials made by Indians to metal replacements made by Europeans. As the gun replaced the bow, hunting and warfare intensified. Chippewa incursions into Sioux hunting territories to the West increased.[1] By the mid-eighteenth century, scattered bands of Lake Superior Chippewas controlled the region west of the Keweenaw Peninsula as far as the upper Mississippi Valley, but they had to fight to maintain their control. Continual warfare with the Sioux in what are today Wisconsin and Minnesota preoccupied the Chippewas as the advancing line of American settlement moved westward following the American Revolution (James 1954, 23; Danziger 1979, Chs. 3-4; Keller 1978, 2; Ritzenthaler 1978, 743-44).

Fig. 2. *Gathering Wild Rice.* An engraving after a drawing by Seth Eastman, from Mary H. Eastman's *American Aboriginal Portfolio* (1853). Courtesy of the State Historical Society of Wisconsin. WHi(x3)25013

The Treaty of Paris, which in 1783 ended the American Revolution, partitioned North America between Great Britain and the United States and its allies. Consequently, the Great Lakes and the Mississippi River became the northern and western boundaries of the independent United States. The Great Lakes region, however, was actually far beyond the area under American control. Chippewas and other Indians living in the region strongly resented having Great Britain and its former thirteen colonies carve up their homelands without consulting them (Jones 1982, 139-42).

Following the Treaty of Paris, the United States used high-handed tactics to secure land cession treaties from Indians in the Great Lakes region. Indian resentment of American methods of acquiring land, together with American efforts to maintain peace on the frontier, led government officials to reexamine their handling of Indian-white relations. Because the United States had failed in its efforts to treat Indian affairs as a domestic problem, government officials found it necessary to treat Indian bands and tribes as if they were foreign nations. As one scholar notes, U. S. officials were "forced to consider relations *with* the Indians, rather than a unilateral policy *for* the Indians" (Jones 1982, 147-48).

On July 13, 1787, American officials adopted a set of principles for dealing with the Indians north of the Ohio River and east of the Mississippi River, a region including the lands of Wisconsin's Chippewa Indians. The Northwest Ordinance declared:

Fig. 3. *Indian Sugar Camp.* This Seth Eastman painting depicts members of a Chippewa village participating in various stages of the process of making maple sugar and syrup. From Francis S. Drake, ed., *Indian Tribes of the United States,* Vol. 1 (1884). Courtesy of the State Historical Society of Wisconsin. WHi(w6)13600

> The utmost good faith shall always be observed towards the Indians, their lands and property shall never be taken from them without their consent; and in their property, rights and liberty, they never shall be invaded or disturbed, unless in just and lawful wars authorised by Congress; but laws founded in justice and humanity shall from time to time be made, for preventing wrongs being done to them, and for preserving peace and friendship with them . . . . (Continental Congress 1787, 10)

Land acquisition by "consent" implied the negotiation of formal treaties.

The Constitution of the United States, drafted in 1787 and ratified two years later, recognized treaty making as the basis for conducting the new republic's relations with Indian bands and tribes. The United States was a small, isolated, agrarian nation with military and financial weaknesses, so its founding fathers placed Indian affairs in the hands of the federal government (Wrone 1986-87, 84-85). John Marshall, one of the nation's most distinguished Supreme Court chief justices, summarized the scope of federal authority in Indian affairs in 1832. The Constitution, he said, "confers on congress the powers of war and peace; of making treaties, and of regulating commerce with foreign nations, and among the several states, and *with the Indian tribes. These powers comprehend all that is required for the regulation of our intercourse with the Indians*" (U.S. Supreme Court 1832, 559). The Supremacy Clause of the Constitution specifically stipulates that treaties with Indian tribes have the same status as those negotiated with foreign nations:

> This Constitution, and the Laws of the United States which shall be made in Pursuance thereof; and all Treaties made, or which shall be made, under the Authority of the United

States, shall be the supreme Law of the Land; and the Judges in every State shall be bound thereby, any Thing in the Constitution or Laws of any State to the Contrary notwithstanding. (Article 6, Clause 2)

As the new American nation inaugurated its first president in 1789, the Northwest Ordinance and the recently ratified Constitution provided it with a basic framework for handling Indian-white relations based on the realities it confronted.

Secretary of War Henry Knox briefed President Washington on the realities of Indian-white relations in the Great Lakes region within a few months of the first chief executive's inauguration. Observing that "the Indians are greatly tenacious of their lands, and generally do not relinquish their right {to them},* excepting on the principle of a specific consideration, expressly given for the purchase of the same" (1789a, 8), Knox advised Washington that "the dignity and the interest of the nation" would best be advanced by recognizing Indian ownership of lands. Considering the number of warriors in the region, Knox urged Washington to adopt "a liberal system of justice" toward the Indians.

> It is highly probable, that, by a conciliatory system, the expense of managing the said Indians, and attaching them to the United States for the next ensuing period of fifty years, may, on an average, cost 15,000 dollars annually.
>
> A system of coercion and oppression, pursued from time to time, for the same period, as the convenience of the United States might dictate, would probably amount to a much greater sum of money . . . but the blood and injustice which would stain the character of the nation, would be beyond all pecuniary calculation.
>
> As the settlements of the whites shall approach near to the Indian boundaries established by treaties, the game will be diminished, and the lands being valuable to the Indians only as hunting grounds, they will be willing to sell further tracts for small considerations. By the expiration, therefore, of the above period, it is most probable that the Indians will, by the invariable operation of the causes which have hitherto existed in their intercourse with the whites, be reduced to a very small number. (1789b, 13-14)

Knox understood that the United States needed peace on its frontiers so it could address other issues facing it, and he believed that acquiring Indian lands by purchase rather than by conquest was in his nation's best interests (Prucha 1984, 1: 49). The first treaty negotiated by the Washington administration with Chippewa Indians and other Great Lakes tribes, the Treaty of Greenville of 1795, specifically declared that in order to promote a "strong and perpetual" peace between the United States and the Indians of the Great Lakes "the Indian tribes who have a right to . . . {unceded} lands, are quietly to enjoy them, hunting, planting, and dwelling thereon so long as they please, without any molestation from the United States." In return for this pledge and for the promise of protection against all white intruders, the Indians agreed to sell lands only to the United States (Kappler 2: 41, 42).

Despite the rhetoric of the Northwest Ordinance and of the Washington administration, the demands of settlers, speculators, and other whites for Indian lands and resources during the early years of the republic were often met by violating the "liberal system of justice" Secretary of War Knox had so enthusiastically

---

*As mentioned in the "Notes to the Reader on Usage," I have used braces { } throughout the book for any information added to a quotation.

endorsed. Knox greatly underestimated the firm attachment Great Lakes Indians had to their lands. As the demand for Indian lands grew, American officials increasingly resorted to bribery, deception, economic coercion, threats, and sometimes brute force to secure Indian signatures on land cession treaties. The treaty-making process served as a convenient means of sanctioning federal land grabs under the guise of diplomacy (Satz 1975, 1-6; 1987, 35-36).

In the early 1800s, the U. S. War Department opened government trading houses at Fort Wayne (Indiana, 1802), Detroit (Michigan, 1802), Chicago (Illinois, 1805), Sandusky (Ohio, 1806), Fort Mackinac (Michigan, 1808), Fort Madison (Iowa, 1808), Green Bay (Wisconsin, 1815) and Prairie du Chien (Wisconsin, 1815) as part of its effort to exert economic influence over the tribes on the northwestern frontier (Prucha 1953, 11; Prucha 1984, 1: 124).[2] As Thomas Jefferson had noted in a private letter in 1803, ''we shall push our trading {ho}uses, and be glad to see the good and influential individuals among them run in{to} debt, because we observe that when these debts get beyond what the individuals can pay, they become willing to lop them off by a cession of lands.'' By following such a policy,[3] Jefferson was confident that ''our settlements will gradually circumscribe and approach the Indians, and they will in time either incorporate with us as citizens of the United States, or remove beyond the Mississippi'' (Jefferson 1803, 10: 370). Jefferson's plan conflicted with the efforts of private traders like John Jacob Astor of the American Fur Company and his lieutenants Ramsey Crooks and Robert Stuart who lobbied hard, especially after the War of 1812, to regain control of the fur trade from the government-run trading houses. Their efforts contributed to the closing of the Green Bay trading house in 1821 and the closing of the one at Prairie du Chien the following year, as the lobbyists succeeded in convincing Congress that the trade should be turned over to private interests (Prucha 1984, 1: Ch. 4).

Following the closing of the trading house at Green Bay in 1821, federal officials anxiously sought other ways to extend their authority over the Indian tribes of the upper Great Lakes region. Yet, the Lake Superior Chippewa continued to depend on British traders and to ignore American claims to their homelands (Keller 1978, 4). As a result, the U. S. War Department established a military post and an Indian agency at Sault Ste. Marie in 1822 for the purpose of countering British influence in the region and extending American control over the Chippewas (Bremer 1987, 53, 56; Hill 1974, 165).

During the mid-1820s, American officials sought to transfer the allegiance of the scattered bands of Lake Superior Chippewa Indians from their British ''Father'' in Canada to their American ''Father'' in Washington through a series of treaty negotiations.[4] The first parley convened on the east bank of the Mississippi River above the mouth of the Wisconsin River at Prairie du Chien on August 19, 1825 (*Fig. 4*). In the resulting treaty (Kappler 2: 250-55), American Commissioners William Clark of the St. Louis Superintendency and Michigan Territorial Governor Lewis Cass called for ''a firm and perpetual peace between the Sioux and Chippewas''; established ''tribal'' boundaries for the Chippewa, Sioux, Sac and Fox, Menominee, Ioway, and Winnebago Indians, as well as for bands living along the Illinois River; recognized Indian title to the newly demarcated ''tribal'' territories; and supposedly placed each of the various Indian peoples under American supervision.

Fig. 4. *View of the Great Treaty Held at Prairie du Chien, September 1825.* A James Otto Lewis painting. By establishing tribal boundaries for the assembled Indians, Treaty Commissioners Lewis Cass and William Clark laid the groundwork for future land cessions. Courtesy of the State Historical Society of Wisconsin. WHi(x3)2812

Not all Chippewa bands were represented by full deputations at Prairie du Chien (Neill 1885, 467-70), and Clark and Cass found it necessary to include the following provision in the treaty under Article 12:

> The Chippewa tribe being dispersed over a great extent of country, and the Chiefs of that tribe having requested, that such portion of them as may be thought proper, by the Government of the United States, may be assembled in 1826, upon some part of Lake Superior, that the objects and advantages of this treaty may be fully explained to them, so that the stipulations may be observed by the warriors. The Commissioners of the United States assent thereto, and it is therefore agreed that a council shall accordingly be held for these purposes. (Kappler 2: 253)

Such a council was assembled a year later on the western end of Lake Superior at Fond du Lac where a treaty concluded by Governor Cass and War Department official Thomas L. McKenney on August 5, 1826, claimed that "the whole Chippewa tribe" had assented to the principles and policies laid out at Prairie du Chien (Kappler 2: 268-73). A year later, at a treaty parley with Chippewa, Menominee, and Winnebago leaders concluded at Butte des Morts near Green Bay, Commissioners Cass and McKenney negotiated the southern boundary line of the Chippewa country (Kappler 2: 281-83). These treaties, as Henry Rowe Schoolcraft of the Sault Ste. Marie Agency on the Upper Peninsula of Michigan noted, were designed "to place our Indian relations in this quarter on a permanent basis, and to ensure the future peace of the frontier" (Schoolcraft 1851, 244-45).

One way in which American treaty commissioners sought to extend American influence into the Great Lakes region was to convince the Indians of America's military strength. To accomplish this goal, soldiers accompanying the commissioners drilled, paraded, and stood inspection on a regular basis. At Fond du Lac, Commissioners Lewis Cass and Thomas L. McKenney emphasized the military strength of the United States by warning the Chippewas, "You have never seen your great father's arm. Only a small particle of it—here on your right—[pointing to the military]—but it is only a bit, and a very little bit, of his little finger." The commissioners told the Chippewas to view agent Schoolcraft as the representative of the president of the United States. "We advise you as friends and brothers, not to offend your great father. He has sent his agent, [Mr. Schoolcraft] among you. He speaks your great father's words, listen to him; then you will be happy—and this is what your great father wishes you to be. It is with yourselves to be so, or not" (Edwards 1826, 475-76).

The American treaty making of the mid-1820s actually had little immediate impact on the daily lives of Wisconsin Chippewas for nearly a decade. Americans generally viewed the Chippewa country in the Lake Superior region as "sterile and forbidding" (Schoolcraft 1828, 99), and few ventured into the vast region of approximately twenty-seven million acres including about fifteen million in Wisconsin, seven million in Minnesota, and five million in the Upper Peninsula in Michigan (Wilkinson 1990, 9). Located between and thus remote from the Indian agencies established in 1819 at Fort Snelling near present-day Minneapolis and at Sault Ste. Marie in Michigan Territory in 1822, the Wisconsin Chippewas did not have an American Indian agent residing within their country until the stationing of a subagent at La Pointe in 1837[5] (Hill 1974, 87, 160, 162, 165-66; Danziger 1979, 77).

Despite the efforts of American treaty commissioners to end intertribal hostilities, Chippewa and Sioux Indians continued to fight over the game in Wisconsin and Minnesota largely in response to the prodigious demands of the fur trade system introduced by whites (Hickerson 1962, 28-29, 94 n. 16; 1973, 30). Indeed, surveyors did not actually begin work on the boundary line between the Sioux and the Chippewas called for in the 1825 Treaty of Prairie du Chien until a decade later (Herring 1835, 66). Even though the treaties of the 1820s had little immediate impact on the Chippewas, they set the stage for later negotiations that did have far-reaching effects.

Chippewa leaders had ostensibly recognized American hegemony in the region at Fond du Lac in 1826 since they agreed to a provision allowing the United States the right "to search for, and carry away, any metals or minerals from any part of their country." Although American Treaty Commissioners Lewis Cass and Thomas McKenney gave the Indians no reason to believe that this provision would affect their land title or jurisdiction over the land (Edwards 1826, 458; Kappler 2: 269), the provision would haunt the Chippewas. "The article . . . was so worded," a missionary observed many years later, "that I can conceive the Indians might understand that they gave permission to take specimens of minerals without intending to grant liberty to {the} Gov{ernment} to work the mines, while the Gov{ernment} might understand that they had full liberty to work the mines and this without any intention to deceive the Indians" (Wheeler 1843).

United States treaty commissioners frequently referred to and dealt with the Chippewas as if they constituted a single tribe or nation, as when Cass and McKenney referred to assembling "the Chippewa Tribe of Indians" at the Fond du Lac negotiations in 1826 (Kappler 2: 268). The term *tribe* or *nation,* however, is not applicable to these people because the words connote a single political and social body. In reality, separate Chippewa villages actually carried out ceremonial and political activities as independent, autonomous units (Hickerson 1988, 77-78). As Indian agent Schoolcraft observed:

> Their government, so far as they exercise any, is placed in the hands of chiefs. They have village chiefs and war chiefs. The former are hereditary, the latter elective. Neither are invested with much power in advance. The occasion which calls for action, brings with it an expression of the general voice. The latter is implicitly obeyed; and it is the policy of the chiefs to keep a little in the rear of public sentiment. The power of both orders of chiefs, is only advisory; but that of the war chief predominates during a state of war. No formality is exercised in taking the sense of the village, or nation, as to public men or measures. Popular feeling is the supreme law. They exchange opinions casually, and these are final. Councils generally deliberate upon what has been, beforehand, pretty well settled. (1828, 100)

Many years before Schoolcraft recorded his observations of Chippewa governmental structure and before the negotiation of the 1826 treaty mentioned earlier, Cass had reported to the War Department that the Chippewas were loosely organized into villages headed by chiefs who had only limited power and that "the Government of the Indians, if it deserve that name, is a Government of opinion" (Keller 1981, 2).

Although Chippewa bands shared a common culture and the same Algonquian language, there was no overall political structure binding them together. Individuals from contiguous villages maintained communication links, intermarried, and sometimes participated together in religious ceremonies, peace councils, war parties, and treaty negotiations; but in general, such activities were dealt with by individual villages or bands rather than by united Chippewa communities. There were common law-ways, but these were set and enforced informally through the use of praise and scorn rather than formally through legal institutions tying the bands together (Hickerson 1962, 13; Ritzenthaler 1978, 753; Wilkinson 1990, 7).

By 1830, the Chippewa Indians were deeply in debt to fur traders. Like Thomas Jefferson before him, President Andrew Jackson was eager to use "national" Indian debts as a vehicle for securing "tribal" land cessions. Michigan Territorial Governor Lewis Cass informed the president that the situation among the Indians of the Great Lakes region was ideal for treaty negotiations. "The goods they received were dear," Cass remarked, "and the peltry they furnished was cheap" (1830, 65). This situation played into the hands of federal treaty negotiators.

Andrew Jackson entered the White House in 1829 committed to the removal of Indians from states and territories east of the Mississippi River to locations in the trans-Mississippi West. Years of experience in Indian affairs as an army officer and territorial governor of Florida had led Jackson to the position that American national security demanded the removal of Indians outside the nation's geographical limits in order to provide "a connexion of our territory by the possession of their claims." In 1830, Jackson pushed an Indian Removal Bill through Congress and lost little time in directing eastern Indians to the trans-Mississippi West (Satz 1975, Chs. 1, 3-4).

The Removal Act of 1830 called for the voluntary exchange of lands east of the Mississippi River for lands in an area west of Arkansas and Missouri designated as Indian Country (U. S. Congress 1830). Treaties negotiated under this legislation promised Indian emigrants permanent title to their new lands, rations and transportation to the West, protection en route, medicine and physicians, reimbursement for abandoned property, and assistance in rebuilding their settlements in the West (Satz 1975, 31, 107, 296-98).

Although Jackson's removal policy is associated most frequently with incidents in southern Indian history such as the Cherokee Trail of Tears and the Seminole Indian War, the removal policy was applied to Indians in the Great Lakes region as well[6] (Satz, 1975, 112-15; 1976, 71-93). By the mid-1830s, removal treaties had opened large portions of southern Wisconsin to white settlement, and American policymakers cast covetous eyes on Chippewa lands in the northern part of the state (A. Smith 1973, 131-48).

When President Jackson signed the Removal Bill into law in 1830, Winnebago Indian villages still bordered Lake Mendota, the site of the present-day state capital of Madison. During the following decade, southern Wisconsin witnessed an influx of land speculators and Yankee immigrants who made their way to the western Great Lakes via the Erie Canal. Far from being viewed by settlers as savages as were many Southern Indians, Potawatomis were still welcome in the kitchens of some Milwaukee settlers in 1836 when Wisconsin Territory was organized (Tanner 1987, 146). The territorial seal designed by engraver William Wagner, however, expressed the pervasive belief of the age and pointed the way toward the future of Indian-white relations in the territory. It boldly proclaimed, "Civilitas Successit Barbarum" (civilization succeeds barbarism) and depicted a white settler plowing a field while an Indian faced his destiny in the West (*Fig. 5*).

Fig. 5. *The Great Seal of the Territory of Wisconsin.* William Wagner's territorial seal reproduced from Marcius Willson's *American History* (1855). Courtesy of the State Historical Society of Wisconsin. WHi(x3)45609

2

The 1837
Pine Tree Treaty

Soon after the organization of the new territory, Governor and ex officio Superintendent of Indian Affairs Henry Dodge (*Fig. 6*), played a major role in securing approximately half of the present state of Wisconsin from the Chippewa, Sioux, and Winnebago Indians. The land cessions included all of the western area lying north of the Wisconsin River, except a wide strip bordering Lake Superior (Kappler 2: 491-93, 493-94, 498-500). Wisconsin territorial delegate George W. Jones assured his colleagues in Congress before negotiations began that the Chippewa and Winnebago Indians themselves had asked Governor Dodge to "enable them to dispose of those lands" (Jones 1836).

Treaty negotiations leading to the Chippewa land cession of 1837 (*Fig. 7*) opened at the St. Peters Agency located at the mouth of the Minnesota River on July 20th and lasted ten days. Dodge later informed Commissioner of Indian Affairs Carey Allen Harris that he had "deemed it a subject of the first importance, that as many of the different Bands should be present at the Treaty ground, as could be collected, for the purpose of fully meeting the views of the Government, as well as to produce harmony and concert among the Indians themselves" (*Fig. 8*). Dodge originally reported to Harris that the one thousand Indian men, women, and children in attendance "fully represented" all of the Chippewa bands from present-day Minnesota and Wisconsin (Dodge 1837a), but his later correspondence (Dodge 1838a) and the official proceedings of the treaty[7] demonstrate that this was not the case at the opening of the parley.

Dodge estimated the cession he sought as "containing from nine to ten millions of acres of land, and abounding in Pine Timber." In addition, he reported that "a part of it, is represented, as being well suited to Agricultural purposes; and discoveries are reported to have been made of copper on the St. Croix, and Rum Rivers, and near Lake Courteoreille." The region was "of the first importance to the people of the States of Illinois, Missouri, and the Territory of Wisconsin for its Pine Timber" (Dodge 1837a).

Officials in the administration of President Martin Van Buren sought the land cession not to accommodate white settlers—whites were not demanding Chippewa lands—but to enable lumbering on a large scale along eastern tributaries of the Mississippi River. Demand for cheap pine timber grew rapidly among the new towns of the Mississippi River Valley as the cost of lumber from western New York and Pennsylvania reached prohibitive levels. Transporting timber from the East was both a costly and time-consuming enterprise. When the capitol of Wisconsin Territory was built at Belmont in 1836, for example, the lumber needed for its construction had to be transported from a tributary of the Alleghany River in Pennsylvania down to the Ohio River and up the Mississippi River to Galena, and from there carted by an ox team. Entrepreneurs sought to take advantage of the demand for cheap lumber by exploiting the vast pine forests of northern Wisconsin

Fig. 6. *Henry Dodge, Governor and Superintendent of Indian Affairs for Wisconsin Territory.* Painting by James Bowman. Courtesy of the State Historical Society of Wisconsin. WHi(x28)975

(Bailly 1836, 40; Dodge 1838c, 158; Fries 1951, 8-9), but the federal Indian Trade and Intercourse Acts prohibited Americans from logging on Indian lands without special permission (Prucha 1962a, 2). A land cession treaty would provide legal access to these lands.

In addition to the lumbering interests, other groups would benefit from a land cession treaty. Fur traders had accumulated a large mass of unpaid credits on their

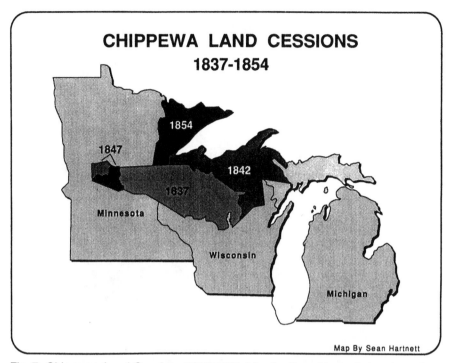

Fig. 7. *Chippewa Land Cessions 1837-1854*. Map by Sean Hartnett. Land cessions associated with the treaties of 1837, 1842, 1847, and 1854 are depicted above. Only the 1837 and 1842 treaties involved cessions in Wisconsin. In 1847, the Wisconsin bands refused to participate in negotiations for the north shore of Lake Superior without a treaty-guaranteed right to remain in Wisconsin. The Wisconsin bands successfully blocked the cession of the north shore until their demands for reservations in Wisconsin were finally met in 1854.

books against the Chippewas, and a land cession would provide an opportunity for them to recover their funds (Babcock 1924, 372-73). Army sutlers[8] at Fort Snelling also needed the cash that was likely to flow from a land cession. The sutlers found themselves in a difficult situation when soldiers from the First Infantry left the area for service in the Seminole Indian War in Florida Territory before paying their debts[9] (Prucha 1966, 29). Beyond economic considerations, fear influenced the decision-making process. Governor Dodge considered the purchase of the timber country an absolute necessity to avoid an Indian war. "I was satisfied in my own mind that if a purchase was not made of this pine region of the country, by the United States," Dodge told Commissioner Harris, "there was great danger of our citizens being brought into a state of Collision with the Chippewa Indians, that would have resulted in bloodshed, and perhaps war" (Dodge 1837a).

War Department officials in Washington had several other reasons to be pleased with Dodge's actions. Traders married to Chippewa women had obtained and monopolized valuable sawmill sites and lumbering rights. Frontier entrepreneurs coveted similar opportunities and worked hard to convince the Indians to lease land for such purposes.[10] Some chiefs and headmen, anxious "to procure some of the necissaries {*sic*} of life" during poor hunting seasons, were willing to grant leases to white "friends" (Chippewa Chiefs {1836}, 53). Such arrangements troubled

Fig. 8. *Ojibwa Portaging Around the Falls of St. Anthony.* Oil on canvas painting, 1835–36, by George Catlin. Courtesy of the National Museum of American Art, Smithsonian Institute, Gift of Mrs. Joseph Harrison, Jr. 1985.66.465

federal officials who were eager to prevent "a complete monopoly of all the advantages of the pine region" (Harris 1836, 1837a; Dodge 1836). Also, since the United States' boundary with Canada on Lake Superior was not settled until the Webster-Ashburton Treaty of 1842, American officials feared British influence in the region. Indeed, there was a war scare along the northern border from Maine to Michigan before the end of 1837. At this time, the American army consisted of only five thousand soldiers stationed at scattered posts, and nearly three-fourths of them were in Florida fighting the Seminole Indians (Van Buren 1838; Bald 1961, 215-18; Prucha 1969, 311-19, 333). Anglophobia encouraged Washington bureaucrats to support actions designed to wean the various Chippewa bands away from British traders and officials (Harris 1837b, 3-4). With these concerns, fears, and hopes in the forefront, the War Department had instructed Dodge to treat with the Chippewas for a land cession (Poinsett 1837).

The official handwritten proceedings of the negotiations recorded in journal format by Secretary Verplanck Van Antwerp of Indiana offer a slightly different interpretation of events than provided by Dodge in his brief letter to Commissioner Harris. Although Dodge did not mention in it in his letter, the proceedings clearly indicate the Chippewa bands living in the desired region of Wisconsin arrived late. Dodge sought in vain to bind the assembled Indians to the cession before the representatives of these bands arrived. Claiming the land in question was "not valuable . . . for its game, and not suited to the culture of corn, and other Agricultural purposes," he promised to provide "full value, payable in such manner, as will be most serviceable to your people." The assembled Indians were mostly from Minnesota, and only a small fraction of their land was involved in the proposed cession; those from the Lake Superior shoreline had no land involved. All refused to discuss the proposal until the arrival of representatives of the interior Wisconsin bands whose lands were the focus of the proposed cession. After the Indians delayed the proceedings for two days, Dodge impatiently requested a reply even though the interior Wisconsin Indians had not yet arrived[11] (Van Antwerp 1837, 0548-550; *App. 1*).

Flat Mouth (Aishkebogekhozo), a member of the Pillager band from Leech Lake reputed "to have more power and control" than any other Chippewa chief (Vineyard 1838, 962), responded. He reminded Dodge that although he was a chief, there was no single chief of the entire Chippewa people. To take action before the representatives of the interior Wisconsin bands arrived, he asserted, "might be considered an improper interference, and unfair towards them" (Van Antwerp 1837, 0550; *App. 1*).

Finally, on July 24, the fifth day of the proceedings, news arrived that La Pointe subagent Daniel P. Bushnell and trader Lyman M. Warren were approaching St. Peters with a large group of Indians from the interior Wisconsin bands. The Wind (Naudin), a chief from Snake River, reminded Dodge that the assembled Indians had to wait until these people arrived, saying: "We are a distracted people, and have no regular system of acting together. We cast a firm look on the people who are coming" (Van Antwerp 1837, 0553; *App. 1*).

Subagent Bushnell and his party arrived on July 25th. Now that the Wisconsin Indians had joined the parley, Dodge directed that Stephen Bonga and Peter (or Patrick) Quinn interpret from the English language into Chippewa and that Scott Campbell and Jean Baptiste DuBay, a Menominee mixed-blood with ties to the

American Fur Company (State Hist. Soc. of Wisconsin 1960, 109), interpret from the Chippewa into English. Dodge then asked the chiefs and headmen from the villages on lakes Flambeau and Courte Oreilles and those along the Chippewa, St. Croix, and Rum rivers to examine a map of the proposed land cession. Chief Buffalo from La Pointe—acknowledged by Dodge to be "a man of great influence among his tribe, and very friendly to the whites" (Dodge 1838b)—immediately protested, "the notice that you have given us is rather too short." Dodge, eager to bring the matter to a close, was reported as saying that "the country which he wished to get from them, was barren of game, and of little value for Agricultural purposes; but that it abounded in Pine timber." He stated he was prepared to give them "a fair price" for the land, and he advised them that in the morning he expected them to be prepared to "act together, as one people" and to select "not more than two" chiefs from the various bands to speak in behalf of all. Dodge, anxious to appease mixed-bloods and traders so they would not oppose the treaty, concluded his remarks by noting he wanted the Chippewas to remember their mixed-blood relatives and to do justice to their traders when they decided on how much and how they were to be paid for the land cession (Van Antwerp 1837, 0556-557; *App. 1*).

On July 27th, the elder Hole-in-the-Day (Pagoonakeezhig) from the Upper Mississippi River region and La Trappe (Magegawbaw) from Leech Lake responded to Dodge. Although the chiefs agreed to cede the land requested, they wished to express their concerns. "We wish to hold on to a tree where we get our living, & to reserve the streams where we drink the waters that give us life," La Trappe said. After the interpreters translated the chief's words into English, Verplanck Van Antwerp wrote a footnote (one of only a handful) in his record of the proceedings, "this of course is nonsense—but is given literally as rendered by the Intrepeters {*sic*}, who are unfit to act in that capacity. I presume it to mean that the Indians wish to reserve the privilege of hunting & fishing on the lands and making sugar from the Maple." Meanwhile, to emphasize the kind of tree he meant, La Trappe walked up to the table on which Dodge had set a map of the proposed cession and placed an oak sprig on it. "It is a different kind of tree from the one you wish to get from us,"[12] he commented, adding, "every time the leaves fall from it, we will count it as one winter past." By this comment, La Trappe declared his willingness to bargain with Dodge over the pinelands in Wisconsin while reserving from any land cession the deciduous forests and the waterways of the Pillager country in Minnesota. Finally, the chief requested that the United States lease the land over a sixty-year period after which the grandchildren of the Chippewas at the present parley would speak to the "Great Father" in Washington about future arrangements. Dodge flatly rejected the offer to lease the lands (Van Antwerp 1837, 0558-559; *App. 1*).

At Dodge's suggestion, the Chippewa chiefs agreed to consult with subagents Daniel Bushnell and Miles M. Vineyard to determine the value of their lands. This provided the United States, through its field officials, an excellent opportunity for helping to determine the value of the land it was attempting to acquire. The chiefs did, however, raise concerns and seek clarification about several other matters. "If I have rightly understood you," La Trappe asserted, "we can remain on the lands and hunt there." He further expressed his expectations for the future of Chippewa-white relations on the ceded lands where nineteen Chippewa villages then existed:

18

"we hope that your people will not act towards ours, as your forefathers did towards our own—but that you will always treat us kindly, as you do now." Finally, the chief corrected Dodge's comments about the alleged agricultural worthlessness of the land being ceded. "We understand you, that you have been told our country is not good to cultivate. It is false. There is no better soil to cultivate than it, until you get up, to where the Pine region commences" (Van Antwerp 1837, 0559; *App. 1*).

Dodge's response contained a summary of the terms being offered by President Martin Van Buren. The Indians, he said, would have "free use of the rivers, and the privilege of hunting upon the lands you are to sell to the United States, during his pleasure." Dodge then assured the Indians, "your Great Father has sent me to treat you as his children; to pay you the value of your land; & not to deceive you in any thing I may do with you, or say to you." The governor concluded by expressing his hope that the Chippewas would agree to use a portion of any funds provided as a result of the land cession for teachers to make their children "wise like those of the white people," for farmers to teach them agricultural pursuits, and for various other goods to help uplift them (Van Antwerp 1837, 0560, *App. 1*).

On Friday, July 28th, Pillager chief Flat Mouth (*Fig. 9*) opened the proceedings, making it clear that he was appointed to speak for all of the chiefs:

> My Father. Your children are willing to let you have their lands, but they wish to reserve the privilege of making sugar from the trees, and getting their living from the Lakes and Rivers, as they have done heretofore, and of remaining in this Country. It is hard to give up the lands. They will remain, and can not be destroyed—but you may cut down the Trees, and others will grow up. You know we can not live, deprived of our Lakes and Rivers; There is some game on the lands yet; & for that reason also, we wish to remain upon them, to get a living. Sometimes we scrape the Trees and eat of the bark. The Great Spirit above, made the Earth, and causes it to produce, which enables us to live. (Van Antwerp 1837, 0560-561, *App. 1*)

Dodge promised to inform President Van Buren of the Chippewa requests regarding continued privileges on the ceded lands. He then reemphasized his earlier statement, "it will probably be many years, before your Great Father will want all these lands for the use of his white Children." Then the governor specified the compensation to be provided for the land cession, including eight hundred thousand dollars distributed as summarized below:

> (1) six hundred and thirty thousand dollars in annuities apportioned over twenty years—specifically earmarked purchases included three thousand dollars a year for blacksmiths and related items; four thousand dollars for cattle and provisions; two thousand dollars for mills and millers; one thousand dollars for farmers and agricultural implements; one thousand dollars for schools; and five hundred dollars for tobacco;

> (2) one hundred thousand dollars to the mixed-bloods as "an act of benevolence;" and

> (3) seventy thousand dollars for debts determined to be "justly due" traders and other creditors. (Van Antwerp 1837, 0561-562; *App. 1*)

Flat Mouth protested payment to the traders from funds provided by the land cession. Instead, he asked that the Great Father pay the debts, noting that many of the debtors had been killed by the Sioux while on excursions for the traders.

Fig. 9. *Ojibwa Chief Flat Mouth, 1855.* From *Minnesota Historical Society Collections,* Vol. 9 (1904). Courtesy of the State Historical Society of Wisconsin. WHi(x3)25050

Furthermore, he said, the traders had no right to speak of debts owed them since these white men had taken fish from the lakes and wood from the forests without ever paying the Chippewas. The chief also questioned the fairness of the proposed twenty-year annuity. "If it was <u>my</u> land you was buying, I would, instead of an annuity for only 20 years—demand one from you, as long as the ground lasted. You know that without the lands, and the Rivers & Lakes, we could not live. We hunt, and make Sugar, & dig roots upon the former, while we fish, and obtain

Rice, and drink from the latter." Following Flat Mouth's remarks, Governor Dodge adjourned the meeting. "Be fully prepared," he advised the Indians, "to finish our business" in the morning (Van Antwerp 1837, 0562; *App. 1*).

Governor Dodge assembled the Chippewas on Saturday morning, July 29th, determined to end the negotiations and to obtain signatures on a land cession treaty. He told them that subagents Vineyard and Bushnell had agreed to the fairness of his offer and had approved of the arrangements with only the question of funds for the mixed-bloods[13] yet to be answered. As the chiefs sat down together in council to discuss this matter, a large contingent of unarmed warriors approached the council lodge singing and dancing in war costume with their war flag flying. The Little Six (Shagobai), a chief from Snake River, spoke for the warriors. He informed Dodge, "the Braves of the different bands have smoked and talked together." Fearing they could not survive the winter without aid from the traders, the braves wanted the traders to be paid, but they did not want "to undo what the Chiefs have done." The warriors requested that the United States pay more money for the lands it wanted to use. Not only should Dodge agree to the sixty-year lease requested by Pillager chief La Trappe, but the traders should also be paid (Van Antwerp 1837, 0563; *App. 1*).

Anxious to win the warriors' support, Dodge agreed to pay an additional seventy thousand dollars toward the traders' debts but said that was all he was prepared to do. He made no mention of extending the annuities from twenty to sixty years. At this point, the elder Hole in the Day, a war chief from the Upper Mississippi, spoke with great excitement and bluntly told the warriors to accept the governor's terms. "Braves! There are many of you—but none of you have done what I have—nor are any of you my equals!!—Our Father wishes us to go home in peace." Pledging that "death alone shall prevent the fulfilment {*sic*} of it on my part," Hole in the Day's words carried the day (Van Antwerp 1837, 0564; *App. 1*).

Before proceeding with the signing of the treaty, Dodge reminded the chiefs and warriors that they were "brethren of the same great Nation." Applause greeted his comment that "it is the duty of the Braves to be obedient to their Chiefs." Dodge concluded his comments by asserting, "both Chiefs & Braves should respect the Traders and treat them justly and kindly, that harmony and good feeling may exist among you all; & that you may be serviceable to each other." The Little Six, the Snake River chief who had previously spoken for the warriors, reminded Dodge that some traders had dealt harshly with the Indians. Dodge was apparently uninterested in pursuing that issue for he turned quickly to another subject (Van Antwerp 1837, 0564-565; *App. 1*)

After Secretary Van Antwerp read the final terms of the treaty, Dodge signed the document (*Fig. 10*). As the governor waited for the Indians to sign, there was silence. There was a great reluctance among the Chippewa chiefs to step forward and sign or make their marks on the treaty. Finally, Dodge offered to give an official copy of the treaty "for all your people to look at" to the first chief to step forward and sign it. Hole in the Day then walked promptly to the treaty table and "with his characteristic intrepidity, offered his signature" (Van Antwerp 1837, 0568; *App. 1*). In his annual report after the conclusion of the negotiations at St. Peters, Dodge predicted the treaty would "attach" the Chippewas to the United States and, "if the proper steps are taken," the Indians could be "easily controlled by their agents" (Dodge 1837b, 538).

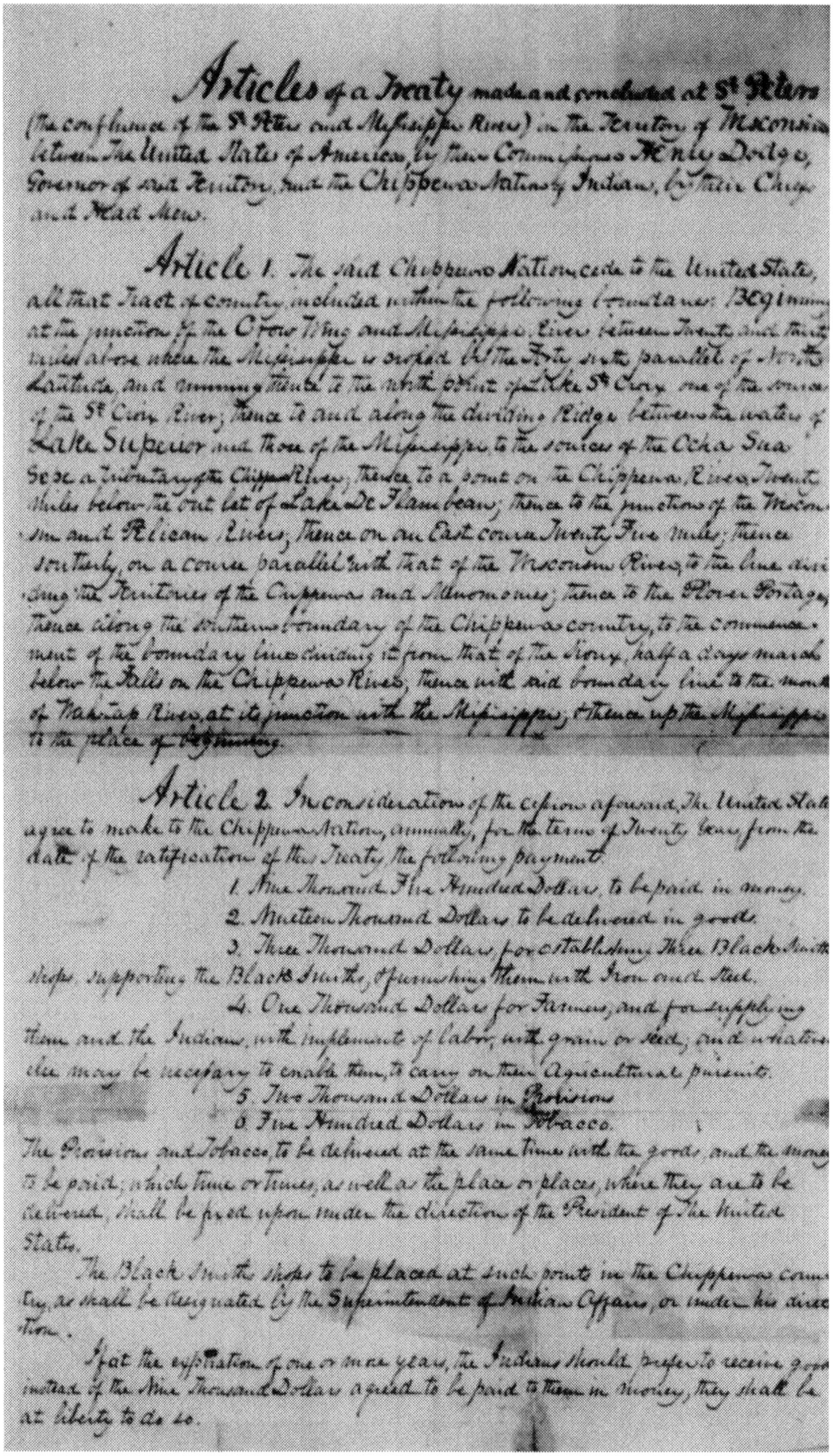

Articles of a Treaty made and concluded at St. Peters (the confluence of the St. Peters and Mississippi Rivers) in the Territory of Wisconsin between the United States of America, by their Commissioner Henry Dodge, Governor of said Territory, and the Chippewa Nation of Indians, by their Chiefs and Head Men.

Article 1. The said Chippewa Nation cede to the United States, all that Tract of country, included within the following boundaries: Beginning at the junction of the Crow Wing and Mississippi Rivers between Twenty and thirty miles above where the Mississippi is crossed by the forty sixth parallel of North Latitude, and running thence to the North point of Lake St. Croix, one of the sources of the St. Croix River; thence to and along the dividing Ridge between the waters of Lake Superior and those of the Mississippi, to the sources of the Ocha Sua Sepe a tributary of the Chippewa River; thence to a point on the Chippewa River Twenty Miles below the out let of Lake De Flambeau; thence to the junction of the Wisconsin and Pelican Rivers; thence on an East course Twenty Five miles; thence southerly, on a course parallel with that of the Wisconsin River, to the line dividing the Territories of the Chippewas and Menomonies; thence to the Plover Portage; thence along the southern boundary of the Chippewa country, to the commencement of the boundary line dividing it from that of the Sioux, half a days march below the Falls on the Chippewa River; thence with said boundary line to the mouth of Wah tap River, at its junction with the Mississippi; & thence up the Mississippi to the place of beginning.

Article 2. In consideration of the cession aforesaid, The United States agree to make to the Chippewa Nation, annually, for the term of Twenty Years from the date of the ratification of this Treaty, the following payments.

1. Nine Thousand Five Hundred Dollars, to be paid in money.
2. Nineteen Thousand Dollars to be delivered in goods.
3. Three Thousand Dollars for establishing Three Black Smiths shops, supporting the Black Smiths, & furnishing them with Iron and Steel.
4. One Thousand Dollars for Farmers, and for supplying them and the Indians, with implements of labor, with grain or seed; and whatever else may be necessary to enable them to carry on their Agricultural pursuits.
5. Two Thousand Dollars in Provisions.
6. Five Hundred Dollars in Tobacco.

The Provisions and Tobacco, to be delivered at the same time with the goods, and the money to be paid; which time or times, as well as the place or places, where they are to be delivered, shall be fixed upon under the direction of the President of The United States.

The Black Smiths shops to be placed at such points in the Chippewa country, as shall be designated by the Superintendent of Indian Affairs, or under his direction.

If at the expiration of one or more years, the Indians should prefer to receive goods instead of the Nine Thousand Dollars agreed to be paid to them in money, they shall be at liberty to do so.

Fig. 10. *Treaty of 1837.* The first page of the handwritten manuscript treaty. Courtesy of the National Archives and Records Service.

Within one month of the signing of the treaty, missionary Reverend William T. Boutwell, who had witnessed the negotiations, reported to his superior in Boston, "the Ind{ian}s have no idea of leaving their country while they live—they know nothing of the duration of a man{'}s pleasure" (Boutwell 1837). This was certainly true of the leaders of the interior bands from Wisconsin. They had arrived late and played only a minor role in the proceedings, according to Van Antwerp's journal. Yet, the portion of the land cession in Wisconsin included their village sites—the area extended from the St. Croix River east to the location of what today are the cities of Crandon, Antigo, and Stevens Point, and from Stevens Point north to Rhinelander, and from Osceola and Eau Claire north to Lake St. Croix. In addition to the village of the interior bands, the cession included a great pine forest region and the headwaters of the Chippewa, Flambeau, Namekagon, Black, and Yellow rivers (Levi 1956, 55-56). As will be demonstrated shortly, the interior bands assumed American use of the timber from ceded lands would not result in permanent white occupation of the region. They steadfastly believed that access to their ceded lands as well as to resources and wildlife (as agreed to in the treaty) would allow them to perpetuate their traditional lifestyle.

Indian agent Henry Rowe Schoolcraft at the Mackinac Island-Sault Ste. Marie Agency in Michigan wondered "why it was that so little had been given for so large a cession, comprehending the very best lands of the Chippewas in the Mississippi Valley." On October 5, 1838, the agent was visited by Lyman M. Warren (Schoolcraft 1851, 611), the La Pointe trader who had arrived with the interior Wisconsin Indians, witnessed the treaty negotiations, and received twenty-five thousand dollars under the provision for the payment of traders' claims under Article 4 (Van Antwerp 1837, 0556-567; *App. 1*). Warren's reflections on the treaty proceedings substantiate Van Antwerp's official version and also offer important insights as to the motivations of the primary players in the drama.

According to Warren, St. Peter's agent Lawrence Taliaferro played an important behind-the-scenes role in the negotiations. Taliaferro, whose primary responsibilities included the Sioux Indians living in Minnesota, signed the treaty as a witness but is not mentioned in the official proceedings (Kappler 2: 493; *App. 2*). Taliaferro had strongly opposed the transfer of the Chippewa of Minnesota to the Sault Ste. Marie agency under Schoolcraft in 1827 and was actively involved in the behind-the-scenes posturing that led to the cession of Sioux claims in Wisconsin shortly after the Chippewa cession (Babcock 1924, 371-74). Warren said Taliaferro promoted the interests of the Minnesota Chippewas of the Upper Mississippi and eagerly sought to thwart those of the interior Wisconsin bands under the jurisdiction of his rival, agent Schoolcraft. Taliaferro had supposedly "loaded" Hole in the Day and another unnamed chief with presents before the proceedings began. Warren claimed (and the proceedings appear to verify) that "the Pillagers, in fact, made the treaty. The bands of the St. Croix and Chippewa Rivers, who really lived on the land and owned it, had, in effect, no voice. So {too} with respect to the La Pointe Indians." Members of the Lac Courte Oreilles and Lac du Flambeau bands also opposed the sale (Schoolcraft 1851, 611). Warren's observations lend a new perspective into the actions noted in the proceedings.

Warren contended that Dodge "really knew nothing of the fertility and value of the country purchased, having never set foot on it. Governor Dodge thought the tract chiefly valuable for its pine, and natural millpower; and there was no one to undeceive him." As a result of Dodge's persistence and Taliaferro's bribery, "the Chippewas managed badly—they knew nothing of *thousands,* or how the annuity would divide among so many." Warren claimed, for example, that the nineteen thousand dollars provided for goods under Article 2 of the treaty "would not exceed a breech-cloth and a pair of leggins apiece." Nevertheless, Warren said, the Indians "were, in fact, cowed down by the braggadocia of the flattered Pillager war chief, Hole-in-the-Day," whom Schoolcraft referred to as "one of the most hardened, bloody-thirsty wretches" among the Chippewas. For these reasons, according to Warren, Dodge obtained the area for much less than he was authorized to offer (Schoolcraft 1851, 611) even though he had promised to pay the Indians the full value of their lands.

In assessing Warren's comments, Schoolcraft recorded in his diary: "I have not the means of testing these facts, but have the highest confidence in the character, sense of justice, and good natural judgment of Gov. Dodge. He may have been ill advised of some facts. The Pillagers certainly do not, I think, as a band, own or occupy a foot of soil east of the Mississippi below Sandy Lake, but their warlike character has a sensible influence on those tribes, quite down to the St. Croix and Chippewa rivers. The sources of these rivers are valuable for only their pineries, and their valleys only become fertile below their falls and principal rapids" (School-craft 1851, 611).

While the official U. S. Government version of the treaty proceedings can be compared with eyewitness accounts like those of Warren and Reverend Boutwell, it is much more difficult to obtain information about the Chippewa perspective of the negotiations. The negotiations were particularly complex since the Chippewas were not organized into any single political entity that could speak with one voice through a recognized leader—even though Dodge acted as if they were. It is unclear as to how the decisions regarding who would speak in behalf of the assembled Chippewas were determined, but the evidence appears to substantiate Warren's claim that the interior bands from Wisconsin remained silent during the meetings with Dodge. Scholars do not know what took place or what was said as the Indians met by themselves between sessions with Dodge. Even so, scholars do know the Indians' silence at the face-to-face meetings with Dodge should not be equated with agreement.

As anthropologists have noted, many Indians customarily remain silent in ambiguous, uncertain, or unpredictable situations. Indian *silence,* which is often interpreted by non-Indians as *stoicism,* is more frequently "based on a caution which is at once related to fear of and to respect for the uncertain status of the other party." This same sense of caution and desire to preserve consensus and avoid conflict may explain the behavior of Indians who refused to attend treaty councils as well as that of those who remained silent or withdrew from treaty councils rather than voicing their opinions (Washburn 1975, 16-17; Wax and Thomas 1961, 306). Methodist minister Chomingwen Pond, a white woman who has served as a pastor for churches on the Lac du Flambeau and Bad River reservations in recent years, has observed that the Chippewas's reticence is often wrongly interpreted by whites as unfriendliness or even a lack of intelligence (*Wisconsin State Journal* 1990c, 25).

Also helpful in understanding Chippewa behavior at the 1837 treaty proceedings is what scholars have referred to as the Indian "ethic of non-interference," which most Indians follow unconsciously. As Rosalie H. Wax and Robert K. Thomas have observed, "the white man has been and is torn between two ideals: on the one hand, he believes in freedom, in minding his own business, and in the right of people to make up their own minds for themselves; but, on the other hand, he believes that he should be his brother's keeper and not abstain from advice, or even action" in his brother's behalf. In contrast, "the Indian society is unequivocal: interference of any form is forbidden, regardless of the folly, irresponsibility, or ignorance of your brother" (Wax and Thomas 1961, 308-09).

Flat Mouth's refusal to begin the treaty negotiations before the arrival of the interior bands because "to do so . . . might be considered an improper interference, and unfair towards them" (Van Antwerp 1837, 0549; *App. 1*) exemplifies the ethic of non-interference. Similarly, the ethic helps to explain Chippewa expressions of their fear of Governor Dodge at the negotiations. From earliest childhood, Indians are trained to "regard absolute non-interference in interpersonal relations as decent or normal and to react to even the mildest coercion in these areas with bewilderment, disgust, and fear" (Wax and Thomas 1961, 310). The Wind's expression of fear may well have represented such a reaction to Dodge's coercive efforts. After repeatedly refusing to negotiate with Dodge until the Wisconsin bands arrived, The Wind told Dodge: "when I look at you it frightens me. I cannot sufficiently estimate your importance, and it confuses me" (Van Antwerp 1837, 0551; *App. 1*).

It is also important to remember that the Chippewas, like other non-English-speaking Indians, often understood words and events in different terms than their white counterparts. Linguistic research reveals there was no single word in the nineteenth-century Chippewa language for *fishing,* so it is very likely that the convenient catchall Ojibwa word meaning "general foraging" with *any* kind of a device for *any* purpose was used by interpreters to translate the meaning of the treaty wording, "hunting and fishing" (Lurie 1987, 59-60). Such substitutions could render an Indian's understanding very different from a white person's understanding of treaty stipulations. And although most whites would see written words as taking priority over spoken, this is not true in Chippewa culture.

Since oral rather than written communication was the typical mode of Indian negotiations, the final written document to which Indians affixed an "X" or their symbols was not as important to them as their understanding of the verbal agreements made, a direct contradiction to most white people's assumptions. The following comment by ethnohistorian Wilcomb E. Washburn aptly describes some of the difficulties Indians had in dealing with American treaty commissioners:

> The white man as officeholder is, in many ways, a more perplexing and perverse figure to the Indian than the individual conqueror, or fur trapper, or explorer. Under the panoply of European formality the government representative communicated with Indian leaders, but too often the form and spirit were not in close juxtaposition. The Indian, valuing the spirit rather than the recorded form, which in his letterless society was, for the most part, superfluous, could not cope with the legalisms of the white man. Nor could an alien government sympathize with, let alone understand, the plight of a race organized into categories that had no parallels in the white bureaucratic machinery. (Washburn 1964, xiii)

As Washburn indicates, Indians left treaty negotiations with understandings based on the dialogue that had taken place while whites left with a written document confirming their intentions and goals if not their actual words as understood by the Indians. Several years before the parley at St. Peters, French visitor Alexis de

Tocqueville witnessed the U. S. government's conduct of Indian affairs and observed the impact of federal policy on the Indians, including the Chippewas in the Great Lakes region (1831-32, 134-45). Tocqueville maintained that there was a tremendous gulf between appearances and reality, and he argued that American Indian policy was skillfully designed to acquire Indian lands "with wonderful ease, quietly, legally, and philanthropically, without spilling blood and without violating a single one of the great principles of morality in the eyes of the world." While the American public might be fooled, Tocqueville believed "it is impossible to destroy men with more respect to the laws of humanity" (1848, 324-25, 339). In 1837 at St. Peters, Governor Dodge used the formalities of the treaty-making process to benefit the national interest, but he did not treat with the Chippewas in the same manner that an American diplomat would have been obliged to handle negotiations with a European power.

Interpreters played a key role in treaty negotiations. "The right understanding and successful issue of every negotiation depend upon their fidelity and ability," Indian Commissioner Harris informed Secretary of War Joel R. Poinsett in 1837 (Harris 1837c, 528). Appointed and paid by the Indian Office, interpreters were in fact representatives of the United States government who, as Commissioner Harris poignantly observed, helped to shape the outcome of each treaty negotiation (Satz 1975, 196). For that reason, even the interpreters whom modern readers might assume to have been unbiased were paid to act in the best interests of the U. S. government, not of the Indians.

Further complicating matters, interpreters sometimes had to use several languages in their attempts to convey the words of one negotiator to another. During the 1837 Chippewa parley, for example, an eyewitness reported, "it appeared as though neither the Governor or Indians understood the interpretation properly at the time, it having to pass from Indian into French and then into English before the Governor got the meaning & a high wind blowing at the time in an exposed place but after some time and one or two Repetitions The secretary was directed" what to write (Baker 1838). According to a missionary eyewitness to the 1837 treaty proceedings, government interpreter Peter Quinn was "a thick-mouthed, stammering Irishman" who was unable "to speak intelligibly" in either English or Ojibwa (Brunson 1872-79, 2: 83).

Although the Chippewas did not maintain their own written record of the 1837 proceedings, a number of disgruntled Indian participants sent messages to President Van Buren through missionary Frederick Ayer. Their complaints included inadequate compensation for ceded lands and the loss of fish, rice, sugar, and timber taken by a local trader without providing compensation. In one of these messages, The Wind of the Snake River area charged, as did Lyman Warren in his conversation with Agent Schoolcraft, that Hole in the Day played a leading role: "There were many Chiefs who spoke with the Gov. at St. Peters, at the Treaty. But only one however sold the land (the hole in the day). He does not own the land where I dwell, he is a mere Child" (The Wind 1837). These words could just as easily have been spoken by any of the Chippewas from the interior Wisconsin bands whose lands were ceded at St. Peters. In June of 1839, when Hole in the Day protested the transfer of annuity payments from St. Peters to La Pointe, he reminded Agent Taliaferro that he was the chief to whom Governor Dodge had given a copy of the 1837 treaty to hold because he was "the Ch{i}ef of all the Indians that sold their land'' (Hole in the Day 1839). By 1839, as the commissioner appointed to pay traders' claims against Chippewa mixed-bloods under Article 3 of the treaty noted, it was well known that ''the 'Leech Lake' Indians{,} a very warlike band of the Chippewas who took an active part in making the Treaty{,} had no interest or right whatever in the country ceded'' (Lyon 1839a).

Twenty-seven years after the signing of the 1837 treaty, a delegation of Chippewa chiefs, headmen, and warriors—including men from the bands at Lac Courte Oreilles, Lac du Flambeau, and La Pointe (Bad River and Red Cliff) in Wisconsin as well as from Fond du Lac in Minnesota and Ontonagon in the Upper Peninsula of Michigan—recalled the events of the meeting at St. Peters (Chippewas of Lake Superior 1864). The occasion was the drafting of a petition they signed and took to Washington for presentation to Commissioner of Indian Affairs William P. Dole. The bilingual petition refers to the 1837 treaty proceedings and the U. S. government's failure to fulfill various stipulations of that agreement. Leaders of the Bad River Reservation dictated the petition during the winter of 1864, and U. S. Interpreter Joseph Gunroe, a Chippewa mixed-blood from Bayfield, transcribed it verbatim in a two-column format, one column in Ojibwa and the other in English. This document contains a brief statement about the 1837 treaty proceedings from the Chippewa point of view.[14]

According to the bilingual petition, ''Great Father'' Martin Van Buren in Washington had assembled representatives of the Chippewa bands at St. Peters in July of 1837 to acquire the pinelands in order to provide timber for his people. The Indian response to Dodge's demand for a land cession in 1837 was supposedly as follows:

> So then Father, Our Great Father requests me to sell him my Pine Timber, our Great Father is mighty, therefore whatever he says would not be in vain, and whatever he promises to do he will fulfill.
>
> Very well, I will sell him the Pine Timber as he requests me to. From the usual height of cutting a tree down and upwards to top is what I sell you, I reserve the root of the tree. Again this I hold in my hand the Maple Timber, also the Oak Timber, also this Straw which I hold in my hand. Wild Rice is what we call this. These I do not sell.
>
> That you may not destroy the Rice in working the timber. Also the Rapids and Falls in the Streams I will lend you to saw your timber, also a small tract of land to make a garden to live on while you are working the timber.
>
> I do not make you a present of this, I merely lend it to you. This is my answer, My Great Father is great, and out of respect for him I will not refuse him, but as an exchange of civility I must see and feel the benefits of this loan, and the promises fulfilled.
>
> This was the Indians answer. (Chippewas of Lake Superior 1864)

Members of the 1864 delegation claimed, ''we do not get, receive what was promised, which was part of the pay for the Timber I sold. For instance the employees, three years was all they worked, also Beef and Working Cattle were promised us but we did not see any, we think they were never given to us.'' The very reason for the presence of the delegation in Washington was that, with regard to the Treaty of 1837 and other agreements with the United States, ''certain it is that the Indian has failed to see the promises made to him fulfilled'' (Chippewas of Lake Superior 1864).

27

There are several discrepancies between the Indians' remembrance of the 1837 proceedings in 1864, the official proceedings of the treaty, and the signed treaty. For example, the number of years for the annuity was actually twenty not twenty-five as claimed by the delegates in 1864. Yet the paragraphs quoted above reflect the substance, albeit not the exact wording, of the comments of the Chippewas who spoke during the negotiations based on Van Antwerp's journal and the comments of trader Lyman Warren. As Warren's son, interpreter William Warren[15] noted some years later, "in order to arrive at the truth of a fact obtained of an Indian, respecting their past history, a person must go from one old man, to another of different villages or sections of the tribe, and obtain the version of each; if they all agree in the main fact, even if they disagree in the details, you can then be certain that the circumstance has happened, and the tale has a substantial origin"[16] (Warren 1851, 47). Chippewa Indians memorized the details of important events such as treaty negotiations and taught them to their young who in turn passed the information on to the next generation with remarkable accuracy (Keller 1981, 3).

Anthropologist Mary Druke reminds us that among Indian peoples the spoken word was weighted more heavily than the written word. While oral traditions of treaties may not be verbatim accounts of the treaty proceedings, they "convey an accepted interpretation of relationships based on agreements made in council negotiations" (Druke 1985, 90-91). Indian memory, as one scholar has noted, is very reliable. "For a person who can't run to a bookshelf or a notebook to look up either vital or trivial information, reliance on memory becomes very important in everyday life." As a result of having to learn "by heart" multitudes of details about rituals, kinship and other social relationships, and the names and uses of hundreds of plants and animals, for example, "nonliterate people have more finely developed memories than do literate people" (Allen 1986, 66).

Oral traditions of treaties were open to criticism by Indian listeners who either were present at the time of a recounted occurrence or heard other accounts of the tradition against which to judge the narrative. Although the 1837 Chippewa treaty did not, for example, specifically mention anything about reserving the right to make maple sugar, the reference to the maple trees in 1864 by Indians from various Chippewa bands is understandable given the number of times the Indians mentioned making sugar during the proceedings in 1837 and given Dodge's promise to discuss the matter with the president. When the Chippewas signed the treaty of 1837, they fully expected to continue eating traditional foods—including maple sugar. As one scholar has noted, "maple sugar occupied such a central role in Chippewa culture, commerce and diet that one can argue from historical and anthropological evidence that . . . these Indians, regardless of treaty omissions, must have reasonably expected their access to maple trees to continue long after they had ceded traditional lands. This deduction is confirmed by an array of documents and by specific events during the treaty period" (Keller 1989, 124, 126).

In reviewing the events surrounding the 1837 treaty, it is clear that the Chippewas attempted to explain the importance of their relationship to the natural resources of Wisconsin and that they assumed the whites only wanted access to certain resources, not the land itself (Vennum 1988, 256). Many times during the proceedings the Indians insisted on reserving usufructuary rights.[17] Governor Dodge, anxious to conclude negotiations and concerned about a possible outbreak of hostilities between the Chippewa and the Sioux Indians, agreed to recognize usufructuary rights in the treaty but insisted on adding the phrase ''during the pleasure of the President'' (Van Antwerp 1837, 0566; *App. 1*).

About a year and a half after he negotiated the 1837 treaty, Dodge complained to Indian Commissioner Crawford that the medals and flags he had promised would be distributed among the Indians had still not been procured by the Indian Office. ''The officers of the Government must comply with all promises they may make the Indians,'' he told Crawford, adding, ''if they deceive them once, they never afterwards have confidence in them'' (Dodge 1839, 1187). Dodge was correct. But it was his promise of continued usufructuary rights rather than of medals and flags that would ultimately be the basis by which the Chippewas determined their confidence in officials of the United States government.

Removal of the Chippewa Indians from Wisconsin was not mentioned in the Treaty of 1837. In fact, as already noted, these Indians were told in Article 5 of the ratified treaty that they could continue to hunt, fish, and gather upon the lands, rivers, and lakes in the ceded territory ''during the pleasure of the President'' (Kappler 2: 492; *App. 2*). The interior Wisconsin bands—who as Reverend Boutwell observed ''know nothing of the duration of a man{'}s pleasure'' (Boutwell 1837)—apparently agreed to abide by the treaty only after becoming convinced that they would receive a portion of the goods and money flowing from the agreement without having to abandon their villages, the land upon which they hunted and gathered, or their fishing areas.

The annuities proved to be a mixed blessing to the Chippewas. Governor Dodge predicted shortly after the Senate ratified the treaty that the annuities would ''have a salutary effect'' in helping to control the Indians since they placed ''great reliance'' on the funds (Dodge 1838e, 176). The Chippewas received cash payments and goods as specified in the treaty. War Department officials made a concerted effort after 1837 to convince the Indians to accept guns, ammunition, blankets, and other merchandise as a portion of their annuities in lieu of money so that they would be less dependent upon the traders who tended to ''monopolize'' the cash payment. Viewing federal officials as ''intruders'' in their business relations with the Indians, traders belittled the merchandise supplied by the government (Dodge 1838d, 1029; Dodge 1839, 1186). Sometimes the goods supplied by the government had no value to the Indians. In 1839, for example, the War Department shipped saddles and bridles to the Chippewas at La Pointe who had no horses and no need for them along the forested and roadless south shore of Lake Superior. Despite the subagent's protest that the goods were ''of no earthly value'' to the Indians, another shipment was sent in 1840 (Bushnell 1840a). Guns sent to La Pointe rarely included ammunition, but sometimes this turned out to be a blessing because the weapons were so poorly constructed that many exploded upon firing, crippling Chippewa hunters. Other shoddy government goods such as thin blankets and cheap pots also rankled the Indians and gave weight to the traders' criticism of government efforts to provide goods instead of money (Danziger 1979, 81; U. S. Congress 1849, 537).

Federal efforts to convince the Chippewas to accept goods in lieu of cash did not stop the Indians from buying goods on credit from traders. The purchase of fishing nets on credit from the American Fur Company continued unabated after 1837 as did the whites' demand for Lake Superior fish. A federal official observed in 1839, ''the Indians are encouraged to exertion in this branch of business, by the offer of a fair price for all the fish, they can catch, payable on the delivery of the fish at the different Store houses built to receive them'' (Jones 1838; Lyon 1839b, 97-98).

A large portion of Chippewa annuities continued to end up in the pockets of traders after 1837. Indian agents continued to permit the traders to settle their accounts at the annuity payment grounds. George Copway,[18] an acculturated Chippewa from Canada who witnessed numerous annuity payments in Wisconsin and elsewhere in the Great Lakes region in the years following the 1837 treaty, claimed ''the dissipation, misery, and ruin'' of the Lake Superior Chippewa people was directly related to annuities provided in treaties. According to Copway, annuity payments attracted people having ''white faces (with black hearts),'' unscrupulous white traders and whiskey peddlers as well as other ''unprincipled men and vagabonds'' who were ''no better than pickpockets'' (Copway 1847, 126-28).

Increasingly, the flexible and personalized exchange relationships between the Chippewa trappers and white traders in Wisconsin were replaced by the poorly organized annuity system of the federal government.[19] The system, characterized by ''tedious journeys'' for many to the payment site and long delays once there, interfered with the traditional late fall rice-gathering and the winter hunting patterns of the Chippewa people. The insertion of the annuity system into the Chippewa hunting-fishing-fur trading system not only disrupted traditional economic cycles but also gave the United States increased leverage in dealing with the Indians as they became dependent on the annuities. Indian agents took over many of the functions previously performed by fur traders in Chippewa society (Richmond 1846, 990; Danziger 1979, 79-81; Clifton 1987, 13-14; James 1954, 44).

Another significant impact of the 1837 treaty was the appearance of whites on the ceded lands.[20] American entrepreneurs flooded into the northern Wisconsin pine lands even before the treaty was ratified by the U. S. Senate on June 15, 1838, nearly eleven months after its negotiation. Among the well-known traders who signed the 1837 treaty as witnesses and subsequently exploited the forest wealth thrown open to Americans by that agreement were Henry Hastings Sibley, Hercules L. Dousman, and Lyman M. Warren (Fries 1951, 11; Babcock 1924, 374; Bartlett 1921, 37; Citizens of the Pineries {1840}). Ironically, as the cutting of the pine forests progressed, white-tailed deer flourished and the subsistence value of the ceded land actually increased to the Chippewas, making the old War Department strategy of decreasing Indian hunting grounds by land cession treaties in order to encourage removal ineffective[21] (Clifton 1987, 14).

American officials had plenty of information indicating that any effort to remove the Chippewas from Wisconsin was bound to fail. Six months after the ratification of the 1837 treaty, La Pointe subagent Daniel P. Bushnell advised Territorial Governor Dodge, ''the general policy of our Government in removing the Indians west of the Mississippi can never be carried into effect in relation to . . . {the interior bands of Wisconsin} Chippewas.'' His reasons were twofold: the Indians would ''have to change their habits entirely,'' and they would expose themselves west of the Mississippi River to the Sioux, ''their natural enemies.'' As a result of these circumstances, any effort to remove them would be ''highly improper, and inhumane'' (Bushnell 1839a). In 1840, the subagent reported that the interior bands ''subsist at present by hunting, fishing, and on the wild rice found in the lakes and rivers.'' He again stated that any attempt to remove them and deprive them of their "usufructuary right" under the 1837 treaty would meet strong opposition (Bushnell {1840b}, 339).

The 1837 treaty also had an important impact on the Chippewas along the southern shore of Lake Superior. Chief Buffalo of the La Pointe Band, whom Governor Henry Dodge referred to as "a man of great influence among his tribe, and very friendly to the whites" (Dodge 1838b), spoke the sentiments of the Indians of the region in a message directed to Governor Dodge:

> . . . I have nothing to say about the Treaty, good, or bad, because the country was not mine; but when it comes my turn I shall know how to act. If the Americans want my land, I shall know what to say. I did not like to stand in the road of the Indians at St. Peters. I listened to our Great Father's words, & laid them in my heart. I have not forgotten them. The Indians acted like children; they tried to cheat each other and got cheated themselves. When it comes my turn to sell my land, I do not think I shall give it up as they did.
>
> ....
>
> Father I speak for my people, not for myself. I am an old man. My fire is almost out— there is but little smoke. When I set in my wigwam & smoke my pipe, I think of what has past and what is to come, and it makes my heart shake. When business comes before us we will try and act like Chiefs. If any thing is to be done, it had better be done straight. (Buffalo 1837)

Five years after Buffalo spoke these words, the elderly chief faced American Treaty Commissioner Robert Stuart who was determined to acquire all remaining Chippewa lands in Wisconsin. As Stuart discovered, Buffalo's "fire" was far from out.

3 The 1842 Copper Treaty

As American lumberjacks felled the woodlands of the Chippewa land cession in the late 1830s and early 1840s, reports of vast copper deposits along the shores of Lake Superior and the Isle Royale led federal officials to push for new land cessions from the Chippewa Indians[22] (Bushnell 1839b, 489; Sterling 1840; Jones 1841; Crawford 1842, 379). The reports of rich mineral deposits in the north were well-founded, for the region contained one of the most extensive deposits of surface copper anywhere in the world.[23] Centuries before the birth of Christ, Indians had mined deep copper pits along the shore and used copper in making arrowheads, fishhooks, knives, needles, and bracelets.[24] Chippewa mining was so extensive that scholars claim Indian miners probably worked every modern industrial mining site dotting the shore of Lake Superior (*Fig. 11*). In 1837, the Michigan state legislature appointed geologist Douglas Houghton as director of its newly created Department of Geology. Houghton's surveys in the early 1840s triggered American interest in the entire Lake Superior region (Keller 1978, 16; Nute 1944, 165; Robbins 1960, 141).

Many Americans hoped to profit from the copper deposits. War Department officials wanted to acquire all Indian title to the Lake Superior shoreline, and those who hoped to gain patronage positions from the department offered their services to influence the Indians to remove (Warren 1841). In March of 1841, however, Gouverneur Kemble suggested that American interests could be served without purchasing the ore-bearing lands from the Indians. Kemble, a New York foundry owner[25] and Democratic Congressman, wrote to President Van Buren's secretary of war, Joel R. Poinsett, and then to the new Whig administration's secretary of war, John Bell, recommending employing Chippewa men instead of whites as mine workers and paying the Indians a percentage of the money earned from the copper mining. But Commissioner of Indian Affairs T. Hartley Crawford, who served both the Van Buren and the Harrison-Tyler administrations (Satz 1979b), flatly rejected Kemble's plan of joint Chippewa and American involvement in Lake Superior mining efforts because it would have perpetuated Chippewa ownership of the region's mineral resources (Keller 1978, 17). Instead, Crawford called for the acquisition of all Chippewa lands in the region, noting control of the southern shore of Lake Superior was "very important" to American interests (Crawford 1842, 379).

The Treaty of October 4, 1842 (*Fig. 12*), with the Mississippi and Lake Superior Chippewas accomplished Crawford's purpose by ceding land north of the 1837 cession. Following the cession, copper mining boomed: the region led the world in copper production by 1890 (Keller 1978, 17).

Acting Superintendent of Indian Affairs Robert Stuart of Michigan (*Fig. 13*) negotiated the 1842 treaty at La Pointe. Stuart, a former agent of the American Fur Company (AFC) who was active in Whig political circles in Michigan (Satz 1975, 162), had indicated a strong interest in economic opportunities in the Lake Superior region as early as the 1820s (Nute 1926, 485). The Indians who assembled at the

Fig. 11. *Ancient Mining on Lake Superior.* A drawing by J. C. Tidball, from Henry Rowe Schoolcraft, *Historical and Statistical Information Respecting the History, Condition and Prospects of the Indian Tribes of the United States,* Vol. 5 (1855). Courtesy of the Library of Congress. LC-USZ62-2088

treaty grounds agreed to cede the last of the Chippewa lands in northern Wisconsin (see *Fig. 7*) only after Stuart made oral explanations about the articles he included in the final treaty: the provision for continued hunting, fishing, and gathering privileges in ceded territory; the payments amounting to $75,000 to traders and $15,000 to mixed-bloods; the $5,000 agriculture fund to be expended under the direction of the secretary of war; and the twenty-five year annuity schedule with $31,200 in cash, goods, and services to be "equally divided" between the Mississippi and Lake Superior bands (Kappler 2: 542-45; *App. 4*).

Official documentation for the 1842 treaty is scanty since unlike the 1837 negotiations neither Treaty Commissioner Stuart nor Secretary Jonathan Hulbert kept a journal, or at least neither forwarded one to Commissioner of Indian Affairs Crawford. But historian Mark Keller errs in stating that "government documents are silent on the event" (1981, 10). Stuart corresponded with Commissioner Craw-

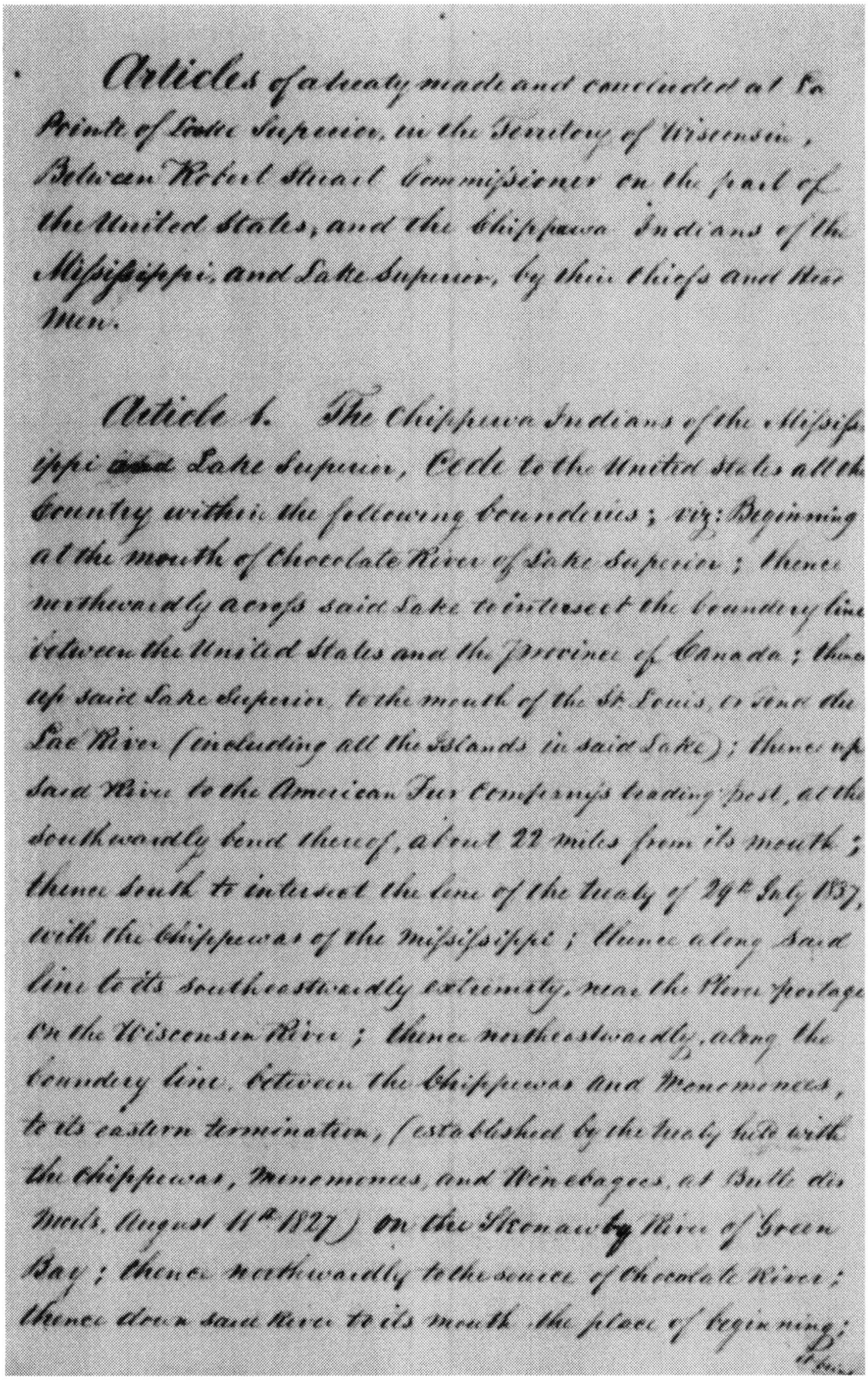

Articles of a treaty made and concluded at La Pointe of Lake Superior, in the Territory of Wisconsin, between Robert Stuart Commissioner on the part of the United States, and the Chippewa Indians of the Mississippi and Lake Superior, by their chiefs and head men.

Article 1. The Chippewa Indians of the Mississippi and Lake Superior, cede to the United States all the country within the following boundaries; viz: Beginning at the mouth of Chocolate River of Lake Superior; thence northwardly across said Lake to intersect the boundary line between the United States and the Province of Canada; thence up said Lake Superior, to the mouth of the St. Louis, or Fond du Lac River (including all the Islands in said Lake); thence up said River to the American Fur Company's trading post, at the southwardly bend thereof, about 22 miles from its mouth; thence south to intersect the line of the treaty of 29th July 1837, with the Chippewas of the Mississippi; thence along said line to its southeastwardly extremity, near the Plover portage on the Wisconsin River; thence northeastwardly, along the boundary line, between the Chippewas and Menomonees, to its eastern termination, (established by the treaty held with the Chippewas, Menomonees, and Winnebagoes, at Butte des Morts, August 11th 1827) on the Skonawby River of Green Bay; thence northwardly to the source of Chocolate River; thence down said River to its mouth, the place of beginning;

Fig. 12. *Treaty of 1842.* The first page of the handwritten manuscript. Courtesy of the National Archives and Records Service.

Fig. 13. *Robert and Elizabeth Stuart.* Acting Superintendent of the Michigan Superintendency Robert Stuart, who negotiated the 1842 treaty, was described by one
contemporary as "a severe man in all things" (Ghent 1936, 176). Courtesy of the
State Archives of Michigan.

ford in Washington regarding the treaty (Stuart 1842a, b; *Apps. 3A, 3B*). He also responded to a letter from Reverend David Greene of the American Board of Commissioners for Foreign Missions[26] in Boston inquiring "whether the later Treaty contemplates the expatriation of the Ojibways, to Queen Victoria's dominions, or some worse place" (Stuart 1842c). In June of 1843, less than three months after ratification of the treaty, Stuart corresponded with Commissioner Crawford about the provision for continued usufructuary rights in ceded territory (Stuart 1843b). Additionally in a letter written two years after the negotiations, Stuart reconstructed the events of the proceedings for Crawford to settle a dispute arising from the treaty (Stuart 1844; *App. 3C*).

Other American eyewitnesses included missionary Reverend Leonard H. Wheeler and his interpreter, Henry Blatchford. Interpreter Blatchford prepared a contemporaneous journal of the proceedings that Wheeler forwarded to his missionary headquarters in May of 1843 (Wheeler 1843). Also present at the parley was La Pointe Subagent Alfred Brunson. He wrote Wisconsin Territorial Governor James D. Doty about the proceedings (Brunson 1843b, c) and later reflected on events in his published reminiscences (Brunson 1872-79, 2: 165, 185-86, 206-07).

The evidence from American eyewitnesses, including that from Stuart, indicates the commissioner used heavy-handed tactics to secure the treaty. Stuart informed the Indians assembled at La Pointe, using language very similar to Dodge's at St. Peters in 1837, that their Great Father in Washington "knows that you are poor, that your lands are not good, and that you have very little game left, to feed and clothe your women & children—He therefore pities your condition, and has sent me to see what can be done to benefit you." Stuart claimed that according to the Treaty of Fond du Lac of 1826, the minerals found on their lands "no longer" belonged to the Indians but to the United States. He also reported, "the whites have been asking your Great Father to give them permission to take away all {minerals} they can find —but your Great Father wishes first to make a new treaty, and to pay you well for these lands and minerals; he knows you are poor and needy." Stuart cautioned the Indians against listening to "some fools {who} have been telling you Squaw stories" that the Great Father was "very anxious to buy your lands & will give you a great price for them" (Stuart 1844, 0061, 0064; *App. 3C*).

Like Governor Dodge in 1837, Stuart used the popular white concept of majority rule to permit the assembled representatives of the Minnesota bands and the Christianized bands from Michigan to outmaneuver those of the Lake Superior Wisconsin bands who were not interested in ceding their lands. "Your Great Father will not treat with you as Bands, but as a Nation," Stuart commented, adding very shrewdly, "treaties are often made when whole Bands are absent, which could not be but on the principle that all your lands are common property, and the majority of the Nation can sell or not as they please, the absentees being entitled to their share of the annuities." Although it was "all right" for the bands to live apart and to choose their own hunting grounds, Stuart told them their lands were "common property" and could be ceded by tribal leaders assembled for that purpose just as annuities "must all be paid at one place" (Stuart 1844, 0067; *App. 3C*).

Stuart informed the Chippewas that the whites "are numerous as the pigeons in the Spring" and that other Indian tribes had already "been sent west of the Mississippi, to make room for the whites." He nevertheless assured the Indians it was the minerals on their lands, not the lands themselves, that the whites desired at this time. "But as these lands may at some future day be required," he stated, "your great Father does not wish to leave you without a home." He proposed that when their ceded lands were required by the president, a "home in common for you all" would be provided in present-day Minnesota (Stuart 1844, 0062, 0064; *App. 3C*).

At first, the chiefs of the Wisconsin bands from the Lake Superior region remained silent. As the Chippewas later recalled the event, "the Chiefs along the Lake Shore did not say a word, not being willing to sell or make any agreement" (Chippewas of Lake Superior 1864). Stuart, failing as did Governor Dodge in 1837 to understand the significance of the silence, attempted to hurry the negotiations to a conclusion. Chiefs from other regions then spoke. Shingoob of Fond du Lac protested Stuart's assertion that the Indians had surrendered all rights to minerals on their lands in 1826. He charged that the Chippewas "had been deceived" by the treaty commissioners at that parley. There were similar complaints about the 1837 treaty at St. Peters being "a lying, cheating concern." Chief White Crow from Lac du Flambeau alluded to prior discrepancies between what the Chippewas understood treaty provisions to be and what the words of the white negotiators actually told other whites when he stated, "We want nothing wrong on Paper. You may think I am troubl{e}some but the way the treaty was made at St. Peters, we think was wrong, we want nothing of the kind again." White Crow informed the assembled Indians he was very reluctant to "touch the pen" to the treaty for fear that "he should be called upon immidiately {*sic*} to remove." Chief Buffalo of La Pointe agreed and complained Stuart was not allowing the Indians enough time to deliberate on the important issues he had presented for their consideration (Wheeler 1843). La Pointe subagent Alfred Brunson, a Methodist missionary and Wisconsin pioneer, bluntly stated, "the Indians did not act free & voluntary, but felt themselves pressed into the measure" by Stuart who according to "several reputable witnesses," had told them "it was no difference whether they signed or not" because "the Gov{ernmen}t would take the land" (Brunson 1843c).

Stuart assured the Lake Shore chiefs, as had Dodge in 1837, that they would not be asked to leave ceded lands for a very long time. When the suspicious chiefs demanded to know the exact length of time, Stuart responded—depending on the individual reporting the event—"as long as we behaved well & are peaceable with our grandfather {in Washington} & his white children" (Martin {1842}), "not probbably {*sic*} during . . . {your} lifetime" (Wheeler 1843), "we and our children after us might be permitted to live on our land fifty years or even a hundred if we lived on friendly terms with the Whites" (Buffalo *et al.* 1851), or "that they were never to be disturbed if they behaved themselves" (Armstrong {1892}, 288). Stuart himself informed Reverend David Greene of the American Board of Commissioners for Foreign Missions in Boston shortly after the treaty negotiations, "I have the pleasure to state, that it is not expected the Indians will have to remove from their present locations, for many years to come. There are a few on and near the mineral district, who, in imitation of Abraham and Lot, may have to move to the right, or left." Nevertheless, Stuart assured Greene that removal of the Wisconsin Indians would not occur in the foreseeable future. As a further inducement to obtaining Greene's support of the treaty, Stuart told the missionary, "I have consulted with your people as to the best locations for schools, Missionaries, Gov{ernmen}t Officers &c; to settle at, and hope to be able to do some good in that way, as well as in nominating good men to the Gov{ernmen}t appointments, should the Treaty be ratified'' (Stuart 1842c). Six months after making these statements, and shortly after the ratification of the treaty, Stuart opposed suggestions that the Indian Office remove the Lake Superior Chippewas to Minnesota. He advised Indian Commissioner Crawford:

> There are those who think that all these Indians should be at once removed to the unceded district; but this would not be in conformity with the spirit of the treaty, nor could it be easily accomplished just now, as they have considerable game, fish, and other inducements to attach them to their present homes; but so soon as they realize the benefits of schools, and the other arts of civilization, which I trust we shall be able to cluster around them, there will be less difficulty in inducing them to renounce their present habits. (Stuart 1843b)

Although Stuart underestimated the Indians' attachment to their ''habits,'' his observation that removal would not be ''in conformity with the spirit of the treaty'' coincided with their understanding of the agreement.

The actual wording of the published treaty provision appears in Article 2:

> The Indians stipulate for the right of hunting on the ceded territory, with the other usual privileges of occupancy, until required to remove by the President of the United States, and that the laws of the United States shall be continued in force, in respect to their trade and inter course {*sic*} with the whites, until otherwise ordered by Congress. (Kappler 2: 542-43; *App. 4*)

There was great controversy following the treaty's ratification as to the exact meaning of this provision and the similar statement in the 1837 treaty (Kappler 2: 492; *App. 2*). The interpretation of these treaty provisions continues to be a source of controversy today.

In 1892, Benjamin G. Armstrong of Ashland, a southerner who moved to Wisconsin during the territorial period, claimed in his reminiscences that Treaty Commissioner Stuart had specifically told the Chippewas they ''were never to be disturbed {in their possession of the ceded lands} if they behaved themselves'' (Armstrong {1892}, 288). Armstrong's reminiscences provide a sympathetic account of the Wisconsin Chippewas. Married to the niece of Chief Buffalo, who had adopted him as his son, Armstrong was a ''sturdy defender'' of the Wisconsin Chippewas (Armstrong {1892}, 175).

Recently, anthropologist James A. Clifton has challenged Armstrong's version of Stuart's alleged promise. Calling Armstrong ''an inconsequential figure,'' Clifton stated unequivocally in an article in the 1987 issue of *Transactions*, ''there is no independent suggestion of the truth of this assertion {by Armstrong}—that continued occupancy and use rights were contingent on good behavior as there is little support for other such claims in Armstrong's reminiscences'' (Clifton 1987, 36 n. 44). In a 1988 Associated Press news release, Clifton attacked recent court rulings restoring Chippewa hunting, fishing, and gathering rights in ceded territory, claiming the rulings relied heavily on Armstrong's memoirs. The Wisconsin news media paid considerable attention to Clifton's assertions because of possible implications on court decisions relating to rights reserved by the Chippewas (*Eau Claire Leader-Telegram* 1988a). Professor Clifton's contention that Armstrong's claims about

Chippewa reserved rights cannot be independently corroborated is erroneous and, as will be noted, is clearly refuted by eyewitnesses to the treaty proceedings.[27]

The Indian recollection of the treaty proceedings as reported shortly after the negotiations supports the conclusion that Commissioner Stuart used harsh measures to secure the agreement. Less than three months after the parley concluded on August 4, 1842, Chief Buffalo of La Pointe sent a message to subagent Brunson through interpreter and treaty witness Lyman Warren indicating the La Pointe band's displeasure with the treaty.[28] Buffalo stated bluntly he was "ashamed" of it, and he charged that Stuart had refused to listen to any Indians opposing the measure. Buffalo personally requested Brunson to ask the Great Father in Washington why he had sought "to oppress his children in this remote country" (Buffalo 1842). Shortly after Buffalo dictated his words of opposition to the treaty and to Stuart's handling of the negotiations, Stuart wrote Commissioner Crawford to assure him that the Chippewas were "highly delighted with the kind and generous dealing of the Government toward them" (Stuart 1842b, 0196; *App. 3B*), but Subagent Brunson sent the War Department ample evidence to refute Stuart's claim (Brunson 1843a, b; Buffalo 1842; Martin {1842}; White Crow 1842).

The correspondence Brunson forwarded to Commissioner Crawford demonstrated that Chief Buffalo was not alone in his criticism of Stuart's handling of the negotiations. Chief White Crow from Lac du Flambeau, for example, also complained about Stuart's insistence that it made no difference whether or not a particular chief signed the treaty since the President would take the land if a majority of chiefs signed (White Crow 1842). Chief Martin of Lac Courte Oreilles, who claimed he had "never touched the pen" to sell lands before, also provided a communication to be shared with Commissioner Crawford. "I & my brother chiefs refused to touch the pen," Martin assured Crawford, until Stuart promised that the Wisconsin Chippewas would be "permitted to live on the land as long as we behaved well & are peaceable with our grand father {in Washington} & his white children" (Martin {1842}). The statements of Chiefs Buffalo, White Crow, and Martin were forwarded to Commissioner of Indian Affairs Crawford on January 8, 1843, a month before the treaty was ratified by the Senate, and more than two months before it was proclaimed by President John Tyler[29] (Brunson 1843b).

Brunson also sent Crawford a report of a council held at La Pointe on January 5, 1843. At the council, Chief Buffalo had refuted Stuart's contention that the Chippewas had signed away their mineral rights to northern Wisconsin at Fond du Lac in 1826. The chief informed the assembled representatives of bands from Wisconsin, Minnesota, and Michigan that the Chippewas had been tricked into ceding land in 1837 at St. Peters "for almost nothing," and he repeated his charge that Stuart had refused to let him speak at the recent treaty parley at La Pointe. Some warriors then stepped forward to speak. Their hearts "pained" by the treaties of 1837 and 1842, they requested a reservation be set aside so their children would have "a resting place" in Wisconsin. Their words as recorded by the subagent, with his parenthetical comments, are as follows (Brunson 1843a):

Our grand father bought our lands for the copper it contains. There is a piece of land where this metal is not found; the trees are not good (pine), & there is nothing there that the pale faces can make use of. We want our Grand father to reserve us this land, where we can make our sugar & plant our gardens. (At this they presented us a piece of birch bark on which was sketched a rough map of Bad River from the falls to the mouth.)

Contrary to Stuart's contention that the Chippewas were "highly delighted" with his dealing with them at La Pointe, there was considerable criticism of the commissioner among the Wisconsin Chippewas, who repeatedly told American officials that their signatures on the treaty were obtained only after assurances that they would be able to remain in Wisconsin.

Pressure from traders had also undoubtedly contributed to the acceptance of Stuart's terms at the 1842 parley. According to the treaty, Stuart was to examine and then approve or disprove claims against the Indians that were to be paid out of funds provided by the United States in payment for the land it was acquiring. The list of approved claimants appended to the treaty by Stuart included his secretary for the proceedings, a majority of the witnesses to the treaty, and Stuart's former employer and close friend John Jacob Astor of the American Fur Company. These individuals had considerable influence among the Chippewas and received the lion's share of the $75,000 set aside for Indian debts (Kappler 2: 544-45; *App. 4*).

Ratification of the Treaty of October 4, 1842, took more than four months (*Fig. 14*). The correspondence of the American Fur Company (AFC) reveals that the company, whose claims were recognized by former company agent Stuart at the negotiations, lobbied hard for ratification. As Michigan Senator William Woodbridge confided to AFC President Ramsey Crooks, the treaty was "in much danger" in the Senate. Opponents raised several objections. Some argued the land was not yet needed. Others believed Commissioner Stuart, who had previously worked for the company, had treated the company's claims too favorably. For some senators, opposition to the treaty was a means of venting their "vindictive hostility" toward Governor James Doty, a longtime friend of Commissioner Stuart and a strong supporter of the treaty. Finally, there were objections to the treaty provision continuing U. S. laws (prohibiting the introduction of liquor and such) in the ceded territory as a violation of the principle of state rights. Senator Woodbridge, cautioning Crooks to burn his letter after reading it, urged the AFC official to redouble his lobby efforts against the treaty before it assumed "a party character" (Woodbridge 1843).

Whatever political machinations secured ratification of the treaty, the Chippewas had a clear understanding of what they had accepted at La Pointe. Chief Martin's contention that the Chippewas had been assured they could remain on their lands as long as they behaved was repeated to federal officials years later in 1864 by the Chippewa delegation from Lac Courte Oreilles, Lac du Flambeau, and La Pointe (Bad River and Red Cliff) visiting Washington that year. Although exact identification of the members of the delegation is difficult to determine because the Chippewas reuse names in different generations and because names reappear in several locales, Canadian scholar John D. Nichols has concluded that at least three members of the delegation may have been signers of the 1842 treaty (Nichols 1988, 3). According to the statement made by the delegation, the 1842 proceedings ended as follows:

Then it was that the Chief White Crow spoke, he spoke in regard to every thing, and all the business being transacted at the time.

> And said to . . . {Stuart}, My Father I understand you to say that you want the Mineral, well then I will comply with the wish of our Great Father in asking me to sell him the Mineral which he wants.
>
> I do not give you the land, it is the Mineral only that I sell if there is any to be found on my land. I do not cede the Land, as he cried with a loud voice turning to his fellow Indians in which they all responded, with Eh! Eh!
>
> And as my Great Father promises and agrees I accept. I agree with the proposition that the payment should be for Twenty Five Years, and also that I shall see the end of my payments here.
>
> Then he was answered back, and told that he any how had the privilege of remaining on the land for Fifty Years, and even for a Hundred Years, as he owned and had possession of the land, he has a right to live on it.
>
> But then there may be a time that your Great Father will call you to a Council and ask you to sell him the land you live on. (Chippewas of Lake Superior 1864)

In 1864, as in 1842, Chippewa leaders from the Lake Superior country were convinced that they would not be asked to leave their lands as long as they remained at peace with the Americans.

Several years after the bilingual petition was presented in Washington, La Pointe Agent John H. Knight forwarded to Indian Commissioner Ely S. Parker a speech made in 1869 by Chippewa orator Black Bird[30] to a council held at Bad River. The speech (with comments added in brackets by Knight) was sent as a "specimen of Chippewa oratory furnished for . . . information and entertainment." In his comments, Black Bird said the Chippewas had been "robbed" of their lands by the treaties of 1837 and 1842.

> My name is Black Bird in whose mouth there is no lie. A lie never has had a place in my mouth since I was born. What these speakers have said is as true as everybody in these parts will testify to. The man who acted for us when the first treaty was made was named Magegawbaw and the man that acted for us when the mineral lands were ceded was named Obiskawgawgee (the White Crane). [The speaker was here referring to what previous speakers had stated that only the minerals and timber were ceded at the St. Peters treaty & treaty of '37; the lands, birch, oak & maple timber were reserved by them also the rice fields.] Who was it that put in the treaty a cession of our lands? It must have been the Commissioner. We utter nothing against our Great Father nor his Agent. But it is our Great Father's place to put these things right. His arms are long and strong, he has much power, he is great.

Black Bird concluded his remarks by noting, "the lands still belong to us. We have never sold the lands. When our Great Father shall have made these things right with our people, we will be satisfied, then and not until then" (Black Bird 1869). Thus, as late as 1869, oral tradition about Chippewa reserved rights was consistent with the views of the band leaders present at the actual negotiations in 1842.

The negotiations of 1842, along with those of 1837, created the basis for a later, prolonged dispute over the meaning of Chippewa reserved hunting, fishing, and gathering rights and the meaning of the phrase "during the pleasure of the President of the United States." More than two months before the ratification of the 1842 treaty in March of 1843, La Pointe Subagent Alfred Brunson raised serious questions about the agreement (Brunson 1843b).

JOHN TYLER,

PRESIDENT OF THE UNITED STATES OF AMERICA,

TO ALL AND SINGULAR TO WHOM THESE PRESENTS SHALL COME, GREETING:

WHEREAS, a Treaty was made and concluded at La Pointe of Lake Superior, in the Territory of Wisconsin, between Robert Stuart, Commissioner on the part of the United States, and the Chippewa Indians of the Mississippi and Lake Superior, by their chiefs and headmen, on the fourth day of October, in the year of our Lord, one thousand eight hundred and forty-two, which Treaty is word for word, as follows, to wit:

Articles of a Treaty made and concluded at La Pointe of Lake Superior, in the Territory of Wisconsin, between Robert Stuart Commissioner on the part of the United States, and the Chippewa Indians of the Mississippi, and Lake Superior, by their chiefs and headmen:

ARTICLE I. The Chippewa Indians of the Mississippi and Lake Superior, cede to the United States all the country within the following boundaries; viz: beginning at the mouth of Chocolate River of Lake Superior; thence northwardly across said lake to intersect the boundary line between the United States and the Province of Canada; thence up said Lake Superior, to the mouth of the St. Louis, or Fond du Lac River (including all the islands in said lake); thence up said river to the American Fur Company's trading post, at the southwardly bend thereof, about twenty-two miles from its mouth; thence south to intersect the line of the treaty of 29th July, 1837, with the Chippewas of the Mississippi; thence along said line to its southeastwardly extremity, near the Plover portage on the Wisconsin River; thence northeastwardly, along the boundary line, between the Chippewas and Menomonees, to its eastern termination, (established by the treaty held with the Chippewas, Menomonees, and Winebagoes, at Butte des Morts, August 11th, 1827) on the Skonawby River of Green Bay; thence northwardly, to the source of Chocolate River; thence down said river to its mouth, the place of beginning; it being the intention of the parties to this treaty, to include in this cession, all the Chippewa lands eastwardly of the aforesaid line running from the American Fur Company's trading post on the Fond du Lac River to the intersection of the line of the treaty made with the Chippewas of the Mississippi July 29th 1837.

ARTICLE II. The Indians stipulate for the right of hunting on the ceded Territory, with the other usual privileges of occupancy, until required to remove by the President of the United States, and that the laws of the United States shall be continued in force, in respect to their trade and intercourse with the whites, until otherwise ordered by Congress.

ARTICLE III. It is agreed by the parties to this Treaty, that whenever the Indians shall be required to remove from the ceded district, all the unceded lands belonging to the Indians of Fond du Lac, Sandy Lake, and Mississippi Bands, shall be the common property and home of all the Indians, party to this Treaty.

ARTICLE IV. In consideration of the foregoing cession, the United States, engage to pay to the Chippewa Indians of the Mississippi, and Lake Superior, annually, for twenty-five years, twelve thousand five hundred (12,500) dollars, in specie, ten thousand five hundred (10,500) dollars in goods, two thousand (2,000) dollars in provisions and tobacco, two

Fig. 14. *Proclamation of 1842 Treaty by President John Tyler.* From *Documents Relating to the Negotiation of Ratified and Unratified Treaties with Various Indian Tribes, 1801-1869,* Microcopy T494, Roll 9, Record Group 75, the National Archives and Records Service. Courtesy of the University of Wisconsin-Eau Claire Media Development Center.

Shortly after Stuart negotiated the treaty, Brunson—arguing that "economy should never impair justice"—informed Wisconsin Territorial Governor and Superintendent of Indian Affairs John Doty and Secretary of War John C. Spencer that the Chippewas had been shortchanged by their treaties with the United States. The Indians, he claimed, received less than eight cents an acre for eleven million acres in 1837 and only seven cents per acre for twelve million acres in 1842—a trifle for excellent port sites and land rich in copper, fish, and timber (Brunson 1843b; Smith 1954, 285; Keller 1978, 5-6).

Superintendent Stuart assured Indian Commissioner Crawford that Brunson's "crude and visionary" perception of "alleged" injustices against the Chippewas were an "absurdity." He advised Crawford that the subagent should be "strictly admonished" and made to acknowledge the "wise and humane policy" of the federal government that Stuart had carried out at La Pointe in 1842 (Stuart 1843a). "It is the duty of every public officer to sustain with his best exertions the views and policy of the Government," the commissioner informed Brunson (Crawford 1843). Then, upon Crawford's recommendation, Secretary of War James M. Porter dismissed the subagent (Porter 1843; Smith 1954, 285; Keller 1978, 5-6).[31] "The {War} Department did not remove Mr. Brunson any too soon," Stuart assured Crawford several months later. According to Stuart, Brunson was "not only deficient in head, but depraved in heart" for making "false and absurd accusations" with regard to Stuart's conduct at the 1842 negotiations (Stuart 1844).

Not until two years after the ratification of the 1842 treaty in early 1843 did the federal government issue mining permits for the ceded territory in an organized fashion. Indeed, the special agent sent by the War Department to reconnoiter the area was overwhelmed by the "unexpected magnitude of the Cession" (Cunningham 1844, 677). Enterprising miners had entered the region, however, even before President Tyler signed the treaty and there was considerable pressure on the War Department to grant permits (Robbins 1960, 141; Doty 1843; Talcott 1845).

During the copper boom of the 1840s, the Lake Superior Chippewa remained on their ceded lands enjoying, to quote Article 2 of the Treaty of 1842, their reserved "right of hunting on the ceded territory, with the other usual privileges of occupancy." Few white settlers had any interest in the pinelands of northern Wisconsin with their harsh winters and short growing seasons, so the Indians continued to follow age-old patterns of hunting, fishing, and gathering without interference by whites (Danziger 1979, 88). The Indians assumed that under the 1842 treaty they had only granted whites the *use* of their lands (Vennum 1988, 257). In reviewing the circumstances surrounding the Chippewa treaties of 1837 and 1842, economists Daniel W. Bromley and Basil M. H. Sharp assert that "the Indian conception of *property* would easily have allowed them to believe the land in question could be shared, but that the land could not be alienated." The Chippewas believed that as long as they behaved themselves and were orderly, they could continue to hunt, fish, and gather while whites cut pine trees and searched for minerals on the same lands (1990, 14-15). As Chief Martin commented shortly after signing the agreement, "we have no objection to the white mans {sic} working the mines, & the timber & making farms. But we reserve the Birch bark & Ceder {sic}, for canoes, the Rice & the Sugar tree and the priviledge of hunting without being disturbed by the whites" (Martin {1842}).

Many Chippewa Indians and whites in Wisconsin enjoyed a good relationship during the years immediately following the 1842 treaty according to anthropologists Charles Cleland and James Clifton. Lake Superior Chippewa men increasingly engaged in commercial fishing, either with their own equipment or as seasonal laborers for white Americans, and Chippewa women cleaned the fish before packing it in salt as American entrepreneurs sought to create a national market for this product from the Lake Superior country. As mining developed, numerous Chippewa men transported supplies, acted as guides, cut and supplied mine timber, or delivered fish, venison, furs, hides, rice, and maple sugar (the major sweetener used in the United States before 1860). Chippewa women traded surplus fruits and vegetables to miners. In the interior, some Chippewa men and women became attuned to the labor and material requirements of the lumber industry. Both along the southern shore of Lake Superior and in the interior of Wisconsin, the Chippewas delivered services and goods that created economic and social bonds, which in turn created potential allies. In addition, removal of the Chippewas from Wisconsin would have deprived many loggers and miners of female companions (Cleland 1985, 14-17; Clifton 1987, 18-19).

While contemporary evidence suggests that Wisconsin Chippewas participated in the kinds of activities described by Cleland and Clifton (Ramsey 1850, 53-54), some may have tried to avoid contact with whites whenever possible. In September of 1843, for example, White Crow from Lac du Flambeau and chiefs from several other interior bands requested their annuity payments be made at the falls of the Chippewa River rather than at Bad River to the north. "If we go to Bad river {sic}," they protested, "we are near to the white men, who work the copper mines—we sold twelve moons ago. We do not wish to be near them. Whenever we are near white men we are sure to have trouble." Yet the chiefs understood that total isolation from whites was not the answer. Although they asserted that "the great Spirit never made the Red men and white men to live together," the chiefs nevertheless acknowledged their dependence on whites for some things by pleading for the restoration of the blacksmith shop and the model farm that had been moved from Chippewa Falls to distant northern locations (Chippewa Chiefs 1843). Whether they sought to avoid contact with whites or whether they enjoyed a good working relationship with them, the Chippewas had no intention of leaving Wisconsin. Events of the mid- and late-1840s, however, brought considerable pressure for removal reminiscent of Andrew Jackson's handling of the Southern tribes in the 1830s.

The return of the Democrats to the White House in 1845 elevated avowed expansionist William Medill to the position of commissioner of Indian affairs. Medill soon began planning for the establishment of a northern "Indian colony" on the headwaters of the Mississippi River. He argued that the creation of such a colony, together with the concentration of Indians on the desirable lands north of the Kansas River to the area west of Missouri and Kansas, would permit a safe corridor for emigrants to the west coast (Satz 1988; Medill 1846a, 1848, 388-90).

Territorial acquisitions in the Far West after the Mexican War had led many American officials including Medill to realize the Indian removal policy so vigorously pursued by Andrew Jackson and his successors had ironically established by the mid-1840s what Napoleon in the 1790s and the British at the Treaty of Ghent in 1814 had failed to achieve—namely, the construction of an Indian barrier to American continental expansion. This barrier stretched from Canada in the North to Texas in the South and from the Rocky Mountains in the West to the Arkansas-Missouri-Iowa-Wisconsin line. Medill hoped to break open this barrier, and his strategy hinged on the relocation of northern Indians. Wisconsin statehood (1848) and the territorial organization of Minnesota (1849) were both still a few years in the future as Medill sought to remove Indians still in Wisconsin to northern Minnesota and particularly to remove the Chippewas from the mineral-rich south shores of Lake Superior that were "exciting much interest" among American entrepreneurs (Medill 1846b, 219-20; Dodge 1847a, 1056; Satz 1975, 231-36; 1988; Trennert 1979c, 33-34).

Although the Chippewa bands in Wisconsin viewed any effort to relocate them near "the wandering and vicious tribes which infest the plains and the mountains stretching from the Mississippi to the Pacific" as synonymous with a death sentence[32] (Head Chiefs 1849, 2), Medill sent Isaac A. Verplanck of Bativia, New York and Charles E. Mix of the Indian Office staff in Washington to the south shore of Lake Superior in the summer of 1847 to arrange for the resettlement of the Chippewas across the Mississippi River. Medill told the commissioners that the Chippewa bands in Wisconsin are "widely scattered and lead a roving & unsettled life, & obtain subsistence principally by fishing & hunting." As a result, "their concentration in a section of country as far as possible beyond the reach of a white frontier population, is requisite to enable the Government to give them the benefit of the benevolent course of policy it is now pursuing for the civilization & moral improvement of the red race." Medill reasoned it would be less expensive in the long run if the federal government moved the Chippewas across the Mississippi at one time rather than if the government acquired a land cession in Wisconsin and allowed the Indians to congregate on their remaining lands only to be moved again later. He told the treaty commissioners, "considering the expenses to which the government is subjected in surveying and disposing of lands purchased of Indians, ten cents per acre has been found to be a full price for those occupied & valuable to Indians, & which are important for settlement & cultivation by a white population" while "unoccupied & unused" lands should cost no more than five cents per acre. Medill stressed that "it is a leading object with the Department to consider the Chippewas, and to have them think themselves one United people with possessions and interests in common" rather than the separate bands claiming "exclusive interest" in different portions of their lands. "Should you succeed in effecting a treaty with them," the commissioner cautioned Verplanck and Mix, "it should as far as possible be made clearly & unequivocally to express the meaning & intention" of the War Department (Medill 1847).

The treaty commissioners obtained land cessions in present-day Minnesota (see *Fig. 7*), but the Wisconsin bands on the south shore of Lake Superior resisted their efforts. The Wisconsin Chippewas had no intention of relocating as part of Indian Commissioner Medill's grand design to rid Wisconsin, Iowa, and southern Minnesota of Indians so as to provide a safe corridor for westward-bound American travelers between the Indian country southwest of the Missouri River and a new northern counterpart to be established in north central Minnesota. Treaty Commissioner Verplanck informed Indian Commissioner Medill that the Indian Office was "mistaken" if it thought that the Lake Superior Chippewas were willing to relocate. "When I said in council that I would talk no more about their lands," Verplanck reported, "they at first understood me to say that they would never again be asked to sell their lands and they expressed themselves much pleased that they were to be left alone'' (Verplanck 1847).

Medill, using arguments similar to those of President Jackson in his efforts years earlier to promote Indian removal to the West,[33] suggested evicting the Chippewas from northern Wisconsin as a means of promoting their ''civilization.'' In 1846, for example, he had reported that ''the principle means of subsistence of these Indians is the chase: they are widely dispersed, so that but little supervision can be exercised over them, and hence ardent spirits can be introduced among them with facility and little risk of detection. While they remain in their present situation, but little if anything can be done to give them the benefit of the benevolent policy of the government for the improvement of the Indian race.'' Removal across the Mississippi River and concentration on a reduced land base would supposedly force the Chippewas ''to resort to agriculture and other pursuits of civilized life'' while permitting the federal government to provide better enforcement of its laws against the importation of liquor into Indian country (Medill 1846b, 219-20).

Although Commissioner Medill used the control of liquor in Indian country as a reason for promoting the removal of the Wisconsin bands, the Indians' conduct does not seem to have warranted removal. A group of forty-four whites from Eagle River complained in February of 1847 that traffic in ''Ardent Spirits'' on the southern shore of Lake Superior ''materially impeded'' mining operations, ''effecting also the Society, and interest of all concerned,'' but they blamed the federal government for failing to ''enforce the law'' against the sale of liquor to Indians (Residents Near Lake Superior 1847). An altercation in September of 1847 between Chippewa Indians—from the Wisconsin River and Pelican Lake bands returning home from an annuity payment at Bad River—and whites who had sold them whiskey elicited a very revealing commentary from La Pointe subagent James P. Hays. When the whites refused to provide the intoxicated Indians with more liquor, the Indians shoved the whites off their boats and fired upon them. Subagent Hays reported the incident to Governor Henry Dodge:

> This is the first instance of an Indian raising his hand against a white man on Lake Superior, which has ever come within my knowledge; but it is no more than I would expect under the circumstances. If {white} men will pursue this {whiskey} traffic, they must look for such results, and have no right to complain or receive sympathy. The Chippewas as individuals, and as a nation, are well disposed, and will continue to be so as long as the cupidity and heartlessness of the whiskey dealer will permit. I fear that in our accounts of outrages and crime, we have done the Chippewas, if no other tribe, injustice in many cases; for I find on comparing them with almost any civilized community of the same size, for four years, there will be found the smaller aggregate of crime on the part of the savage; and every crime of any magnitude which has been committed may be traced to the influence of the white man. (Hays 1847, 825)

According to Hays, there was much more need to control the activities of greedy whites like the whiskey traffickers than there was to decry Chippewa behavior (*Fig. 15*). The attempted rape of a Chippewa woman by a lumberjack near Chippewa Falls on July 4, 1849, is an example of violence inspired by drunken whites. The incident resulted in the lynching of the woman's husband by a white mob when he tried to rescue her. Three lumberjacks were arrested, but they escaped on their way to stand trial at Prairie du Chien (Current 1976, 154). Six years before this incident

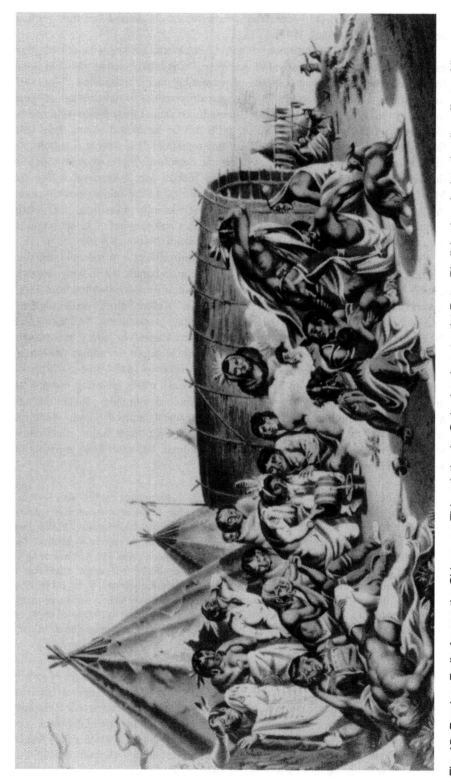

Fig. 15. *Drunken Frolic Among the Chippewas.* This painting by Swiss immigrant-artist Peter Rindisbacher depicts the dire effects of liquor on a Chippewa community along the Canadian-American border. Because alcohol was storable, immediately consumable, and addictive, white traders found it to be a particularly effective inducement in encouraging Indians to hunt more intensively for them. Courtesy of the West Point Museum Collections, United States Military Academy, West Point, New York.

and just months after the ratification of the 1842 treaty, one of the nation's highest ranking Army officers warned that the real culprits responsible for inciting tension and disputes between Indians and whites in northern Wisconsin were the "worse than savage white men" who sold liquor to the Indians (Gaines 1843).

During the late 1840s, Wisconsin Chippewas had done nothing to trigger removal under the treaties of 1837 and 1842. Nevertheless, persistent rumors of their impending eviction troubled them and led them to take direct action to prevent such a disaster (*Detroit Daily Free Press* 1848).

4 The Removal Order and the Wisconsin Death March

In late fall of 1848, a contingent of Chippewa Indians including chiefs representing sixteen Lake Superior bands traveled to Washington to try to end any additional talk about their removal to the West (*Detroit Daily Free Press* 1848). Early in 1849, they presented a petition to the members of Congress (*Fig. 16*). "Our people," they said, "desire a donation of twenty-four sections of land, covering the graves of our fathers, our sugar orchards, and our rice lakes and rivers, at seven different places now occupied by us as villages." The chiefs requested the establishment of a "permanent home" for their people at Vieux Desert or Old Garden (three sections), at Trout Lake (four sections), at Lac Courte Oreilles (four sections), at La Pointe (four sections), at Ontonagon (three sections), at L'Anse (three sections), and at Pequaming[34] (three sections). "We do not wish," they declared, "to be driven north of the British line, nor West among the wandering and vicious tribes which infest the plains and the mountains stretching from the Mississippi to the Pacific" (Head Chiefs 1849, 1-2).

The press in the Great Lakes region kept residents informed of the activities of the Chippewa delegation in Washington (*Detroit Daily Free Press* 1848, 1849; *Green Bay Advocate* 1849a, b). Iowa Senator Augustus Dodge, who heard the Indians address Congress, summarized their presentation as follows:

> They come here . . . to ask of this and the other branch of Congress that the resting-places where the bones of their ancestors repose may be continued to them; that the Government of the United States would grant them a small portion of its vast domain among the fastnesses and marshes of Lake Superior, where their villages are situated, and where they have been enabled to obtain a precarious subsistence by gathering wild rice, cranberries, and other productions of that distant country.

In addition to speaking before Congress, the delegation visited President James K. Polk, Secretary of War William L. Marcy, and Commissioner of Indian Affairs William Medill. According to Senator Dodge, "everywhere their mission was approved by all who became acquainted with them, and everywhere they excited the best sympathies of the human heart" (U. S. Congress 1849, 536). President Polk assured the Indians of "kindly feelings" on the part of the United States government. He promised to read the petition and other documents they presented him and stated, according to one newspaper editor, that "if they behaved themselves they might expect good treatment in {the} future" (*Detroit Daily Free Press* 1849).

When the Chippewas began preparations to return to Wisconsin, they found it necessary to appeal to Congress for financial assistance. Their trip to Washington had not been approved in advance by Commissioner Medill, so no funds were on hand in the Indian Office to cover their expenses. Senator Dodge of Iowa spoke in favor of a joint resolution in their behalf. Claiming that when the Chippewas reached Green Bay on their long journey home it would still take many of them a month

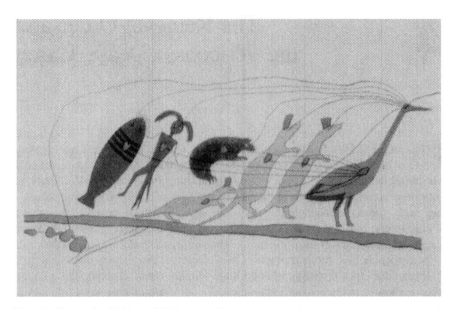

Fig. 16. *Symbolic Petition of Chippewa Chiefs, 1849.* Drawing by Seth Eastman from Schoolcraft, *The Indian Tribes of the United States,* Vol. 1 (1851). The chiefs who went to Washington in 1849 requested a "permanent home" in Wisconsin; they carried this pictograph with them. Animals representing various clans travel eastward along Lake Superior (the dark line across the pictograph). Their unity of purpose is depicted by the lines linking together their hearts and eyes to a chain of wild rice lakes in ceded territory south of Lake Superior. Courtesy of the State Historical Society of Wisconsin. WHi(x3)34127

to snowshoe to their villages, Dodge helped to persuade his colleagues to provide the necessary funds. In doing so, he shared some information:

> . . . If you were to go into a calculation as to the millions of acres of land, the valuable lead and copper mines that you have acquired from these very tribes, specimens of which are to be seen at the War Department, and calculate the cost of these, as compared with their value, there would be a fearful balance against us. These Indians are now many thousand miles from home. Philanthropic gentlemen in Pittsburgh, Philadelphia, and elsewhere, have loaned them sums of money to enable them to reach here. These debts they wish to pay, and to have money enough to pay their way home. (U. S. Congress 1849, 536)

Dodge's efforts assisted the Indians in securing funds for their return trip. As the delegation left Washington, the fate of the Wisconsin Chippewas became entangled with national and state politics.

Chippewa bands in Wisconsin represented a political opportunity to Whig politicians in newly created Minnesota Territory (March 3, 1849). The Minnesota Whigs had helped capture the White House for their party in the presidential election of 1848, and they eagerly awaited the transition to the new administration, which occurred just weeks after the Chippewa delegation met with President Polk.

The idea of removing the Chippewas from Wisconsin to Minnesota Territory had special appeal for some Minnesotans. Removal would mean transferring annuity payments to the new territory where Alexander Ramsey (*Fig. 17*), recently appointed governor and the titular head of the Whig party, would garner a considerable number of patronage jobs from Democratic Wisconsin. After gaining statehood in May of 1848, Wisconsin had cast nearly twice as many ballots for Whig opponents in the presidential election that year than for Whig candidates. President Zachary Taylor was under considerable pressure to open opportunities for loyal, patronage-hungry Whigs. The transfer of the Bureau of Indian Affairs from the War Department to the newly established Interior Department under the direction of Ohioan Thomas Ewing and the selection of Kentuckian Orlando Brown as commissioner of Indian affairs indicated the extent of the politicization of Indian affairs. Ewing had opposed rotation in office while the Democrats were in power and was now thirsting for the opportunity to use his patronage powers to clean house; Brown, with no knowledge of Indian affairs, was little more than a liaison between Kentucky "kingmaker" John J. Crittenden and President Taylor (Hamilton 1951, 113, 132, 151, 173; Satz 1975, 164; Trennert 1979a, 42-46; White 1954, 310).

The 1848 annuity payment at La Pointe may have actually helped to trigger a series of events that played into the hands of Minnesota politicians and traders. A reporter for the *Cleveland Herald* who visited La Pointe in 1848 later charged that there was a direct connection between "the swindle" he witnessed there and the subsequent effort to evict the Chippewas from Wisconsin. The 1848 payment, like many others, began much later than the announced time. As a result, "thousands of Indians traversed many miles of forest, wasted six weeks' time, and lost the crop of wild rice upon which they depended for their winter's subsistence." Traders, who charged what the Ohio reporter called "exorbitant rates" for "the necessaries of life," claimed their profits were "moderate." Yet, for every pound of pork or flour Indians purchased on credit to feed their families, the traders required them to spend an equivalent amount on "dry goods and gewgaws" as well as other "trash" that "had no value for them." By the time the annuity funds arrived, traders "raked" more than eighty-five percent from the payment table; only a few thousand dollars remained to be divided equally among the Indians, who received about one dollar each. According to the reporter, "it was whispered that . . . {the traders} were using all their influence to have the future payments made at some point so far West that competition would not force them to be content with moderate profits." These were the reasons, the reporter observed, "it was necessary to remove the Chippewas further West" (*New York Times* 1851b).

Before the end of 1849, Interior Department officials learned that the newly formed legislative assembly in Minnesota Territory had passed resolutions in favor of revoking the usufructuary rights of the Chippewa Indians on lands ceded in 1837 and 1842. Upon the recommendation of Indian Commissioner Orlando Brown, President Taylor—who had once served as commandant of forts in Wisconsin and Minnesota—issued an executive order on February 6, 1850[35] that revoked the usufructuary rights of Chippewa Indians not only in Minnesota but also in Wisconsin and in the Upper Peninsula of Michigan and ordered the removal of all of the Chippewa Indians in these areas to unceded lands in Minnesota (*Fig. 18*). Indian Office personnel in Washington and in Minnesota Territory offered four reasons for the presidential Removal Order and their emphasis on "prompt action" in carrying it out: (1) the Chippewas had to be removed in order to prevent "injurious contact" with the advancing white population; (2) the Indians had to be removed

Fig. 17. *Alexander Ramsey, Governor and Superintendent of Indian Affairs for Minnesota Territory.* Courtesy of the Minnesota Historical Society.

from areas where there were "ample facilities for procuring ardent spirits;" (3) whites needed to be relieved of the "annoyance" and "evils" of having Indians as neighbors; and (4) removal to the West would provide opportunities for congregating the Chippewas together for purposes of promoting their "civilization and prosperity" (Kappler 5: 663; Lea 1850, 4-6; 1851a; Ramsey 1850, 54-55).

MINNESOTA

The privileges granted temporarily to the Chippewa Indians of the Mississippi, by the Fifth Article of the Treaty made with them on the 29th of July 1837, "of hunting, fishing and gathering the wild rice, upon the lands, the rivers and the lakes included in the territory ceded" by that treaty to the United States; and the right granted to the Chippewa Indians of the Mississippi and Lake Superior, by the Second Article of the treaty with them of October 4th 1842, of hunting on the territory which they ceded by that treaty, "with the other usual privileges of occupancy until required to remove by the President of the United States," are hereby revoked; and all of the said Indians remaining on the lands ceded as aforesaid, are required to remove to their unceded lands.

Z. TAYLOR.

Executive Office
Washington City, February 6th, 1850.

By the PRESIDENT

I. EWING,
Secretary of the Interior.

Fig. 18. *President Zachary Taylor's Executive Order of February 6, 1850.* This typescript copy of President Taylor's Removal Order is reproduced from attorney Charles J. Kappler's compendium of Indian laws and treaties (5: 663), where it appears under the heading "Minnesota" because the order was issued in response to officials from that territory. Courtesy of the University of Wisconsin-Eau Claire Media Development Center.

News of the Removal Order shocked the Lake Superior Chippewa people. According to Subagent Watrous, it "created much excitement and disatisfaction" because the Indians believed "they would not be required to remove until the present generation should pass away" (Watrous 1850, 89). As noted earlier, the Wisconsin Indians understood they had ceded only copper rights—not land rights—in 1842 and that under the 1837 and 1842 treaties they would never be forced to leave Wisconsin unless they acted improperly—i.e., made war or otherwise acted violently against whites. And there were no white demands for Chippewa lands for settlement. In fact, when Daniel H. Johnson of Prairie du Chien attempted to obtain information for the 1850 Census in La Pointe County (later La Pointe and Douglas counties), he found the region "remote and difficult to communicate with" and inhabited primarily by individuals who spoke either French or Ojibwa. The Lake Superior country was, he reported in a certified affidavit, a "thinly settled and half civilized region." Only about five hundred whites had settled in that area (Johnson 1858, 2).

Chief Buffalo of La Pointe and other chiefs who "obstinately" opposed removal responded to the news by sending messengers to every Chippewa village to ascertain if any depredations had been committed against whites. Failing to uncover any incident that might have sparked the president's action, they convened councils throughout the ceded territory to discuss the situation and plan their strategy for opposing "the sudden order" of the U. S. government (Watrous 1850, 89; *Lake Superior News* 1850a, b; Buffalo *et al.* 1852; Armstrong {1892}, 287-88).

A vigorous lobbying campaign of the Wisconsin legislature, various missionary groups, regional newspapers, and many local whites aided the Wisconsin Chippewas in their resistance to the Removal Order (Vennum 1988, 259). The Sault St. Marie *Lake Superior News and Mining Journal,* for example, responded on May 22, 1850, to reports that agent Watrous had told the Indians they would lose their annuities if they remained in Wisconsin and Michigan by observing, "this is a new and ingeniously contrived way of effecting the removal of the natives." As far away from the La Pointe Agency in the Great Lakes region as Detroit, this editorial comment received support from regional editors (*Detroit Daily Free Press* 1850). A follow-up article in the Sault Ste. Marie newspaper on June 12, 1850, referred to the Removal Order as "uncalled for by any interest of the government—uncalled for by any interest of the Indians." The editor of the paper concluded that "this unlooked for order has brought disappointment and consternation to the Indians throughout the Lake Superior Country, and will bring upon them the most disastrous consequences." The paper issued reports highly favoring the continued residence of the Chippewa Indians in the Lake Superior region (*Lake Superior News and Mining Journal* 1850b). Cyrus Mendenhall, an eyewitness to the 1842 treaty parley and mining entrepreneur associated with the Methodist Episcopal Mission Society (Kappler 2: 544; Clifton 1987, 21), rallied ministers, physicians, local officials, merchants, mine foremen, lumbermen, and other influential citizens between Sault Ste. Marie and La Pointe for support of the Chippewas. Ohio Whig Congressman Joshua R. Giddings forwarded to President Zachary Taylor a petition circulated by Mendenhall and signed by him and many other men "of high moral Character and respectability." Declaring any removal of the Chippewas from the lands ceded in 1842 "uncalled for by any interest of the Government or people of the United States, and . . . in a high degree prejudicial to the welfare of the Indians," the petitioners urged the president to rescind his order (Giddings 1850).

Mendenhall's petition arrived at the White House after President Taylor's unexpected death on July 9, 1850. Millard Fillmore, who had served as president for only a few weeks, replaced the entire cabinet (Hamilton 1951, 401-02) and then referred the petition to the Interior Department. On August 3, 1850, the Secretary of the Interior Ad Interim asked Commissioner of Indian Affairs Luke Lea,[36] who was just finishing his first month in office, to prepare a report on the issue (Giddings 1850). In the meantime, regional newspapers reported that "arrangements to remove the Chippewa Indians from Lake Superior are producing much dissatisfaction among the Indians and the Whites. The Indians are loth to remove, and the Whites to let them go" (*Detroit Daily Free Press* 1851). Sympathetic eastern newspapers reprinted articles from Great Lakes newspapers accusing Agent Watrous of perpetrating an "iniquitous scheme" to remove the Indians against the wishes of "the entire population of the Lake Superior country" (*New York Times* 1851a, b). Northern Wisconsin mine owners and whites who employed the Chippewas as fishers, sailors, guides, and hunters raised what Minnesota Governor Ramsey called "almost insuperable" obstacles to their removal (Ramsey 1851, 162).

Not all non-Indian residents of the Lake Superior country openly opposed the government's efforts to remove the Chippewas to Minnesota Territory. Missionaries residing among the Indians found themselves in a vulnerable position. As happened in the Indian removal crisis in the South during the Jacksonian era, they were torn between their interpretation of their duty to their Indian charges and their obligation to civil authorities. In the early 1850s, as in the 1830s, federal officials used the fierce competition for government subsidies for Indian mission schools to their advantage (Satz 1985, 395-401; 1975, 55). The withdrawal of federal funds for the support of Indian mission schools in Wisconsin and the prospect of the restoration of those funds in Minnesota led some missionaries to resign themselves to accepting the inevitability of the removal of the Chippewas (Watrous 1852b, 48; Armstrong {1892}, 291 n. 6).

During the summer of 1851, *Copway's American Indian,* a new weekly newspaper published in New York by Canadian-born Chippewa George Copway[37]—one of the best-known Indians in the eastern United States—carried a report from the American Board of Commissioners for Foreign Missions (ABCFM) about the operations of missionaries Leonard Wheeler at La Pointe and Sherman Hall at Bad River in Wisconsin. While hoping that "no compulsory means" would be used to evict the Indians from the state, the ABCFM governing board in Boston envisioned some benefits that relocation might bring the Wisconsin Chippewas. The board had learned valuable lessons during the removal crisis of the 1830s in the South and predicted the removal of the Chippewas "will cause considerable excitement among them," but "their removal will concentrate them more, and render them more accessible to the means of instruction and improvement" (*Copway's American Indian* 1851, 1; Berkhoffer 1965, 104-05). Missionary Hall had already advised ABCFM officials to make the best of the situation and to seek federal funds for a mission boarding school in Minnesota Territory before other Protestant or Catholic missionary societies secured them. "Whatever we may think of this policy," Hall wrote in 1850 shortly after President Taylor had issued his Removal Order, "if we wish to continue our missionary efforts for the Ojibwas, we had better conform to it" (Hall 1850a, b; 1852).

Hall's conversion to "conformity" with the presidential order was the result of the efforts of officials in the Interior Department in Washington: Minnesota Territorial Governor Ramsey who openly argued that in dealing with Indians "it would be indisputably the duty of government to impose such terms as should seem proper, and by duress or otherwise compel their observance" (Ramsey 1850, 49); and La Pointe subagent John Watrous. These men actively conspired to lure the Chippewas to Minnesota from northern Wisconsin and Michigan's Upper Peninsula. To accomplish their goal, they had moved the payment site for the 1850 annuity from La Pointe to Sandy Lake on the east bank of the Upper Mississippi River, a location that was some three to five hundred difficult canoe and portage miles from the various Chippewa villages in Wisconsin. They had also refused to provide services required under the 1837 and 1842 treaties at any location other than at Sandy Lake. In the fall of 1850, Watrous urged the Chippewas to bring their families to Sandy Lake for the payment, but neither he nor other federal officials made adequate arrangements to feed, shelter, or otherwise provide for the Indians there. Indeed, deliveries of annuity goods and rations were delayed until the "pelting rain and snows of autumn" nearly trapped the several thousand Chippewas who had traveled to that remote location (Watrous 1850, 89; Armstrong {1892}, 288; Buffalo *et al.* 1851; Buffalo *et al.* 1852; Watrous 1852b, 48; Pitezel 1859, 298-300; Clifton 1987, 1, 19-25).

In his annual report of November 27, 1850, Indian Commissioner Lea claimed he sought the removal of the Chippewas from Wisconsin in order to isolate them in the West from "injurious contact" with whiskey peddlers and the like and to prevent them from suffering "destitution and want" in Wisconsin as the game on which they depended became exhausted (Lea 1850, 4-5). But many Wisconsin Chippewas were destitute and in want by the end of 1850 precisely because Lea lured them to Sandy Lake in Minnesota by transferring the payment of their annuities to that location.

Governor Ramsey, who boasted that a removal plan had been "fully matured" in his office, acknowledged that any such efforts undertaken after the first of November would lead to "much hardship" for emigrants (Ramsey 1850, 60-61). By forcing the Chippewas to reach Sandy Lake in October in order to collect their annuities, Ramsey set into motion a series of events culminating in what anthropologist James Clifton has recently called "The Wisconsin Death March" of 1850-1851. The Indians waited six weeks at Sandy Lake for the arrival of their subagent only to discover that he had come empty-handed because Congress failed to appropriate funds in a timely manner (Clifton 1987, 24-25). Seemingly trapped in Minnesota as the winter weather made travel back to Wisconsin extremely difficult, the Wisconsin Chippewas suffered what Governor Ramsey conceded was "a distressing mortality" (Ramsey 1851, 161).

According to missionary eyewitnesses, the federal government's "unwise course" of action in handling the annuity payment at Sandy Lake, especially its failure to provide adequate provisions for the Chippewas who traveled there, had serious consequences. Infectious diseases appeared in the makeshift Chippewa camps and spread rapidly when food supplies ran out shortly after the arrival of the first contingent from Wisconsin. The Indians traded their annuity claims for spoiled food and other shoddy provisions merchants sold at highly inflated prices. As winter set in, many Indians burned their canoes for firewood and returned to Wisconsin carrying their belongings on their backs (Hall 1850b; Pitezel 1859, 299-301).

Although the mortality figures cannot be determined precisely, Chippewa eyewitnesses from La Pointe and from the interior bands reported that some four hundred Indians, mostly able-bodied men, died from illness, hunger, and exposure—170 at Sandy Lake[38] and another 230 on the return trip (Buffalo *et al.* 1851; Buffalo *et al.* 1852; Clifton 1987, 1, 25). Methodist Episcopal missionary John Pitezel, who traveled to Sandy Lake from Michigan and recorded his observations some months later, saw "evidences of a terrible calamity every-where" as he approached the annuity payment site. "All over the cleared land graves were to be seen in every direction, for miles distant, from Sandy Lake; they were to be found in the woods {too}. Some, it is not known how many, were interred by their friends on the way home." Sickness and death were everywhere. "So alarming was the mortality," Pitezel commented "that the Indians complained that they could not bury their dead" (Pitezel 1859, 300-01).

Anxious to deflect any criticism of his handling of the annuity payment at Sandy Lake, Governor Ramsey wrote a long defense of his actions to Indian Commissioner Lea. "Far from famine or starvation ensuing from any negligence on the part of Government officers," he claimed, "the Chippewas received all that Government was under treaty obligations to furnish to them, except their money; and this, as every one is aware, who is at all familiar with the thriftless habits of the Indians, and the fatal facility with which they incur debts whenever opportunity presents, is usually all of it due to their traders." Ramsey, who had directed the Indians to travel to Sandy Lake for their annuity money in the first place, told Lea that he had found it necessary to spend half of the funds on provisions for the Indians. "Had the residue been so invested, which the scarcity of supplies rendered impossible," he asserted, "it would not have subsisted the large number congregated at the payment an additional fortnight" (Ramsey 1851, 162).

Subagent Watrous admitted a "great mortality" had occurred as a result of the circumstances surrounding the annuity payment and reported that the Chippewas referred to Sandy Lake as a "grave yard" and that they had "a particular dread and horror for the place" (Watrous 1852a). According to a recent study of the incident, "the Ewing-Brown-Ramsey-Watrous plan to lure the Lake Superior Chippewa west and trap them there successfully removed some twelve percent, by killing them." The tragic loss of such a large number of people weakened the Wisconsin bands. Many of their able-bodied men had died. They had also lost capital equipment—their canoes, as well as valuable time that could have been devoted to subsistence work and other productive economic activities. Dependent upon traders for food, the Chippewas who returned to Wisconsin found it necessary to encumber their unpaid and future annuity funds in order to survive the winter of 1851 (Clifton 1987, 25). The tragic events associated with the annuity payment at Sandy Lake strengthened the resolve of the leaders of the Wisconsin bands to resist all efforts to remove them to Minnesota.

5   Reservations Replace Removal

News of trauma inflicted upon the Wisconsin Chippewas as a result of the scheme to lure them to Sandy Lake aided the Indians in their opposition to removal. The intense lobbying effort on behalf of the Lake Superior Chippewas described earlier eventually proved successful. Early in June of 1851, Indian Commissioner Lea informed Interior Secretary Alexander H. H. Stuart that citizens in Wisconsin and in the Upper Peninsula of Michigan strongly opposed the removal of the Chippewas. According to Lea:

> When the extent of this order became known, communications from sources of the highest consideration—embracing petitions from the Legislature of Wisconsin and the citizens resident in the ceded country; letters from the Authorities of Missionary establishments, among the Chippewas of Lake Superior and other highly respectable individuals were received at this office—remonstrating in strong terms against the application of the order to these Indians.

In view of "the Weighty reasons" provided in the communications from prominent citizens received in the Indian Office—that the removal of the Lake Superior Chippewas was "not required by the interests of the citizens or Government of the United States, and would in its consequences in all probability be disastrous to the Indians''—Lea recommended in early June that the presidential order "be so modified as to permit such portions of those bands as may desire it to remain for the present in the country they now occupy" (Lea 1851a). Then, in late August of 1851, he announced the suspension of the order "until the final determination of the President, as to whether they (the Ojibwas) should be permitted to remain, or their removal resumed" (Treat 1851).

News of the suspension of the Removal Order encouraged newspaper editors from the Great Lakes region. An editorial from the *Cleveland Herald* reprinted in the East, for example, said the order was "uncalled for, useless, and abominable; and we are glad, for the sake of humanity and justice, that the Administration have resolved that for the present the edict shall not be enforced. We trust it may never be" (*New York Times* 1851b). Another widely circulated editorial from the Sault Ste. Marie *Lake Superior News and Mining Journal* claimed efforts to remove the Chippewas were unlike any other attempt to relocate an Indian people ever undertaken by the U. S. government.

> We believe we express the conviction of the entire population of the Lake Superior country in regarding this removal as uncalled for by the best interests of the Government, the whites, or the Indians. This is not a case of removal like any other that has taken place in this country. Generally, there has been some show of reason for this painful resort . . . . But it is far different in the case of the Chippewas. They occupy a remote portion of the country . . . that would not, in all probability, have been settled for a

61

hundred years to come, had it not been for the rich deposits of minerals lately discovered in its rocky hills.

From time immemorial this people have occupied the northern region, and have become acclimated to its cold and rigorous climate; and by hunting and fishing, and the cultivation of their small patches of soil, they have lived comfortably and contentedly, causing little or no trouble to the United States and their neighbors. Until their little fields are needed for the accommodation of their white brethren, why should they be driven to strange places, a prey to the designs of their worst enemies {the Sioux}? They can live comfortably where they now are, but they will starve to death, as hundreds did last winter, in the miserable region {in Minnesota} to which the Government would remove them.

Unlike Indians affected by other instances of government-sponsored Indian removal efforts, asserted the Sault Ste. Marie editor, the Chippewas were not an impediment to "the tide of civilization constantly sweeping in from the East." In the East, the editor of the *New York Times* agreed with and reprinted this assessment (*New York Times* 1851b).

Despite the positive public reaction to Commissioner Lea's temporary suspension of the Removal Order, Governor Ramsey and newly promoted Agent Watrous[39] continued their efforts to entice the Indians to emigrate from Wisconsin. They insisted that annuity payments and educational funds be paid only in Minnesota. In addition, Watrous recommended that a company of infantry be dispatched to La Pointe to assist in promoting "a general removal" (Watrous 1851, 1852a, b, 48; Hall 1852a; Clifton 1987, 26-27). Ramsey informed Washington officials that the best way to handle Chippewa "stragglers" in Wisconsin was to follow "a rigid adherence . . . to the rule of paying annuities to those only who remove to, and remain in, their proper country" (Ramsey 1851, 163; 1852, 44).

In late November of 1851 after issuing his temporary suspension of the Removal Order, Indian Commissioner Lea came to the support of Ramsey and Watrous. After reading their reports in preparation for his own annual report, Lea urged administration officials to proceed with efforts to "concentrate" the Chippewas west of the Mississippi River. Lea claimed he proposed the measure for humanitarian reasons. It was "calculated to promote the future welfare of this large and interesting tribe" and "to save them from actual starvation; as the game on which they mainly depend for the means of living is fast disappearing, and cannot much longer afford them a support" (Lea 1851b, 4).

Meanwhile, continued pressure for their removal led Chief Buffalo of La Pointe (*Fig. 19*) and twenty-eight other Chippewa chiefs and headmen to dictate a petition to Lea. Charging that Watrous had "aggrieved and wronged" them, the Chippewa leaders complained about the "great deception" that had been used to promote their removal to Sandy Lake. Reciting Commissioner Stuart's 1842 promise that they could remain on their land as long as they "lived on friendly terms with the Whites," the chiefs and headmen charged Watrous with misconduct.

We are not satisfied that it is the President that requires us to remove. We have asked to see the order, and the name of the President affixed to it, but it has not been shewn us. We think the order came only from the Agent and those who advise with him, and are interested in having us remove.

Since the Chippewas of Lake Superior had "never shed the blood of the Whites; nor killed their cattle; nor done them any injury; and . . . are not in their way,"

Fig. 19. *Portrait of Chief Buffalo.* The head chief of the La Pointe band is depicted dressed in a military uniform and wearing a peace medal. From the Madeline Island Historical Museum Collection. Courtesy of the State Historical Society of Wisconsin. WHi(x3)41266

the Indians asked, "why is {it} that we now hear this order to remove?" Claiming to be totally "in the dark" about the reasons for the order, Buffalo and the other leaders of the Lake Superior Chippewas called for an end to all efforts to remove their people and for the resumption of the payment of annuities at La Pointe as promised in the 1842 treaty. The Indians ended their petition with a request that they be allowed to send a delegation to Washington in order to review their grievances with American officials there (Buffalo *et al.* 1851).

The Chippewas waited for a response to their petition, but their patience wore thin by the spring of 1852. Chief Buffalo, who was then in his early nineties, decided to travel to Washington without prior approval. In early April, Buffalo together with Oshoga, a young chief of "rare promise and merit" (Morse 1857, 348), several other chiefs, and interpreter Benjamin Armstrong left La Pointe en route to Washington. "To return {from Washington} without anything accomplished," commented Armstrong as the delegation traveled eastward, "would be to rekindle the fire that was smouldering into an open revolt for revenge" (Armstrong {1892}, 294).

Chief Buffalo led the delegation to Washington armed with a petition supporting the Chippewa cause. As they passed through white communities, Armstrong circulated the document among the residents and asked them to sign it (Armstrong {1892}, 293). "We are satisfied," the petition said of the Indians, "that they have been hardly and injuriously used by the Agents appointed to make them their payments during the past Two Seasons, & by the removal of their usual place of payment Conceeded {sic} to them in their treaty to a place farther west where they are exposed to the cold & starvation." The petition referred to the Chippewas as "a peaceable and inoffensive race living chiefly by hunting & fishing" (*Fig. 20*). Included among the residents of Lake Superior communities signing the petition were bankers, merchants, and traders. Eager to keep the Chippewas and their annuities nearby, these men had little difficulty in signing the document, which concluded that "while their removal West would in Our Opinion be a great damage to them it would in no manner benefit the white population of the Country" (Citizens of Lake Superior 1852).

When the Chippewa delegation finally reached Washington during the latter part of June (*Fig. 21*), both Indian Commissioner Lea and Interior Secretary Stuart ordered the Indians to return home immediately since they had not received permission to make the trip. Only the intervention of Whig Congressman George Briggs of New York, who encountered the delegation by accident while dining, led to a meeting with Briggs's fellow New York Whig, President Fillmore (Armstrong {1892}, 296-97).

In preparation for the meeting with "Great Grand Father" Fillmore, Buffalo had dictated a document that reviewed all of the outstanding grievances against the United States. The chief began by informing the president that Chippewa men, women, and children of northern Wisconsin were "deeply grieved" by the way in which they had been treated since 1850. Buffalo protested the violation of Chippewa reserved rights and urged Fillmore to remember the promises made at the 1842 treaty parley. "All who were present at that treaty listened to your words, which you sent to us," the memorial stated, adding that "Commissioner {Stuart} promised . . . that if we were good men, that we should not only be permitted to remain on our lands for fifty, but one hundred years to come." Explaining that his band had "at all times acted in obedience" to American laws and had advised other Indians to "lead a quiet and peaceable life," Buffalo requested an explanation for the Removal Order and for the subsequent efforts to evict his people from Wisconsin (Buffalo *et al.* 1852).

Buffalo especially complained about the indignities the Chippewas had suffered as a result of having to go to Sandy Lake to receive their annuities in 1850. He spoke of the "very bad flour," which "resembled green clay," and the other "rotten provisions" American officials had issued, and the loss of "so many" young people due

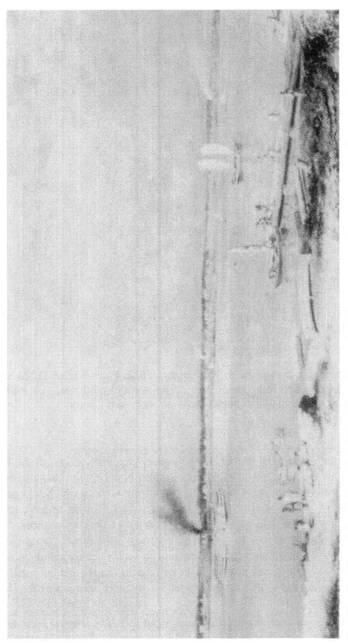

Fig. 20. *The City of Superior, 1856.* This lithograph by P. S. Duval and Son shows Chippewas and whites fishing and sharing the shoreline of Lake Superior. Courtesy of the Library of Congress. LC-USZ62-50524

Fig. 21. *Chippewa Delegation in Washington, 1852.* From Bartlett (1929, 69). Benjamin Armstrong and four unidentified chiefs are depicted here. Courtesy of the University of Wisconsin-Eau Claire Media Development Center.

to the remote location and lateness of the annuity payment, which left the Indians at the mercy of the "incliment" weather. Buffalo also charged that recent annuity payments were inadequate. "I obtained part of my annuity which was paid to me by My Agent, with one arm he paid me that, which I ought to have had in full with both arms." Buffalo requested redress for all of these grievances. "Is it not the obligation of white men to fulfill their contracts," he asked. "And should they not fulfill them, their contracts become null & void{,} consequently a misunderstanding exists, which can and ought to be adjusted to the mutual satisfaction of the parties concerned." Buffalo concluded his remarks with a plea for "justice":

It is generally the case with the white men, when they have selected a spot to dwell at, that they begin to consider and look around them, to see what obstacles are in their way. They begin to cut away the underbrush and bad trees, in order to make the land level and smoothe so that nothing will come in contact to hurt their feet, they see good trees and they are allowed to stand & live, & they are not cut down. We beseech you to do towards us as you do, allowing the good trees {—the Wisconsin Chippewas—} to stand and live in your domain. And furthermore we pray, that in accordance to that, we so fully understood that our annuities should be paid to us at La Pointe & that they may be continued there. (Buffalo *et al.* 1852)

Thanks to the efforts of Congressman Briggs, Buffalo soon received an opportunity to present the grievances of his people to President Fillmore.

According to interpreter Armstrong, the Chippewa delegation presented Chief Buffalo's petition to President Fillmore in the White House after everyone present at the meeting, including Congressman Briggs, Commissioner Lea, and Secretary Stuart, had smoked the peace pipe passed to them by Buffalo. In reading the petition, the president acknowledged that he recognized some of the signatures of leading citizens of the Great Lakes region. After deliberating a day, Fillmore agreed to rescind the Removal Order, to cease all efforts to remove the Chippewas, and to pay back, current, and future annuities at La Pointe. As news of the delegation's success reached Wisconsin, the Chippewas celebrated their great victory. Upon his return, Buffalo convened a "grand council" of Chippewa bands at La Pointe where an interpreter translated the message President Fillmore had given him (Armstrong {1892}, 297-98; Buffalo *et al.* 1852; Levi 1956, 60-61; Clifton 1987, 27).

President Fillmore's decision to allow the Chippewas to remain in Wisconsin has been the subject of recent controversy between supporters and critics of continued Indian usufructuary rights. Scholars have not located a decree by Fillmore specifically rescinding President Taylor's Removal Order. As noted earlier, the Interior Department ordered a temporary suspension of the order while Fillmore reviewed the status of the Chippewas (U. S. District Court 1978, 1328-330, 1350 n. 17; U. S. Court of Appeals 1983, 348; Lea 1851a; Treat 1851). Several contemporaneous events shed light on the president's motivation for undertaking such a review, reinforce Armstrong's contention that Fillmore revoked Taylor's order, and demonstrate that such a suspension by Fillmore is consistent with his handling of Indian affairs.

Chief Buffalo and white missionaries residing among the Chippewas had presented the Fillmore administration with strong accusations about the conduct of Agent Watrous (Fillmore 1852a; Buffalo *et al.* 1852; Treat 1852). At the same time, opposition to the Removal Order by distinguished white citizens of the Great Lakes region may have influenced the president (Citizens of Lake Superior 1852). By the end of 1852, Fillmore had definitely shown more interest in the well-being of Indians than had his immediate predecessors. For example, he had granted the Menominees an extension of the date of their removal from Wisconsin and had ordered the Indian Office to search for a suitable home for the tribe *in* Wisconsin (Ourada 1979, 118-19). He also expressed concern that "justice" to the Indians in the states of Texas and California as well as those in the Territory of Oregon required the establishment of "particular districts" or reservations so that they would not be "tenants at sufferance, and liable to be driven from place to place at the pleasure of the whites" (Fillmore 1852b, 171; Knobel 1984, 188-89; Trennert 1975, 86). There is some basis, therefore, for Chippewa editor George Copway's recollection several years after Fillmore left office that the New Yorker's administration was "kind to the Indians" (Copway 1856). Whatever Fillmore's motivation, the Chippewas were elated by his decision to allow them to remain in Wisconsin.

Two years after Chief Buffalo's meeting with President Fillmore, the Wisconsin legislature informed federal officials that ''the Chippewa Indians in the region of Lake Superior are a peaceable, quiet, and inoffensive people, rapidly improving in the arts and sciences: that they acquire their living by hunting, fishing, manufacturing maple sugar, and agricultural pursuits: that many of them have intermarried with the white inhabitants, and are becoming generally anxious to become educated and adopt the habits of the 'white man.' '' Wisconsin legislators urged the Indian Office not to impose removal upon the Chippewas and recommended that laws be adopted to ''encourage the permanent settlement of those Indians as shall adopt the habits of the citizens of the United States.'' Finally, and probably an important consideration for some of the legislators with ties to the traders in northern Wisconsin, they requested that all future annuity payments be made at La Pointe (Wisconsin Legislature 1854, 397).

In negotiations at La Pointe in September of 1854, United States treaty commissioners found it necessary to assent to the insistent demands of the Lake Superior Chippewa for the demarcation of permanent reservations in Wisconsin. George Manypenny, who had replaced Luke Lea as commissioner of Indian affairs following the inauguration of Democrat Franklin Pierce as president in March of 1853, had hoped to secure the mineral wealth of unceded areas in the Lake Superior region by concentrating all Chippewa Indians west of the Mississippi River (Manypenny 1853, 245). A year later, however, Manypenny conceded:

> There are . . . within the limits of Wisconsin, and also within the northern peninsula of Michigan, a few small bands of the Chippewas of Lake Superior, who still occupy their former locations on lands ceded by the treaties of 1837 and 1842. It has not, thus far, been found necessary or practicable to remove them. They are very unwilling to relinquish their present residences, as are all the other bands of the same Indians; and it may be necessary to permit them all to remain, in order to acquire a cession of the large tract of country they still own east of the Mississippi, which, on account of its great mineral resources, it is an object of material importance to obtain. They would require but small reservations; and thus permanently settled, the efforts made for their improvements will be rendered more effectual. (Manypenny 1854, 212-13)

The Wisconsin Chippewas acceded to American acquisition of the rich mineral lands along the north shore of Lake Superior only after American officials promised to establish permanent reservations. Treaty Commissioner Henry C. Gilbert informed Commissioner Manypenny that ''the points most strenuously insisted upon'' by the Wisconsin Chippewas were ''first the privilege of remaining in the country where they reside and next the appropriation of land for their future homes. Without yielding these points, it was idle for us to talk about a treaty. We therefore agreed to the selection of lands for them in territory heretofore ceded'' (Gilbert 1854, 0137; *App. 5*).

Wisconsin's Chippewa Indians had learned several valuable lessons from the 1837 and 1842 treaty parleys. They absolutely refused to agree to the land cession sought by the Americans in 1854, as they had done in 1847, until *permanent* reservations were provided *in* the state. Furthermore, according to Benjamin Armstrong, when the U. S. interpreter began to translate the remarks of the American negotiators, Chief Buffalo interrupted him and insisted that the Indians appoint their own interpreter. "We do not want to be deceived any more as we have in the past," asserted the chief (Armstrong {1892}, 301).

The 1854 treaty (*Fig. 22*) provided for American acquisition of the north shore (see *Fig. 7*) and the establishment of four Chippewa reservations in Wisconsin (*Fig. 23*): *Bad River* located directly east of Ashland on the shore of Lake Superior with two hundred acres on Madeline Island for a fishing ground; *Red Cliff* situated at the northern tip of Bayfield County, which was established as a result of the 1854 treaty and an 1856 executive order by President Franklin Pierce;[40] *Lac Courte Oreilles* in Sawyer County southwest of Ashland; and *Lac du Flambeau* to the east in Vilas County along the Flambeau Lake, known to the Indians as "Lake of the Torches," because of the traditional practice of spearing fish by torchlight (Kappler 1: 933-34, 2: 648-52, *App. 6;* Danziger 1973, 178-79; Royce 1899, 796-97).

Approximately one year after the negotiations at La Pointe, Commissioner Manypenny[41] commended the people of Wisconsin for supporting the establishment of reservations in their state for the Chippewas. "They have not interposed any objection, but, on the contrary, have seemed willing that the Indians might be permitted to remain," Manypenny said of Wisconsinites in 1855. The commissioner reported that he was undertaking "the necessary steps" to survey the boundaries of the reservations and to provide the Chippewa bands with "the means of education, and in all other respects to fulfill the beneficial stipulations of their treaty" (Manypenny 1855, 322-23). The following year, Manypenny issued a glowing report about the condition of the Chippewas in northern Wisconsin. He informed Secretary of the Interior Robert McClelland in 1856 that the reservation Indians of the missionary settlement at Bad River had received "a liberal supply of farming implements, carpenters' tools, household furniture and cooking utensils; and every Indian having a house and residing in it, has been supplied with a good cooking stove and the usual cooking utensils, a table, bureau, chairs, bedstead, looking-glass, and many other articles for household use. The effect of this policy is quite perceptible and salutary, and has stimulated many to erect and provide for erecting new houses at Bad river {*sic*} and several other places" (Manypenny 1856, 554-55).

Manypenny's glowing report did not reflect reality for many of the Chippewa people of Wisconsin. Bad River had better soil conditions than the other areas designated for reservations, and it took some twenty years before all of the reservations granted in the 1854 treaty were selected and surveyed (Kappler 1: 928-36; *Madison Weekly Democrat* 1878a). Many Indians continued to roam throughout the ceded area engaging in their traditional pursuits. Without clearly marked boundaries for their reservations, the Lac du Flambeau and Lac Courte Oreilles Indians found it especially difficult to protect many of their resources (Vennum 1988, 260). The St. Croix Chippewas, who were left out of the 1854 negotiations, remained landless for eighty years. They lived as squatters on cutover lands or on tax-delinquent lands belonging to various counties, eking out a living as best they could deep in the forests just west of Lac Courte Oreilles. The Sakaogan Chippewas, who were also left out of the 1854 negotiations, signed a treaty with American officials in 1855, which promised them a reservation of twelve square miles of land. Left landless since the U. S. Senate refused to ratify the treaty, they lived as squatters near Crandon. Not until after the enactment of the Indian Reorganization Act in 1934 did the St. Croix and Sakaogan bands, the so-called Lost Bands, obtain legal title to the lands they had occupied for centuries—the Sakaogan Chippewas

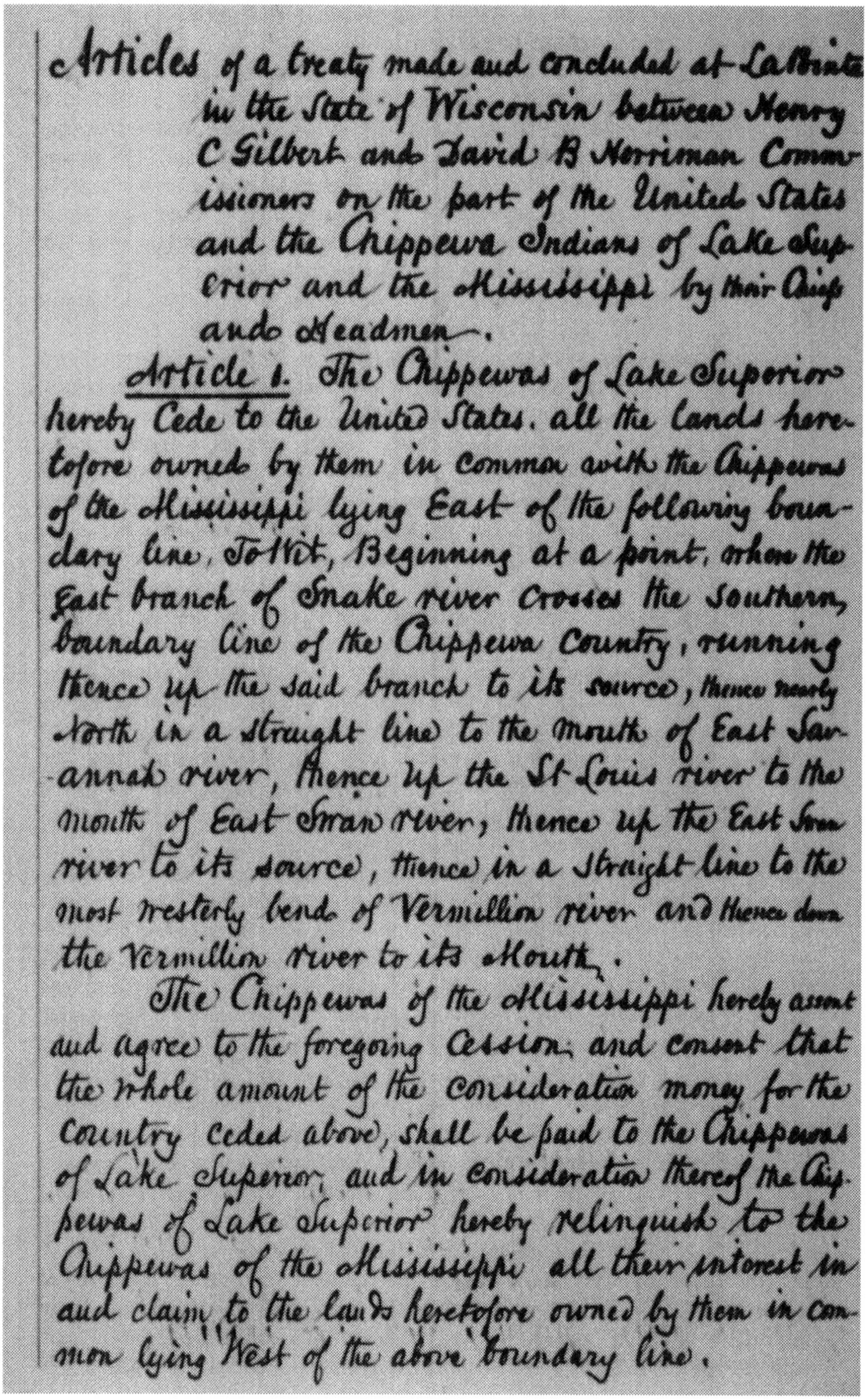

Articles of a treaty made and concluded at LaPointe in the State of Wisconsin between Henry C Gilbert and David B Herriman Commissioners on the part of the United States and the Chippewa Indians of Lake Superior and the Mississippi by their Chiefs and Headmen.

Article 1. The Chippewas of Lake Superior hereby Cede to the United States. all the lands heretofore owned by them in common with the Chippewas of the Mississippi lying East of the following boundary line, To Wit, Beginning at a point, where the East branch of Snake river Crosses the Southern boundary line of the Chippewa Country, running thence up the said branch to its source, thence nearly North in a straight line to the mouth of East Savannah river, thence up the St Louis river to the mouth of East Swan river; thence up the East Swan river to its source, thence in a straight line to the most westerly bend of Vermillion river and thence down the Vermillion river to its Mouth.

The Chippewas of the Mississippi hereby assent and agree to the foregoing Cession; and consent that the whole amount of the consideration money for the country ceded above, shall be paid to the Chippewas of Lake Superior, and in consideration thereof the Chippewas of Lake Superior hereby relinquish to the Chippewas of the Mississippi all their interest in and claim to the lands heretofore owned by them in common lying West of the above boundary line.

Fig. 22. *Treaty of 1854.* The first page of the handwritten treaty manuscript is reproduced above. Courtesy of the National Archives and Records Service.

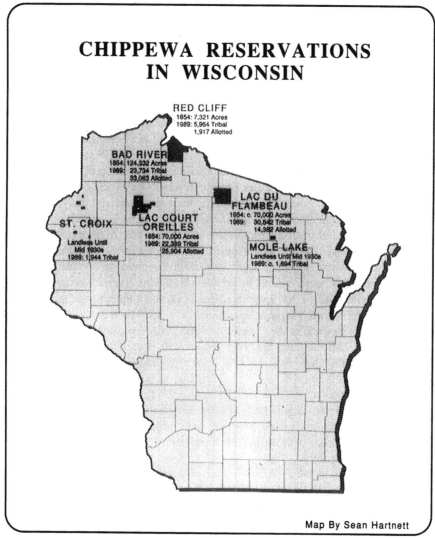

CHIPPEWA RESERVATIONS IN WISCONSIN

RED CLIFF
1854: 7,321 Acres
1989: 5,964 Tribal
1,917 Allotted

BAD RIVER
1854: 124,332 Acres
1989: 23,734 Tribal
33,063 Allotted

LAC DU FLAMBEAU
1854: c. 70,000 Acres
1989: 30,542 Tribal
14,382 Allotted

ST. CROIX
Landless Until Mid 1930s
1989: 1,944 Tribal

LAC COURT OREILLES
1854: 70,000 Acres
1989: 22,389 Tribal
25,904 Allotted

MOLE LAKE
Landless Until Mid 1930s
1989: c. 1,694 Tribal

Map By Sean Hartnett

Fig. 23. *Chippewa Reservations in Wisconsin.* Map by Sean Hartnett. Data from Lurie (1987, 10) and the Bureau of Indian Affairs, Great Lakes Agency in Ashland, Wisconsin. Compare tribally held acres in 1989 to the acreage originally provided and the number of acres alloted after the establishment of each reservation. Although federal officials promised in 1855 to establish a twelve-square-mile reservation at Mole Lake, the 1,700 acre reservation was not provided until the Indian New Deal of John Collier. The St. Croix Chippewa, who were also landless until they received 1,715 acres under Collier, are scattered in five small parcels of land across three counties. Today each reservation is a checkerboard of white-owned property equal to or exceeding the amount of Indian land held in trust under federal jurisdiction. Also, some Indian land is held by individual Indians rather than by the bands.

took possession of a small reservation barely comprising 1,700 acres known as Mole Lake in southwestern Forest County near Crandon, and the St. Croix Chippewas received a slightly larger reservation for their five scattered communities at Danbury, Webster, and Hertel in Burnett County and at Luck and Balsam Lake in Polk County (see *Fig. 23*). Nevertheless, the Wisconsin Chippewas had at least retained a portion of their homeland at Bad River, Red Cliff, Lac du Flambeau, and Lac Courte Oreilles as a result of the 1854 agreement (Lurie 1987, 21; Levi 1956, 95-101; Erdman 1966, 24, 27; Danziger 1979, 153-55; *Masinaigan* 1985; *Wisconsin State Journal* 1990c, 10).

The reservations proved to be small in terms of the traditional Chippewa hunting-fishing-gathering practices. Efforts to concentrate the Lac Courte Oreilles and Lac du Flambeau bands at the Bad River Reservation in the early 1870s failed. Although their lands were unsuitable for agriculture and they were plagued by trespassing lumbermen, settlers, railroaders, and white "sharpers" who defrauded them, the members of these bands refused to abandon their reservations (*New York Times* 1871; Campbell 1898, 317; Royce 1899, 857; Danziger 1973, 182-83).

Reports from the Indian agent at Red Cliff in 1861 and those of the agent stationed there in 1891 indicate that the Indians near Lake Superior were experienced sailors and active fishers who sold their surplus to white communities (Webb 1861, 74; Leahy 1891, 468). A Bureau of Indian Affairs official who traveled through northern Wisconsin in the early 1870s noted that Chippewa men opposed the federal government's efforts to train them as "agriculturalists." He reported that, although the men considered farming to be "squaws work," they were eager to undertake "mans" work. "All the Lake Superior Indians will work if only somebody will find something for them to do," the official assured Indian Commissioner Edward P. Smith (Day 1873).

During the second half of the nineteenth century, Chippewa men found temporary employment as sawyers, log drivers, graders for railroads, and packers of survey equipment. But, such wage labor positions were unstable and unpredictable. The Chippewas found it necessary to live by a mixture of traditional pursuits such as hunting, and fishing, and gathering, as well as wage labor, the sale of wood and other products, and annuity payments until they expired in the mid 1870s (Day 1873; Shifferd 1976, 19; Danziger 1979, 96). For many years after the establishment of the reservations, so many Chippewa men found it necessary to fish, hunt, and look for employment away from the areas reserved for them that not until 1892 could Indian Bureau officials state assuredly that a majority of the Wisconsin Chippewas were permanent reservation residents (Danziger 1973, 182).

The presence of Chippewa Indians near white communities sometimes alarmed the residents. During the summer of 1878, for example, Norwegian and Swedish immigrant settlers in Burnett County in northwestern Wisconsin misinterpreted the intentions of Chippewa Indians at a nearby encampment and triggered an "Indian panic." Wild rumors of Chippewa warriors from Wisconsin and Minnesota joining Sioux braves on the warpath caused what one observer referred to as the "timid Swedes" of Burnett County to abandon their farms and flee for their lives. Telegraph messages reporting that local officials had joined the exodus crossing over to Minnesota led Governor William E. Smith to seek assistance from the U. S. War Department (Forsyth 1878; Bryant 1878; *Madison Weekly Democrat* 1878b; *Barron County Chronotype* 1878; *St. Paul Pioneer Press* 1878).

Wisconsin Adjutant-General Edward E. Bryant and Lieutenant Colonel James W. Forsyth, aide-de-camp to U. S. Army General Philip Sheridan, investigated the situation and found no cause for alarm. As a Minnesota editor reported, rumors of an impending attack were "absurd." Noting that the Chippewas in both states were at peace and that the Indians in Burnett County had not taken anything from the abandoned farms, the editor commented:

> The Chippewas of Wisconsin . . . are not only utterly dependent upon the whites, but they are surrounded upon all sides by a wide cordon of white settlements. War would simply drive them from their ancient retreats in the pine woods and rice lakes out of the two States, into the arms of their old and merciless enemies, the Sioux, across the Missouri. But not only the physical conditions render a Chippewa war on the whites impractable, but the moral conditions render it absurd. Such a panic as that in Burnett county, Wisconsin, could only arise from a profound misconception of the habits and character of the Chippewa Indians of that section. All their traditions bind them to peace with the whites. Their utter dependence on the whites guarantees it. (*St. Paul Pioneer Press* 1878)

A newspaper editor in Rice Lake, Wisconsin, agreed with his Minnesota colleague but expressed the hope that the incident in neighboring Burnett County would "result in obliging the Indians to keep on their reservations" (*Barron County Chronotype* 1878). General Bryant and Colonel Forsyth supported this position.

General Bryant lost little time in assuring Governor Smith that the situation was under control. Seemingly oblivious of the Chippewa usufructuary rights in ceded territory including Burnett County, Bryant recommended that the innocent Chippewas make way for the needs of the white settlers:

> While the Indians undoubtedly meditate no mischief, certainly no hostility to the whites, they are a nuisance to the settlers; they stroll about, beg, pester timid women, pick cranberries before ripe, shoot off the deer, and by their presence retard the growth of those portions of the State which they frequent. They ought to be kept on their reservations. As long as they are allowed to roam about in bands, so long will they cling to the lazy habits of Indian life. Penned up on their reservations, they would be compelled to resort more to agriculture, and it certainly would be a relief to the settlers in our northern woods, if these disagreeable bands were kept out of their neighborhoods.

Colonel Forsyth agreed and informed General Bryant that he intended to recommend that the Bureau of Indian Affairs (BIA) adopt stricter regulations for the Chippewa bands in order "to keep them on their reservations, and to drive them by all politic measures into industrial pursuits" (Bryant 1878). Also ignoring Chippewa off-reservation usufructuary rights, BIA officials responded by encouraging the Indians to earn their living *within* their reservations under federal guidance (Danziger 1979, 96).

In the 1870s, federal officials not only actively sought to prevent the Chippewas from "clinging" to such "lazy habits of Indian life" as hunting, fishing, and gathering off-reservation on ceded lands, they also reexamined the policy of negotiating treaties with the Indian tribes. In ending treaty making for domestic political reasons in March of 1871, however, congressmen specifically recognized the validity of existing treaty obligations[42] (Kappler 1: 8; Priest 1942, 96-102, 244; Cohen 1982, 128). Chippewa usufructuary rights in ceded territory as reserved in the treaties of 1837 and 1842 remained in effect. There was little legal impact on the continuing relationship between the United States and the Chippewas as a result of the 1871 enactment, but the BIA and residents of Wisconsin increasingly undermined Chippewa usufructuary rights during the ensuing decades.

Among those questioning the soundness of treaty making with Indians were some prominent residents of Wisconsin. In 1870, a committee of the Old Settler's Club of Milwaukee County, composed of Increase A. Lapham—a charter member of the Wisconsin Academy of Sciences, Arts and Letters and of the American Ethnological Society whose numerous achievements earned him the titles of "the first Wisconsin scientist" and "the first scholar of Wisconsin" (Kellogg 1933; Sherman 1876, 60-61; Quaife 1917)—and colleagues Levi Blossom and George G. Dousman, praised the federal government's earlier decision to establish reservations in Wisconsin for the Chippewas rather than to remove them from the state. They quoted approvingly from Commissioner Manypenny's 1856 report (cited earlier) and referred to the government's reservation policy for the Chippewas as "a move in the right direction, and one that might have been adopted with advantage at an earlier date." While the members of the Old Settler's Club viewed the removal policy as "at best a temporary, a short-sighted policy," they had even harsher words for the government's policy of "regarding a mere handful of poor, miserable Indians as a distinct *nation*." Calling the idea of dealing with Indians in Wisconsin as sovereign states an "absurdity," they commented, "why the Indians, any more than the Chinese, the Mormons, or any other people should be allowed to maintain a distinct government within our own, it is difficult to understand." The solution was clear to them. "Let us at once cease this absurd and ridiculous policy, and treat every Indian, as we do all others, according to his individual rights; allow him the same privileges, and require of him personally, and individually, the same duties; and subject him to the same laws, as other citizens and residents within our borders, and very much of our Indian trouble will be avoided" (Lapham *et al.* 1870, 10, 13-14). Lapham, Blossom, and Dousman, like other Americans of their generation, had come to view Indian treaties as an obstacle to an effective Indian policy. Indeed in 1871, when Congress prohibited further treaty making with Indian tribes, the three Wisconsinites—like others who advocated making the Indians citizens—undoubtedly viewed the change as only the first step toward eventual citizenship (Mardock 1971, 105).

The precarious economic position of the reservation Indians made them vulnerable to the Bureau of Indian Affair's educational and assistance programs, which were designed to promote acculturation. No longer in a position to choose from white culture those features that appealed to them, the Wisconsin bands found themselves increasingly dependent on the white man's largesse. Chippewa agriculture, following white practices, was still in its early stages by 1900 and provided only a minor source of food and income. The Indians were also exploited by unscrupulous logging companies who cheated them while transforming their forests into cutover lands and by white trespassers who stripped timber from their reservations without much fear of capture and prosecution since they were often aided by conniving Indian agents (*New York Times* 1888b, c; Danziger 1979, 89-91, 94, 100, 103; Fries 1951, 202; Levi 1956, 242). In 1872, for example, La Pointe Agent Selden N. Clark negotiated a "give-away" contract for timber from Lac Courte Oreilles with an Eau Claire entrepreneur[43] (Shifferd 1976, 22). Not until 1888 did Congress extend anti-trespass legislation to Indian reservations and the Senate launch an investigation into the logging practices on Chippewa lands (*Fig. 24*) that exposed numerous

Fig. 24. *Logging Scene on Lac Courte Oreilles Reservation, 1909.* Courtesy of the State Historical Society of Wisconsin. WHi(x3)37336

frauds committed against the Indians (*New York Times* 1888b, c; 1889; Fries 1951, 202; U. S. Secretary of the Interior 1889).

From the ratification of the 1854 treaty until the turn of the century, the Lake Superior Chippewas tried repeatedly to convince American officials to faithfully execute the financial provisions of their treaties (Shifferd 1976, 21). They especially complained about overdue annuity payments (*Fig. 25*) and funds owed them as a result of the federal government's use during the Civil War of inflated paper currency instead of the hard coin required by the treaties. During a visit to Washington in 1864, the members of a delegation from Wisconsin recounted their recollection of the manner in which Chippewa reserved rights had been incorporated into the treaties of 1837 and 1842. The bilingual petition of 1864 cited earlier in this study was preceded by a memorial stating, "we have always kept our promises made to our Great Father, and we have the right to expect him to keep his promises made to us."[44] The petition may have contributed to the Bureau of Indian Affair's decision in 1865 to pay the annuities at Red Cliff and Bad River in coin, but the arrearages went unpaid in spite of the contributions of Chippewa warriors to the Union cause during the Civil War (Nichols 1988, 3-5; Current 1976, 366).

One administration after another found excuses for denying the Indians an audience to discuss the overdue payments (Danziger 1979, 230 n. 19). In 1867, for example, Acting Commissioner of Indian Affairs Charles E. Mix rejected a Chippewa request for a conference in Washington on the basis that travel through American cities would have a bad moral influence on the Indians. Yet, Mix did not meet them in Wisconsin either (Mix 1867). For the next twenty-five years, the Chippewas persisted in their efforts to secure their overdue funds; but, as an eastern newspaper editor observed in 1888, "no one {was} willing to listen" (*New York Times* 1888a). In 1878, after reporting that rumors of Chippewa hostilities in Wis-

Fig. 25. *Annuity Payment Scene at La Pointe.* Photograph by Charles A. Zimmerman. Courtesy of the Minnesota Historical Society.

Fig. 26. *Indian School in the Vicinity of Hayward, 1880s.* Courtesy of the State Historical Society of Wisconsin. WHi(x3)23295

consin were groundless, La Pointe Indian agent Isaac L. Mahan informed Indian Commissioner Ezra A. Hayt that "the Chippewas have grievances that would make white men tear their hair and howl from one end of the country to the other, but they prefer to submit quietly and peaceably to the powers that be, praying without ceasing, hoping continually that the good men of the Great Father's household will yet hear and answer their petitions by the necessary legislation." In particular, Mahan urged Hayt to convince Congress to pay the funds the United States owed the Chippewas. "If the government would pay these poor people half what is justly their due under former treaties," the agent asserted, "they could and would live comfortably for many seasons to come." In the meantime, Mahan stressed the necessity of securing "large appropriations for net-twine and hooks" so Chippewa fishers could provide adequate subsistence for their families (Mahan 1878, 147-48). Despite such pleas, when the members of the U. S. Senate Committee on Indian Affairs examined the records of the U. S. Treasury Department in 1892 they discovered that the federal government still owed the Chippewas more than ninety-two thousand dollars. "The breach of faith to these unfortunate people," the Senators asserted, "is a greater reproach to the Government by reason of the fact that, while so many tribes and bands of western Indians have resorted to war in their exasperation, the Chippewas have been uniformly faithful and friendly" (U. S. Senate Committee on Indian Affairs 1892, 2-4). Nevertheless, a thorough examination of the federal statute books for the 1890s led historian Edmund Danziger, Jr. to conclude that Congress never appropriated funds to pay the Chippewas (Danziger 1979, 230 n. 19-231, n. 19).

Throughout the late nineteenth century, but especially after passage of the Dawes Severalty Act in 1887, and continuing during the early 1900s, Bureau of Indian Affairs officials sought to transform the communal Chippewa people into "civilized," capitalistic farmers through programs of coercive education and social

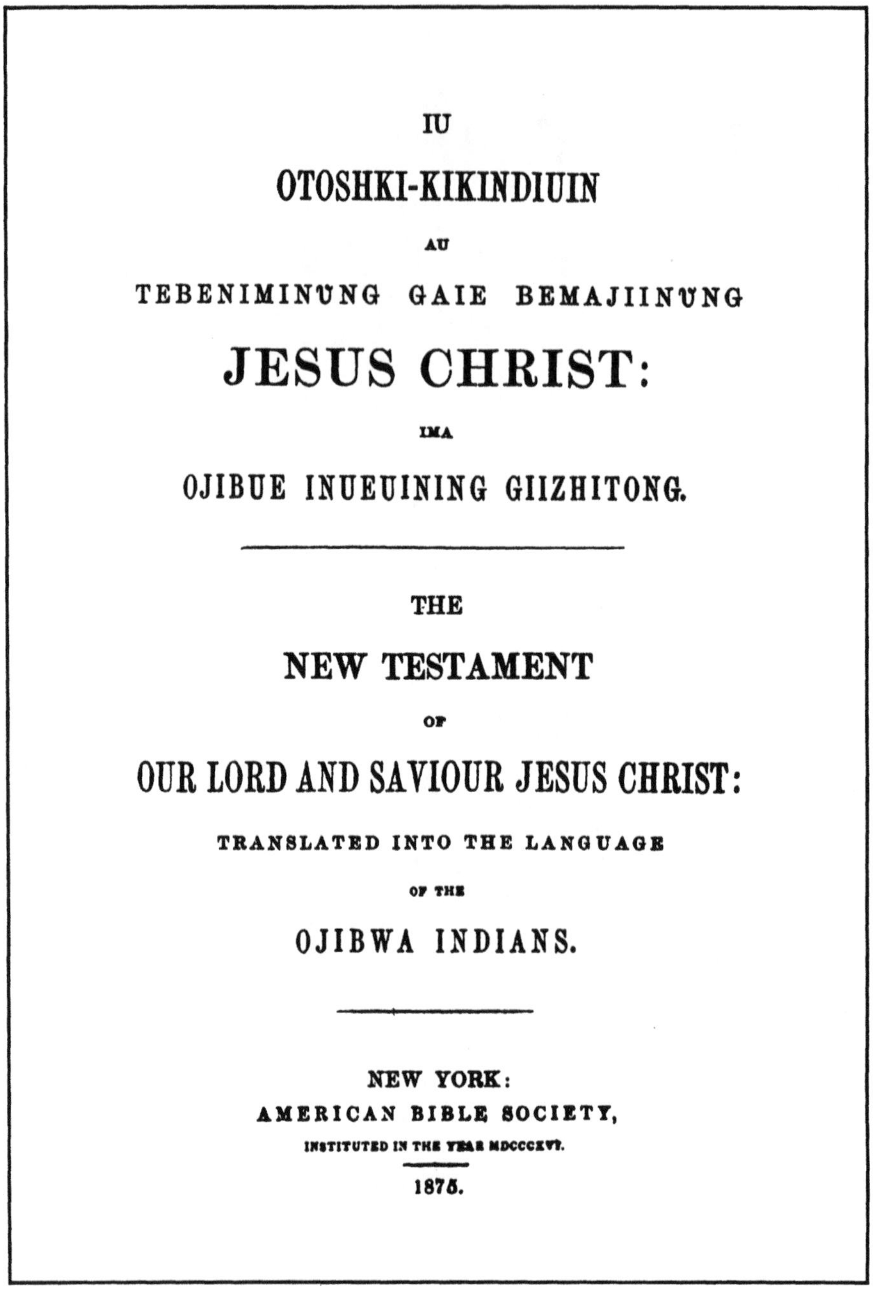

IU

OTOSHKI-KIKINDIUIN

AU

TEBENIMINUNG GAIE BEMAJIINUNG

JESUS CHRIST:

IMA

OJIBUE INUEUINING GIIZHITONG.

THE

NEW TESTAMENT

OF

OUR LORD AND SAVIOUR JESUS CHRIST:

TRANSLATED INTO THE LANGUAGE

OF THE

OJIBWA INDIANS.

NEW YORK:
AMERICAN BIBLE SOCIETY,
INSTITUTED IN THE YEAR MDCCCXVI.

1875.

Fig. 27. *New Testament in Ojibwa Language, 1875.* The conversion of Chippewas to Christianity was one of the ways non-Indians measured Indian "progress" in becoming "civilized." Courtesy of the State Historical Society of Wisconsin. WHi(x3)24983

control (*Figs. 26-28*). Designed to convert communal tribal property into individually owned lands, the Dawes Act was also intended to isolate individuals from the tribal community so that they could eventually be absorbed into the larger white society (Otis 1973). Whatever the goals of the severalty legislation, lands allotted

Fig. 28. *An Indian Farmer Preparing a Seed Bed, c. 1930.* Federal officials encouraged the Chippewas to farm, but small family farms on the cutover lands available to the Indians proved inadequate for making a living. Courtesy of the State Historical Society of Wisconsin. WHi(w6)6290

to Indians became easy targets of lumber companies or were lost through forfeiture when taxes could not be paid (Danziger 1979, 97-109; Glad 1990, 486). As one scholar has commented, "a Wisconsin county tax sale notice can be mightily confusing when you do not understand ownership to begin with, when you have never heard of taxes, and when you speak only Chippewa" (Wilkinson 1990, 17-18). Although they congregated together on an increasingly diminished land base and were under tremendous pressure to abandon tribal affiliations and identity as well as traditional communal ways, the Chippewas tried to follow their traditions as best they could (*Figs. 29-30*). They developed cooperative strategies for hunting, fishing, and gathering under existing conditions (Haskins 1909; Shifferd 1976, 18, 26-38; Vennum 1988, 264; Glad 1990, 486-87).

Beginning during the latter part of the nineteenth century, Chippewa fishers and hunters (*Fig. 31*) faced increasing competition for fish and game from commercial fishers, market hunters, and white sportfishers and hunters. Northern towns like Bayfield, a stop on steamer lines, had attracted tourists since the 1860s. As early as 1870, a Bayfield hotel reported that the majority of its registrants during the previous year had been "pleasure seekers" from "down below." All Wisconsin

Fig. 29. *Chippewa Herbalist and Family in Rice Lake, 1916.* The Chippewa woman depicted here had a wide knowledge of herb and bark medicines. Courtesy of the State Historical Society of Wisconsin. WHi(x3)36518

railroads terminated in Chicago, and the flow of tourists from that city to Wisconsin was substantial. During the century following 1860, tourism and recreation became the largest combined source of employment and income in many northern counties as more and more city dwellers who enjoyed bird-watching, camping, boating, fishing, hiking, hunting, sight-seeing, and swimming were attracted by the state's more than eight hundred miles of Great Lakes coastline, nearly fifteen thousand lakes, and more than nine thousand miles of trout streams. The promotional efforts of the Wisconsin Central Railroad, which built the rambling Chequamegon Hotel in Ashland that took several trainloads of vacationers as well as sportfishers and hunters to fill, especially contributed to the growing interest in northern Wisconsin as a vacation spot. Meanwhile, the presence of increasingly large numbers of sportfishers and hunters, together with competition for game from commercial sources, made fishing and hunting less dependable sources of food for the Indians by the early twentieth century. The Chippewas also had to contend with the power of the State of Wisconsin as they sought to eke out an existence on and off their reservations (*Wisconsin State Journal* 1990c, 13; Shifferd 1976, 30-31; Nesbit 1985, 194, 529; Thompson 1988, 288).

Fig. 30. *Chippewa Woman Preparing Splints for Basket-making, c. 1925.* Courtesy of the Wisconsin State Historical Society. WHi(x3)18837

Fig. 31. *Hunting in Winter on Snowshoes.* From a stereograph by Charles A. Zimmerman. Courtesy of the State Historical Society of Wisconsin. WHi(x3)15462

6   The Curtailment of Treaty Rights

Between the establishment of their reservations in 1854 and the end of the century, the Chippewas continued to hunt, fish, and gather both on their reservations and off, and the Indians and whites in the region coexisted (*Fig. 32*) peacefully despite occasional misunderstandings as occurred in Burnett County in 1878 (Hanaway 1989, 3-4). The general trend in the Wisconsin legislature as well as in the state court system during this period, however, favored the extension of state jurisdiction over tribal Indians unless federal law specifically prohibited it. For example, an 1849 statute prohibiting the sale of intoxicating liquor to Indians was reenacted in 1858 and again in 1878 (Wisconsin Supreme Court 1916, 354-55). In 1879, the judges of the Wisconsin Supreme Court, arguing that "Indians are included within the laws when not excepted from their provisions," ruled the state's criminal laws applied to the Indians *on* their reservations. This was an ominous portent of things to come for the Chippewas (Wisconsin Supreme Court 1879a, 296-97).

At the end of the nineteenth century and increasingly during the early years of the twentieth century, officials of the State of Wisconsin harassed Lake Superior Chippewa Indians who attempted to exercise their off-reservation rights to hunt, fish, and gather in ceded territory (Wilkinson 1990, 19-20; Strickland *et al.* 1990, 4-5). State efforts to enforce game and fish laws on reservations led to the arrest on April 23, 1901, of John Blackbird, a full blood Chippewa, on the Bad River reservation. The arresting game warden confiscated Blackbird's net and took him to Ashland to stand trial. A municipal court judge found Blackbird guilty of violating state laws and fined him twenty-five dollars plus court costs. In default of payment, Blackbird received a sentence of thirty days imprisonment at hard labor in the county jail at Ashland. U. S. attorneys William G. Wheeler and Henry T. Sheldon arranged a test case challenging the state's authority to convict and imprison Blackbird (U. S. District Court 1901, 140).

In June of 1901, attorneys Wheeler and Sheldon argued before the Federal District Court for the Western District of Wisconsin that state authorities had no jurisdiction to enforce their game and fish laws *on* Indian reservations. The attorneys argued that Congress, in adopting the Major Crimes Act on March 3, 1885 (U. S. Congress 1885), had prescribed which acts constituted crimes when committed by "tribal Indians" on reservations and which courts had jurisdiction in cases involving those crimes. States, they contended, neither had authority to add crimes to the list enumerated by Congress nor to prosecute Indians in state courts for crimes committed on reservations. Wisconsin Attorney General E. R. Hicks's attempt to uphold the state's jurisdiction was soundly rebuffed by Judge Romanzo Bunn (U. S. District Court 1901).

Judge Bunn ruled that the Major Crimes Act had extended *exclusive* Congressional jurisdiction over Indian reservations for specific criminal offenses. "No doubt, if

Fig. 32. *Ojibwa Ceremony at the Wisconsin State Fair, 1906.* Non-Indians watch Chippewas perform a ceremony. WHi(x3)45972

necessary,'' he stated, ''congress would provide for the punishment of lesser crimes committed by the Indians. But so far . . . it has not been found necessary.'' The reason lesser crimes had not been enumerated, at least in the case of the Chippewas, was clear to Bunn:

> These Indians are a quiet, peaceable people, and all the trouble and infractions of the peace that have come among them have arisen from the mercenary acts of white men in selling them intoxicating drink in violation of law. Congress might even provide fish and game laws to restrict the Indians in their natural and immemorial rights of fishing and hunting. But it has not seen fit to do so. It would be intolerable if the state, under these circumstances, should have the power to step in, and extend its civil and criminal codes and police power over these people. It would be an invitation to an early conflict of jurisdiction.

Bunn concluded his strong rebuke of state efforts to enforce fish and game laws on the Chippewa reservations with a reference to the usufructuary rights reserved by the Indians in their treaties with the United States. ''After taking from them the great body of their lands in . . . Wisconsin, allowing them to reserve certain portions for reservations, and stipulating they should always have the right to fish and hunt upon all lands so ceded,'' Bunn stated, ''it would be adding insult as well as injustice now to deprive them of the poor privilege of fishing with a seine . . . upon their own reservation.'' The judge, warning state fish and game wardens that their over-zealousness in arresting Indian fishers for using nets in streams on their reservations was "not justifiable in law," ordered the release of Blackbird (U. S. District Court 1901, 145).

Judge Bunn's ruling in 1901 did not prevent Wisconsin officials from continuing their efforts to extend state authority over the Chippewas. Six years later, an Indian named Morrin, who had become a U. S. citizen under the Dawes Act and had lived in Bayfield for more than five years, was arrested under a 1905 statute for fishing with a gill net in Lake Superior in violation of state fishing regulations. Morrin appealed his conviction on the basis of his alleged reserved usufructuary treaty right to fish in ceded territory. Although Morrin's status as a U. S. citizen added a special nuance to his claim of usufructuary rights in ceded territory, the justices of the Wisconsin Supreme Court used his appeal as an opportunity to reassert state legal authority over tribal Indians on the Chippewa reservations.

> . . . To exempt . . . Indians from state laws regulating hunting and fishing within the borders of a state after its admission to the Union would deprive the state of its sovereign power to regulate the rights of hunting and fishing, and would deny to such state admission into the Union on an equal footing with the original states, upon the ground that a treaty with the national government giving the right to hunt and fish within territory which subsequently is embraced within the limits of a state is a privilege in conflict with the act of admitting the state into the Union on an equality with the other states and is repealed thereby.

According to the justices, the act of Congress admitting Wisconsin into the Union as a state abrogated Chippewa treaty rights pertaining to hunting and fishing within the borders of the state (Wisconsin Supreme Court 1908). Their decision, which ignored Federal Judge Bunn's 1901 ruling, found Morrin guilty and deprived the Chippewa Indians of a major source of food and income for the next seventy-five years until it was reversed by federal appeals court judges in 1983.

In addition to the *State* v. *Morrin* ruling, other dark legal clouds hung over the heads of the Wisconsin Chippewas before 1983. During World War I, while Chippewas were serving overseas in the U. S. army (*Fig. 33*), the Wisconsin Supreme Court continued to encroach upon tribal sovereignty and reserved treaty rights. In 1916, the court cited 1849, 1858, and 1878 statutes to uphold the prohibition of the sale of intoxicating liquor to "all full-blood Indians" whether or not they belonged to a tribe (Wisconsin Supreme Court 1916). In 1927, the court ruled that President Zachary Taylor's Removal Order of 1850 effectively terminated the Chippewa "right of occupancy" in Wisconsin "so far as it would interfere with the lawful occupancy of those claiming patent {land title} from the United States is concerned" (Wisconsin Supreme Court 1927, 473-74) despite earlier U. S. Supreme Court rulings in 1894 and 1918 that no executive order[45] had actually terminated the Chippewa right of occupancy (U. S. Supreme Court 1894, 584; 1918, 137). According to tribal elder James Pipe Mustache of the Lac Courte Oreilles (LCO) Band, state officials began taking a tougher stand toward off-reservation hunting and wild rice gathering by LCO members near Hayward in 1927. Fines, jail terms, car impoundments, and rifle confiscations became common (*Isthmus* 1990, 1). The rise of such incidents during the Great Depression in the 1930s coincided with the state's first appropriation to advertise the resorts and vacation spots of northern Wisconsin and the rise of automobile traffic to that region on the state's increasing number of gravelled and concrete roads (*Wisconsin State Journal* 1990c, 13; Nesbit

Fig. 33. *Chippewa Soldier from Hayward in World War I Uniform.* Courtesy of the State Historical Society of Wisconsin. WHi(x3)37329

and Thompson 1989, 480). As Wisconsin officials courted tourists and harassed Indian hunters, fishers, and gatherers, the Chippewas of northern Wisconsin confronted deteriorating living conditions and suffered from inadequate diet and health care (Danziger 1979, 119-26; Glad 1990, 487).

Not all rulings of the Wisconsin Supreme Court supported efforts to regulate aspects of tribal life and to curtail usufructuary rights. In 1931, for example, in *State* v. *Rufus* the justices of the Court recognized that state courts did not have jurisdiction over criminal actions by an Indian *within* reservation limits, thereby overturning the Court's 1879 decision in *State* v. *Doxtater*. The justices also conceded that Wisconsin had been out of step with federal court rulings regarding the handling of Indian hunting and fishing rights. Wisconsin had not been upholding an 1886 Supreme Court ruling, *U. S.* v. *Kagama,* that said federal jurisdiction over the tribes rested not upon ownership of and sovereignty over the country or reservation in which they reside but upon the fact that the tribes are wards of the federal government. The justices concluded that efforts of state courts to prosecute Indians for violating state hunting and fishing regulations within the confines of their reservations should have ended with the decision in *U. S.* v. *Kagama.* Relying heavily on an article in the *Yale Law Journal* by a University of Wisconsin Law School professor (Brown 1930), the Wisconsin Supreme Court justices ruled that "while prosecutions brought in the state courts against Indians might have beneficial results, such is not sufficient to confer jurisdiction upon state courts in the absence of legislation by Congress authorizing such jurisdiction" (Wisconsin Supreme Court 1931, 335, 339).

In 1933 and again in 1940, attorney Thomas L. St. Germaine of the Lac du Flambeau Band argued before the Wisconsin Supreme Court that Chippewa Indians could not be prosecuted for violating state fish and game laws *off* their reservations either because of the provisions of the treaties of 1837, 1842, and 1854. In both cases, the court conceded the Indians had the right to hunt and fish on their own lands without regard to state regulations but denied them that right on lands that had come under state jurisdiction through sales by Indians to non-Indians (Wisconsin Supreme Court 1933; 1940).

On April 23, 1934, at Hayward near the Lac Courte Oreilles reservation, attorney St. Germaine voiced his concern over the erosion of Chippewa hunting and fishing rights. The occasion was the last of a series of so-called regional Indian congresses called by Commissioner of Indian Affairs John Collier for the purpose of explaining pending legislation (the Wheeler-Howard Bill) to tribal representatives.[46] The Hayward Congress brought together Indians from Wisconsin, Minnesota, and Michigan. St. Germaine was among the delegates from the Chippewa reservations in Wisconsin who raised concerns about the proposed legislation, fearing it might strip Indians of their hunting and fishing rights (U. S. Bureau of Indian Affairs 1934, 28-30; Deloria and Lytle 1984, 119).

Attorney St. Germaine's efforts to preserve the usufructuary rights of the Chippewas are documented in the court cases and in the proceedings of the Hayward Indian Congress mentioned above. The actual day-to-day meaning of state infringements on hunting, fishing, and gathering rights for Indian families may be gleaned from oral histories. Reporter Ron Seely of the *Wisconsin State Journal* recently retold the following remembrance of a member of the Nakomis ("Grandmother") Club on the Lac du Flambeau Reservation:

One winter morning . . . when she was a girl about 12, her father . . . and two friends left early to go deer hunting. The hunting trip was important because the winter had been harsh and the food was low.

After several hours the men spotted a deer. The only problem was that it was off the reservation, just across the creek that forms the eastern boundary. Her father, knowing the family needed food, shot the deer anyway. The men gutted it and took it home.

Later in the day . . . wardens came and arrested her father for violating state game laws by hunting deer off the reservation without a license. He spent six months in jail in Wausau.

The woman remembers she was so mad that she wrote the judge a letter. "Don't you know," she asked, "that deer meant we would have enough food or not?" Her family survived the winter without her father thanks to the generosity of relatives and friends. The woman remains bitter today for what the state did to her family in violation of their reserved treaty right to hunt off the reservation (*Wisconsin State Journal* 1990c, 27-28). Such stories would undoubtedly be repeated many times over if the remembrances of all Chippewa grandmothers were collected. The state's violation of Chippewa usufructuary rights in ceded territory exacted a heavy toll on the lives of Indian families—a cost that cannot be measured solely in terms of fish and game as the above example illustrates.

The years between attorney St. Germaine's efforts in 1933 and 1940 to secure recognition of Chippewa off-reservation usufructuary rights coincided with the "Indian New Deal" under the leadership of Indian Commissioner Collier. A proponent of repealing the Dawes Act and returning lands to the Indians, Collier believed that the communal way of reservation life offered an alternate lifestyle for individualistic white Americans (Philp 1977). His hopes for the future centered around the Wheeler-Howard bill that was designed

> *to conserve and develop Indian lands and resources; to extend to Indians the right to form business and other organizations; to establish a credit system for Indians; to grant certain rights of home rule to Indians; to provide for vocational education for Indians; and for other purposes.* (U. S. Congress 1934)

Collier convened a series of Indian congresses, including the one at Hayward mentioned earlier, to answer questions about the proposed legislation and to win support for it. He responded to criticisms and suggestions by offering amendments to the bill. The U. S. Congress enacted the measure, known as the Indian Reorganization Act (IRA) on June 18, 1934 (Philp 1977, 145-60). Between November 17 and June 15, 1934, voters at each of the Chippewa reservations in Wisconsin overwhelmingly agreed to accept the IRA. Under the act, Collier worked to provide the St. Croix and Sakaogan Chippewas—the so-called Lost Bands—with small reservations (see *Fig. 23*); and he encouraged the Chippewa bands to adopt constitutions and bylaws. Meanwhile, the BIA attempted to provide the tribes with jobs, relief, loans, and educational programs (Danziger 1979, 133-34, 137, 153-54).

The IRA inspired optimism among some Indians. In addition to the cultural and political regeneration it heralded, programs such as the Indian Division of the Civilian Conservation Corps, the Works Progress Administration, and the Civil Works administration brought much-needed job training, jobs, and hard cash to the Chippewa reservations. But Collier's Indian New Deal proved inadequate in meeting the needs of the Chippewas of Wisconsin. The Chippewas survived the Depression and took some steps toward self-determination, but they did not become prosperous or independent. Encouraged by the state's promotion of tourism, whites had already gained title to reservation lands and surrounded the most desirable lakes with cottages and resorts. The Chippewas, who were left with swampy, cutover lands unsuitable for either farming or recreation, faced great difficulties in maintaining tribal cohesion and in providing a sound economic base for their bands during the Depression years. During the 1940s, Congress turned an increasingly deaf ear to Collier's programs for tribal advancement as the war effort drained human and monetary resources. Termination of the New Deal programs mentioned above dealt the Chippewa bands a severe economic blow (Danziger 1979, 168-69; Glad 1990, 489; Lurie 1987, 44).

Following World War II, tourism and recreation became major components of the Wisconsin economy. Increasingly larger numbers of tourists annually spent money in northern Wisconsin on food, lodging, and alcohol. In many counties in the north, they constituted the largest combined source of employment and income. During the 1950s, nearly four million out-of-state people a year vacationed and enjoyed outdoor recreation in Wisconsin as did more than two million state residents annually by the end of the decade. Together, the out-of-state and in-state figures comprised a number half again as large as Wisconsin's total population. Next to sight-seeing, fishing was the most popular attraction. In 1960, the state issued more than 925,000 fishing licenses, two-and-a-half times as many as were issued twenty years earlier. Between 1940 and 1960, the number of hunting licenses issued also grew significantly, from 400,000 to 622,000 (Thompson 1988, 288-89). As the total number of fishers and hunters rose annually in the 1950s, state game wardens increasingly collided with Chippewa fishers and hunters (Wilkinson 1990, 22).

In 1953, the Republican-dominated Congress passed legislation designed to make law enforcement on reservations in Wisconsin a state rather than a federal responsibility. Public Law 280 subjected the Chippewas to state jurisdiction over matters that did not affect treaty rights (U. S. Congress 1953; Brophy and Aberle 1966, 184-85). Enacted at a time when terminating the unique federal relationship with the tribes was national policy, PL 280 was an invitation to Wisconsin to enforce the full gamut of its criminal laws on the reservations. Simultaneously, the state accelerated its crackdown on Indian hunting and fishing (Monette 1990, 276; Wilkinson 1990, 22).

Wisconsin game wardens vigorously applied state conservation laws to Indians *on* the Chippewa reservations during the 1950s. A series of "unjust arrests" of Chippewa fishers and hunters by state conservation officials led the Bad River Band Tribal Council to issue the following *"Declaration of War"* on November 10, 1959:

When, in the course of human events, it becomes necessary to protect the rights and liberties of certain peoples of this great nation from encroachment by other peoples, it is the duty of the Tribal Council, the governing body of the Bad River Band of the Lake Superior Tribe of Chippewa Indians of Wisconsin, to take measures that will protect the members of said Band from unjust arrests by State Conservation officials.

IT IS HEREBY DECLARED, that a state of cold war exists between the Bad River Band of Chippewa Indians and the officials of the Wisconsin Department of Conservation, and that such state shall exist until such time as the State of Wisconsin shall recognize

Federal treaties and statutes affording immunity to the members of this Band from State control over hunting and fishing within the boundaries of this reservation.

During this period, State conservation officials shall be denied access to all tribal and restricted lands within the boundaries of this reservation.

Nothing in this declaration shall be construed to mean that the Tribal Council condones any un-Christian act, or any act of violence upon any person, or to be taken to sanction any riot, or in any manner disturbing the peace. It is known that any such acts are punishable under State Law, such jurisdiction having been given by this Band under {Public Law 280,} the Act of August 15, 1953. (Bad River Tribal Council 1959)

The "cold war" over the enforcement of state regulations *on* Chippewa reservations appeared to have come to an end in 1966 when Attorney General Bronson C. La Follette declared treaty rights were still in force on reservations and that the state's conservation laws only applied to the Chippewas when they were *outside* the boundaries of their reservations (Erdman 1966, 62-63). The controversy over state regulation of usufructuary rights on reservations in the 1950s, however, was but a precursor of other problems for the Indians.

7

The Continuing Pursuit of Justice

During the 1950s and 1960s, the Chippewas and other reservation Indians across the United States confronted numerous efforts to abrogate their treaties and to seize tribal lands for dams and other purposes. Indians responded by turning to the federal courts for protection of rights reserved under treaties. The State of Wisconsin provided an early example of this trend. In 1962, the Menominee Indians contested the arrest of a tribal member by state wildlife authorities for hunting out of season (Lurie 1987, 59; U. S. Court of Claims 1967, 998-1010). When the case finally reached the Supreme Court several years later, the justices ruled that nineteenth-century Menominee treaty rights relating to hunting were still valid since they had never been explicitly extinguished by the United States government (U. S. Supreme Court 1968, 404-12).

The Court's contention that treaty rights must be *explicitly* extinguished by the federal government and just compensation provided in order for the United States to abrogate them is one of a series of legal precedents referred to by scholars of Indian law as ''canons of construction.'' Four such canons have emerged since the nineteenth century (Cohen 1982, 221-25). A brief review of them is essential to our understanding of the legal context and the results of recent Chippewa efforts to protect their treaty rights.

Judicial canons or standards of interpreting Indian treaties evolved during and after the treaty-making era of American history. This period lasted from the 1778 treaty with the Delaware Indians until Congress ended treaty making in 1871. The following four canons or principles have emerged from a number of Supreme Court decisions:

1) treaties must be liberally construed to favor Indians;
2) ambiguous expressions in treaties must be resolved in favor of the Indians;
3) treaties must be construed as the Indians would have understood them at the time they were negotiated; and
4) treaty rights legally enforceable against the United States should not be extinguished by mere implication, but rather explicit action must be taken and 'clear and plain' language used to abrogate them.

These standards of dealing with cases involving Indians represent an acknowledgement by the federal judiciary of the unequal bargaining position of the Indians at the time of treaty negotiations. This acknowledgement is based, among other things, on the federal government's employment of interpreters and its superior knowledge of the language in which the negotiations were conducted. Fundamentally, the canons reflect the fact that justices of the U. S. Supreme Court have acknowledged Indians did not bargain with the federal government from a position of equal strength (Cohen 1982, 221-25).

The reason for the emergence of the canons is rooted in the special trust relationship between the Indian people and the United States (Cohen 1982, 220-22). This relationship was outlined in an 1831 U. S. Supreme Court case involving a dispute between the Cherokee Nation and the State of Georgia. Chief Justice John Marshall declared Indian tribes to be "domestic dependent nations" whose relationship to the United States resembled that of "a ward to his guardian." Marshall viewed Indian tribes as self-governing entities, but he recognized that their location *within* states of the Union established a "peculiar" relationship with the federal government (U. S. Supreme Court 1831). The concept of the federal trust responsibility to Indians evolved judicially from Marshall's rulings (Satz 1987, 34-49; Cohen 1982, 220-21) and has played an important role in the efforts of Wisconsin's Chippewa Indians to protect their hunting, fishing, and gathering rights.

The primary question of concern to federal judges and legal experts in reviewing treaty rights controversies is this: what reasonable expectations did the Indians have as a result of treaty negotiations? Although federal judges have recognized the duty of the United States to carry out the terms of treaties as they were understood by Indians, it is not an easy task to determine today what the understanding of an Indian tribe or band was more than a hundred years ago. Among the most important documents used for this purpose are the proceedings that were usually recorded during the treaty councils. Copies of those documents that have been preserved in the National Archives and Records Service in Washington, D.C., are available on microfilm (Hill 1981, 44-45). The proceedings contain the official minutes of the treaty negotiations as recorded by representatives of the U. S. government. Together with related correspondence to the commissioner of Indian affairs and other government officials, the proceedings often help to clarify the motives, concerns, and perceptions of U. S. treaty commissioners and Indians. Since the proceedings were written by government employees and thus undoubtedly are biased in favor of the United States government, federal judges have carefully noted those instances in which these documents support the Indians' recollection of events and treaty provisions as opposed to the government's written version of the treaty. In instances where the proceedings reinforce the Indians' version (see, for example, those noted in Chapters 2-4 of this study), the courts have ruled in favor of the Indians in interpreting the provisions of the treaties (Kickingbird *et al.* 1980, 34).

During the last two decades, the descendants of all of the Lake Superior Chippewa bands have increasingly turned to the federal courts for assistance as some white Americans have challenged their efforts to continue to enjoy the rights their ancestors reserved in the treaties they signed with the federal government. Events of the mid- and late 1960s set the stage for the legal actions of later decades. The Great Society programs of the Lyndon B. Johnson administration opened up new links between Indian leaders and the federal government (Prucha 1984, 2: 1092-095). Office of Economic Opportunity (OEO) funds were used, among other things, to establish legal services programs. Wisconsin Judicare, for example, was established to assist low-income people in the state's northern counties, which also happen to contain all of Wisconsin's Chippewa reservations (Lurie 1987, 51, 54; Wilkinson 1990, 23). Although the programs of the Johnson administration had an important impact on the lives of many American Indians, the following events related to the rising Indian militancy[47] of the late 1960s and early 1970s captured the attention of the news media[48] and spotlighted Indian grievances: the organization of the American

Indian Movement (AIM) in Minneapolis in 1968, the seizure and occupation of Alcatraz Island in San Francisco Bay in 1969, the Trail of Broken Treaties that resulted in the occupation of the Bureau of Indian Affairs building in Washington, D.C., in 1972, and the seizure of the hamlet of Wounded Knee on the Pine Ridge Reservation in South Dakota in 1973 (Prucha 1984, 2: 1116-120).

Such militancy had its counterpart in Wisconsin as well. In addition to the Indian students who badgered university administrators for Indian counselors and programs in Indian studies and languages, there were such events as the three-day occupation of the Northern States Power Company dam site near the town of Winter in Sawyer County in late July and early August of 1971 by a group of about a hundred Lac Courte Oreilles Chippewas and some twenty-five AIM supporters[49] and the occupation on New Year's Eve 1974 of a vacant Catholic novitiate near the reservation town of Gresham in Shawno County by the Menominee Warrior Society.[50] By the mid-1970s, however, most Indian activists in Wisconsin—like their counterparts across the United States—had turned to the legal system for assistance in redressing their grievances (Lurie 1987, 54-56, 58).

Wisconsin Indians looked to the federal courts and organizations such as the Native American Rights Fund and Wisconsin Judicare to seek the benefits of the federal government's trustee relationship to the tribes without the burden of federal domination (Lurie 1987, 54). As Indian activists Russel Lawrence Barsh and James Youngblood Henderson have noted, in the American constitutional system of checks and balances "the ultimate security of a minority excluded from or too few to take advantage of majoritarian political processes lies in the Constitution and constitutional courts" (Barsh and Henderson 1980, 138).

The rising militancy of the 1960s and 1970s gave many Indians a new sense of pride in being Indian, and a new generation of leaders sought legal redress for their grievances. "The legal weapon is especially potent in the Indian situation," a student of the new Indian politics reminds us, "because the relationship of Native Americans to the United States, unlike that of any other group in American life, is spelled out in a vast body of treaties, court actions, and legislation" (Cornell 1986, 128).

As early as 1971, Wisconsin Judicare had undertaken a test case involving Chippewa fishing rights in Lake Superior under nineteenth century treaties (*Capital Times* 1972). In two cases reviewed together, the Wisconsin Supreme Court ruled on January 6, 1972, that the Red Cliff and Bad River Chippewa Indians had fishing rights in Lake Superior by virtue of the establishment of their reservations on the lake's shores in the 1854 treaty, but the majority decision recognized the state's right to "reasonable and necessary" regulations to prevent a substantial depletion of the fish supply and declared that Indian methods of gathering fish had to "reasonably conform to the aboriginal methods." In a concurring opinion, Chief Justice E. Harold Hallows upheld the right of the Chippewas to fish in Lake Superior but disagreed with his colleagues on state regulation of Indian fishing. Hallows argued that the needs of whites should not determine the extent of Chippewa fishing rights nor should the Indians be limited to using aboriginal methods. As Hallows commented:

> The majority opinion states to the Indians you have your historic and traditional fishing rights, but the state of Wisconsin 'who did not grant you those rights in the first place' is going to regulate them. The regulation of the Indians' right to fish could reduce them to the status of privileges of the white inhabitants of Wisconsin. I cannot agree that the

needs of the white inhabitants of Wisconsin must determine the extent of the Indians' fishing rights. Nor can I agree that the methods of fishing by the Indians must be by aboriginal methods.

Hallows concluded his remarks by stating, "the Indians should be allowed a spinning rod as well as a bone hook or spear" (Wisconsin Supreme Court 1971, 410-12).

The most famous court case involving Chippewa hunting, fishing, and gathering rights in Wisconsin is *Lac Courte Oreilles Band of Chippewa Indians* v. *Voigt*. In early March of 1974, Wardens of the Wisconsin Department of Natural Resources (DNR) arrested Frederick and Michael Tribble, members of the Lac Courte Oreilles (LCO) Band, for spearfishing on Chief Lake, located south of Hayward in ceded territory in Sawyer County. Charged and found guilty of possessing a spear for taking fish on inland off-reservation waters and for occupying a fish shanty without a proper tag, the brothers were defended by the LCO Band, which filed suit in 1974 against DNR Secretary Lester P. Voigt, DNR Conservation Wardens Larry Miller and Milton Dieckman, Sawyer County District Attorney Norman L. Yackel, and Sawyer County Sheriff Donald Primley for interfering with Chippewa off-reservation hunting and fishing rights (*Capital Times* 1974; U. S. District Court 1978).

In 1978, Federal District Court Judge James Doyle ruled against the Chippewas. Doyle concluded that "when the boundaries of the Lac Courte Oreilles reservation were finally determined pursuant to the 1854 treaty, the general right of the Lac Courte Oreilles Band and its individual members to hunt, fish and gather wild rice and maple sap in the area ceded by the treaties of 1837 and 1842, free of regulation by state government, was extinguished, except as to reservation lands, and except as to special hunting and fishing rights on limited parts of the ceded territory adjacent to the treaty reservations which might properly be inferred from the language of the 1854 treaty setting apart the reservations 'for the use of' the Chippewa" (U. S. District Court 1978, 1361).

After initial rejection of their arguments by Judge Doyle, the Chippewas turned to the U. S. Court of Appeals for the Seventh Circuit, which in 1983 reversed Judge Doyle's decision and reaffirmed the sanctity of the treaties and the right of the Indians to hunt, fish, and gather on and off their reservations on public lands[51] in ceded territory in the so-called *Voigt Decision* or what has come to be known as LCO I.[52] In deciding in favor of the Indians, a three-judge panel reviewed historical and ethnographical evidence and concluded the Indians had been led to believe they could continue to hunt, fish, trap, and gather on ceded lands as long as they refrained from molesting white settlers. Further, the judges ruled that the usufructuary rights were not withdrawn by the 1850 Removal Order because the order was invalid; they concluded the 1854 treaty did not specifically revoke those rights either (U. S. Court of Appeals 1983).

In reversing Judge Doyle's 1979 decision, the U. S. Court of Appeals was upheld by the U. S. Supreme Court, which refused to review the case (U. S. Supreme Court 1983; *Milwaukee Sentinel* 1983). The Court of Appeals remanded the case to Judge Doyle with instructions to "enter judgment for the LCO band . . . and for further consideration as to the permissible scope of State regulation over the LCO's exercise of their usufructuary rights" (U. S. Court of Appeals 1983, 365).

Soon after the Supreme Court refused to review LCO I, the other five Chippewa bands recognized as successors to the Chippewa Indians who signed the 1837 and 1842 treaties—the Red Cliff Band, the Sokaogon Chippewa Indian Community/Mole Lake Band, the St. Croix Chippewa Indians, and the Lac du Flambeau Band joined the Lac Courte Oreilles Band in the lawsuits that followed (Bichler 1990b, 2).

Meanwhile, Governor Anthony S. Earl, a Wausau attorney who had served as secretary of the Department of Natural Resources from 1975 to 1980, was anxious to promote harmony in the northern part of the state where the *Voigt Decision* had stunned many non-Indians. On October 13, 1983, just ten days after the U. S. Supreme Court refused to hear the appeal of the *Voigt Decision* by the State of Wisconsin, Earl issued *Executive Order 31* which stated:

> WHEREAS, there are eleven federally recognized Tribal governments located within the State of Wisconsin, each retaining attributes of sovereignty, authority for self-government within their territories and over their citizens; and
>
> WHEREAS, our Nation, over the course of two centuries has dealt with American Indian tribes through the application of international common law, negotiation of treaties, and constitutional interpretation of law, each recognizing the special government-to-government relationship as the basis for existance {*sic*}; and
>
> WHEREAS, the Supreme Court has consistently upheld this unique political relationship developed between Indian tribes and the United States government; and
>
> WHEREAS, the State of Wisconsin was established in 1848 with a continuous vested interest in service to all of its citizens regardless of specific jurisdiction, ethnic or cultural background, religious affiliation or sex; and
>
> WHEREAS, it is in the best interest of all units of government, federal, tribal, state and local to recognize the pluralistic diversity of our government and society;
>
> NOW, THEREFORE, I, ANTHONY S. EARL, Governor of the State of Wisconsin, order my administration, state agencies and secretaries to work in a spirit of cooperation with the goals and aspirations of American Indian Tribal Governments, to seek out a mutual atmosphere of education, understanding and trust with the highest level of tribal government leaders.
>
> AND, FURTHERMORE, all state agencies shall recognize this unique relationship based on treaties and law and shall recognize the tribal judicial systems and their decisions and all those endeavors designed to elevate the social and political living conditions of their citizens to the benefit of all. (State of Wisconsin Executive Department 1983)

Earl called for cooperation between state agencies and tribal governments, but the state and the Chippewa bands continued to confront each other in federal court.

When Judge Doyle entered a partial judgment in favor of the Chippewas as specified by the Seventh Circuit of the U. S. Court of Appeals, the Wisconsin Department of Justice appealed that ruling. State officials claimed usufructuary rights could not be exercised on any land that had at any time been privately owned. A three-judge panel of the Seventh Circuit ruled in 1985 (LCO II) on the availability of private and public lands subject to the exercise of treaty rights. "It is appropriate once again to say," the judges stated, "that the whole thrust of LCO I was that the usufructuary rights survived after the treaty of 1854 and that those rights must be interpreted as the Indians understood them in 1837 and 1842." The judges also ruled that "Wisconsin's obligation to honor the usufructuary rights of the Indians is no more or less than was the federal government's obligation prior to Wisconsin's statehood" (U. S. Court of Appeals 1985, 182-83).

During the 1986 gubernatorial campaign, Republican Tommy G. Thompson, the Assembly minority leader from Elroy, attempted to woo voters away from Democratic incumbent Governor Earl in northern Wisconsin by openly speaking against Chippewa reserved treaty rights during campaign swings in the region. At a Protect Americans' Rights and Resources (PARR) banquet in Minocqua near the Lac du Flambeau reservation where the most active spearfishers reside, for example, Thompson spoke to about two hundred and thirty anti-treaty activists:

> A very major difference between Tony Earl and me is that I believe in treating all people equally. I believe spearing is wrong regardless of what treaties, negotiations or federal courts may say. The exercise of these special privileges has hurt our tourism industry, created an image problem and has hurt real estate and land values . . . . If I am governor, the state of Wisconsin will defend your right and your title to your lands. (*Milwaukee Journal* 1986a; *Wisconsin State Journal* 1989a)

Thompson told a meeting of the Northwoods Realtors in Rhinelander that "spearing is wrong, period" and that "we cannot stand by and let our fishing areas, hunting grounds and tourism industry be threatened" (*Ashland Daily Press*, 1986).

Governor Earl took a different approach to the treaty rights issue. In June, he appointed a sixteen-member commission to "review alternatives for resolving concerns about the exercise of treaty rights, improving understanding between Indians and non-Indians and addressing the social needs of the region." Commission members included the tribal chairs of the Chippewa bands and non-Indians. Among the latter were local government officials, representatives of the tourism industry, conservationists, a minister, and a college instructor. Earl named Jeff Long, chair of the town of Boulder Junction in Vilas County, and Stockbridge-Munsee tribal chair Leonard Miller, president of the Great Lakes Inter-Tribal Council, as co-chairs. The governor urged the commissioners "to explore ways to resolve disputes stemming from the Indian treaties, to encourage better race relations and to promote tourism and economic development." Earl urged the commission to engage in "positive thinking about Wisconsin's Northland and its resources." In response to reporters' questions about proposals to abrogate treaties, Earl replied, "I'm not going to join the chorus of abrogating the treaties. Politically, it's the easy way, but hell, I know that's kidding the people" (*Milwaukee Journal* 1986b; *Message Carrier* 1986).

Candidate Thompson criticized the governor for failing to appoint critics of off-reservation hunting and fishing rights to the tribal-community relations commission (*Milwaukee Journal* 1986c). Following his victory at the polls in November, Thompson was confronted with growing opposition to Chippewa treaty rights—a problem political opponents claimed his own campaign had helped to inflame. Paul DeMain, editor of *News from Indian Country* (Hayward, Wis.) and a former aide to Governor Earl, claims that Thompson's courting of PARR and Stop Treaty Abuse (STA) since 1986 gave those groups a legitimacy they did not deserve and emboldened them to mount large boat-landing protests against spearfishers. "Tommy Thompson pumped those people up," DeMain argues (*Wisconsin State Journal* 1989a, e; *Milwaukee Journal* 1989f). Evidence to support DeMain's contention that Thompson played into the hands of PARR and STA may be gleaned from the promotional literature of these organizations. *PARR Issue*, for example, regularly informs dues-paying and potential members in words and in photographs of the frequent meetings between PARR officers and the governor and his aides (*PARR Issue* 1991q, v). Such tactics undoubtedly assisted the development of anti-treaty sentiment as Judge Doyle addressed the various issues emerging from the *Voigt Decision*.

After LCO II, Doyle divided the court proceedings on Chippewa treaty rights in Wisconsin into three phases:

Phase I: The Declaratory Phase was to result in the determination of the nature and scope of Chippewa treaty rights.

Phase II: The Regulatory Phase was to lead to a determination of the permissible scope of regulation by the State of Wisconsin.

Phase III: The Damages Phase was to lead to the determination of the amount of damages, if any, to which the Chippewas are entitled for interference by state officials with the exercise of their off-reservation treaty rights. (Bichler 1990a, 254; *Masinaigan* 1990a)

After dividing the proceedings into these phases, Doyle began to address the various issues.

On February 18, 1987, on what treaty rights opponents referred to as "Doomsday for Wisconsin" (*Milwaukee Journal* 1987a, 22A), Doyle ended Phase I of the court proceedings by affirming in LCO III the right of the Chippewa bands to exercise their usufructuary treaty rights to harvest nearly all varieties of fish, animal, and plant life available in ceded territory necessary to maintain a "modest living" free from state interference. The state may, however, impose restrictions upon the Chippewas provided restrictions are "reasonable and necessary to conserve a particular resource." Doyle ruled that the Chippewas could employ any means of harvesting resources used at the time of the negotiation of the treaties or any developed since then, the Chippewas could trade and sell harvested goods to non-Indians using modern methods of distribution and sale,[53] and that "appropriate arrangements" must be made to allow the Chippewas to exercise their usufructuary rights on private lands *if* public lands were insufficient to support a modest living. The judge further explained his reasoning:

I have found, and now repeat, that the Chippewa understanding in 1837 and 1842 was that in the absence of a lawful removal order or in the absence of fresh agreement on their part, settlement and private ownership of parcels by non-Indians would not require the Chippewa to forgo anywhere or in any degree exercise of their reserved usufructuary rights necessary to assure that, when the exercise of those rights was combined with trading with non-Indians, the Chippewa would enjoy a moderate living within the entire ceded territory. (U. S. District Court 1987a, 1432, 1435)

Republican Governor Tommy Thompson responded to Doyle's rulings by announcing that the state would appeal (*Milwaukee Journal* 1987a, 1A).

Following Doyle's death in June of 1987, Judge Barbara Crabb took over the case and began Phase II of the court proceedings. Judge Crabb ruled in August of 1987 (LCO IV) that the modest living standard did not restrict the Chippewas to an upper limit during their harvesting of resources. She also established the legal standards for permissible bounds of state regulation, maintaining that the State of Wisconsin could regulate Chippewa off-reservation usufructuary rights in the interests of conservation, public health, and safety, provided the regulations were reasonable and necessary to conserve a particular species, did not discriminate against the Chippewas, and were the least restrictive alternative available. Effective tribal self-regulation, however, would preclude state regulation (U. S. District Court 1987b).

Less than two weeks after Judge Crabb announced her ruling in LCO IV, the U. S. Court of Appeals for the Seventh Circuit criticized the legal team the Thompson administration had assembled to challenge the *Voigt Decision* and to protest the awarding of interim attorney's fees to the Chippewas. Not only did the judges dismiss the state's appeal on August 31, 1987, but they also imposed sanctions for "inexcusable" errors in filing the appeal. Pointing out that this was Wisconsin's third error concerning appellate jurisdiction in the litigation resulting from the 1983 case, the judges expressed concern about the state's "serious lack of understanding of the basic principles of federal appellate review." In assessing sanctions for the "frivolous appeal" the judges stated, "we are entitled to expect better from the State of Wisconsin" (U. S. Court of Appeals 1987).

Following the rulings in LCO IV and in the appeal case, state and tribal officials sought a delineation of the Chippewas' harvesting rights. In 1988 (LCO V), Judge Crabb determined the Chippewas could not maintain "a modest living" of slightly more than $20,000 per family from the available harvest within ceded territory (U. S. District Court 1988). Crabb in 1989 (LCO VI) established Chippewa walleye and muskellunge rights using a plan proposed by Chippewa tribal conservation officials in the Great Lakes Indian Fish and Wildlife Commission modified by a "safe harvest" calculation methodology supplied by the state. The judge prohibited state officials from interfering in the regulation of treaty rights with regard to the harvesting of walleye and muskellunge except insofar as the Indians had otherwise agreed by stipulation (U. S. District Court 1989).

On May 9, 1990 (LCO VII), Judge Crabb ruled on Chippewa off-reservation deer harvest rights within the ceded territory. She recognized the state's right to prohibit deer hunting by Indians in the summer and during evenings based on safety concerns and decided that Indians and non-Indians were each entitled to one half of the game harvest[54] (U. S. District Court 1990a, 1401-02, 1413-27). Attorney General Hanaway reacted positively, noting that the decision put the Chippewas and non-Indians on an equal footing. "The decision is in a sense equal rights for everyone," he said. Stop Treaty Abuse leader Dean Crist, however, summed up the anti-treaty rights position by observing, "the bad thing is you still have less than 1 percent of the population with 50 percent of the resource." Crist accused Crabb of "trying to court-appoint co-management" (*News from Indian Country* 1990c, d)

Judge Crabb ruled on October 11, 1990 (LCO VIII), that the Chippewa Indians could not sue the State of Wisconsin for an estimated $300 million in damages for denial of treaty rights over the years. In an opinion that shocked treaty rights advocates and brought loud cheers from the Thompson administration and anti-treaty spokespersons, Crabb argued that recent U. S. Supreme Court interpretations of the Eleventh Amendment[55] indicate that states have "sovereign immunity" from lawsuits by Indian tribes. As a result, the Chippewa bands must persuade the federal government to sue the State of Wisconsin on the bands' behalf if the Indians are to have any hope of collecting damages for the state's past denial of their treaty rights. Meanwhile, as attorneys for the various bands contemplated appealing Crabb's ruling in Phase III of the proceedings, the judge reviewed the state's power to regulate Chippewa harvesting and selling of timber in ceded territory (*Eau Claire Leader-Telegram* 1990i, j).

Crabb, who had earlier barred the state and its counties from challenging the Chippewas' treaty right to harvest and sell timber, reviewed these rights in a four-week trial held in early 1991. About 1.8 million acres of county forests lie on ceded lands, and the Wisconsin Counties Association and the Wisconsin County Forests Association have vigorously argued for many years that timber rights on county forest lands are not covered by the Chippewa treaties. In the mid-1980s Wisconsin counties earned in excess of 3 million dollars annually from timber sales. In addition to the counties, the state, which was represented in the trial independently, has about 370,000 acres of land, generating approximately $800,000 annually, involved in the timber rights dispute. Many Chippewa leaders, facing unemployment rates exceeding fifty percent on their reservations, view logging as a way to boost their economies (Wisconsin County Forests Association *et al.* 1990, 1, 6; State of Wisconsin *et al.* 1990, 2-3; *Milwaukee Journal* 1984b, 1989d; *Green Bay Press Gazette* 1990; *Milwaukee Sentinel* 1990f; Hazelbaker 1984, 6; Mulcahy and Selby 1989, 24; *Eau Claire Leader-Telegram* 1990h, i, 2a, 1991). Federal Indian policy scholar Robert H. Keller recently suggested that the Chippewas "could be granted special if not exclusive access for sugaring," or they "could be paid royalties on all commercial sugar collected from their traditional lands." Since Chief Flat Mouth had specifically told Governor Henry Dodge at the treaty negotiations in 1837 that the Indians wanted to "reserve the privilege of making sugar from the trees," Keller argued the Chippewas reserved the right to take maple syrup from ceded territory just as they reserved the right to harvest fish, game, and wild rice (Keller 1989, 118, 124, 128).

On February 21, 1991, Judge Crabb simultaneously issued opinions and orders relating to the Chippewas' timber harvesting claims and to the state's right to enforce its civil boating regulations against tribal members engaged in the exercise of their usufructuary rights. Observing that neither Judge Doyle nor she had previously addressed explicitly the Indians' usage of tree resources at the time of the nineteenth-century treaties, Crabb concluded that the harvesting and selling of timber were not among the Chippewas' "usual and customary activities." Crabb also argued that "logging cannot be characterized as simply a modern adaptation of a traditional harvesting activity engaged in by the Chippewa." Conceding that the Chippewas have "a somewhat stronger argument to the effect that . . . {they} never understood they were selling timber resources other than pine," Crabb nevertheless ruled that the state and county governments could impose "reasonable and necessary" regulations for conservation of forest products so long as they do not discriminate against Indians (U. S. District Court 1991a). Crabb also ruled that the State of Wisconsin could enforce and prosecute violations of safe boating laws committed by tribal members engaged in treaty activities provided that the regulations did not "infringe, restrict, hinder, impede or prohibit the time, place or manner of treaty fishing rights (or limit the quantity or types of fish or other resources harvested) and are reasonable and necessary for purposes of public safety and conservation" (U. S. District Court 1991b). Barring appeals or the raising of other issues by the tribes or the state, Crabb concluded that all of the issues in the seventeen-year-old litigation had now been adjudicated (U. S. District Court 1991c). In mid-March, Crabb responded to efforts by the Lac du Flambeau spearfishers to stop what they allege to be "a racially-motivated campaign of violence and intimidation . . . to make it difficult or impossible for them to spear fish" by prohibiting treaty protesters from interfering with the exercise of spearing rights (U. S. District Court 1991d). Several days later, on March 19, 1991, Crabb issued her "Final Judgment," summarizing and clarifying the court's decisions, which evolved from the lengthy litigation. Crabb advised all parties involved that they had two months to review the document and to determine whether or not they wished to file appeals (U. S. District Court 1991e; see *App. 7*). Two months later, on May 20, the six Chippewa bands and Attorney General James E. Doyle, Jr. announced in separate statements that they would not appeal the rulings. The litigation resulting from the state's interference with the reserved treaty rights of the Chippewas, which had come to a head with the arrest of the Tribble brothers in 1974, had finally been resolved. In announcing their decisions not to appeal, the Chippewa leaders and Attorney General Doyle alluded to their hopes for a new era of cooperation and improved tribal-state relations (See *Apps. 8-9*).

During the years between LCO I in 1983 and Judge Crabb's Final Judgment in 1991, while the Chippewa bands and the State of Wisconsin litigated the extent of Chippewa treaty rights, the two sides worked out a series of interim agreements.[56] The agreements dealt with such issues as the exercise of treaty rights off the reservations, the measures necessary to protect natural resources, and the role of tribal and state game wardens. The Chippewas agreed to temporarily limit the exercise of their rights, and Wisconsin officials agreed not to arrest Indians harvesting natural resources within the agreed-upon guidelines. The Indians and the state reached the first such agreement on the issue of harvesting white-tailed deer in November of 1983 shortly after Governor Earl issued *Executive Order No. 31* calling for state-tribal cooperation. While working with leaders of the Earl administration to establish interim agreements, the six Wisconsin Chippewa bands joined with other tribes in Minnesota and Michigan to form the Great Lakes Indian Fish and Wildlife Commission and set about adopting a conservation code, hiring tribal fish and game wardens to regulate Indian fishers and hunters, assessing and managing natural resources, and publishing data to counteract propaganda from white backlash groups (*Milwaukee Journal* 1984a; Strickland *et al.* 1990, 7-8; Great Lakes Indian Fish and Wildlife Commission {c.1988}, {c.1989}; Busiahn 1989a; Busiahn *et al.* 1989; *Masinaigan* 1990b; Bichler 1990b).

8　　The White Backlash and Beyond

The 1983 *Voigt Decision* evoked bitter denunciations from white hunting and fishing groups. Supported by generally anti-Indian whites, these groups claimed the Indians would wantonly wipe out all fish and game. Especially objectionable to sportfishers and hunters are the traditional practices of spearing, gill-netting, and "shining" (night hunting) employed by the Chippewas who are more concerned with following their traditions and with efficient harvests than with sport. Opponents of the *Voigt Decision* consider it "unjust" for the Chippewas to have "special privileges" denied other Wisconsin residents—like longer hunting seasons and the right to shoot deer from vehicles—just because of some "old treaties." Charging that Indians have "more rights" today than white citizens, irate critics of treaty rights argue Indians and whites should enjoy "equal" rights, that treaty rights must be abolished. As far away from the reservations as Milwaukee, one hears stories about drunken Indians peddling deer from their pickup trucks at taverns "up north." Anti-Indian sentiment oozed from bumper stickers proclaiming "Save a Deer, Shoot an Indian" and "Spear an Indian, Save a Muskie." An unofficial notice circulated in the Ashland County Courthouse declared "open season on Indians" with "a bag limit of 10 per day." A 1984 newspaper headline summed up the situation this way, "North Woods Steaming with Racial Hostility" (*Milwaukee Journal* 1984c; O'Conner and Doherty 1985).

Strong opposition to federal court pronouncements on Chippewa hunting and fishing rights spurred protest and violence at boat landings throughout northern Wisconsin during every fishing season since 1983. Some whites, fearing Indians would destroy all fish and ruin tourism, have argued that Indian treaties and reservations are relics of the past. Such fears have been exacerbated by the fact that per capita income in the region has lagged behind the rest of the state by as much as twenty percent, and northern Wisconsin's unemployment rate has nearly doubled the statewide average during some months. In addition, the efficient Chippewa methods of harvesting fish for subsistence—using gill nets and spears—upset many non-Indian sportfishers who find themselves limited by very strict state regulations. Bait shops in northern towns have sold "Treaty Beer" with labels protesting Indian spearfishing and claiming to be the "True Brew of The Working Man" (*Fig. 34*), and many restaurants and taverns display and dispense literature attacking spearfishing and calling for the abrogation of Chippewa treaties (*Fig. 35*). The peaceful harvesting of fish by Chippewa spearfishers has been disrupted by non-Indians hurling rocks, insults, and racial epithets like "timber niggers," waving effigies of speared Indian heads and signs with slogans like "Save Two Walleye, Kill a Pregnant Squaw," and using large motorboats trailing anchors to capsize Indian boats. Treaty protesters have also placed concrete fish decoys in lakes to break the spears of Chippewa fishers. Chippewa women singing religious songs in support of the spearers have faced what one reporter has aptly called "a gauntlet of hate"

Fig. 34. *Treaty Beer.* Distributed for the Stop Treaty Abuse (STA) organization in Minocqua, this beer has been sold in northern Wisconsin taverns as the "True Brew of the Working Man." Called "racism in a can" by treaty supporters, the product label protests Indian spearfishing. Photograph by Jason Tetzloff. Reprinted with permission.

as some demonstrators jeer and shout vicious taunts, racial slurs, and threats while others blow whistles in continuous shrill blasts in their ears. Even Indian schoolchildren have been harassed. One school with a large Indian enrollment has received bomb threats (Fixico 1987, 498-507; Vennum 1988, 276-77; O'Conner and Doherty, 1985; Wilkinson 1987, 72; Strickland *et al.* 1990, 1; *Milwaukee Journal* 1989a, b; *Milwaukee Sentinel* 1990d; *Masinaigan* 1991c, 8; *Wisconsin State Journal* 1990c, 11; *Eau Claire Leader-Telegram* 1990g).

Non-Indian eyewitnesses including members of the U. S. Civil Rights Commission, the state's Equal Rights Council, and state legislators have compared the acts of violence against spearfishers at boat landings in northern Wisconsin in recent years to the racial violence against blacks that rocked Milwaukee in the 1960s *Capital Times* 1986a; *Milwaukee Sentinel* 1989b; *Masinaigan* 1990d). Protesters in

Fig. 35. *Spear This!* A poster found in a tavern in the Eagle River, Wisconsin, area before the 1987 Chippewa spearfishing season. From Great Lakes Indian Fish and Wildlife Commission ({c.1989}, 15). Reprinted with permission.

Vilas County near the Lac du Flambeau Reservation have been so unruly that some Indians refer to it as "Violence County" (*Wisconsin State Journal* 1990a). U. S. Interior Department official Patrick Ragsdale said he was "appalled" and "disgusted" by the language protesters used at the boat landings (*Milwaukee Sentinel* 1989a). Archbishop William Wantland of the Episcopalean Diocese of Eau Claire observed, "of all the states I've lived in{,} in this Union, Wisconsin is the most racist. I grew up in the South. And I said that before the *Voigt Decision* was handed down.

It's obvious—the racism, the hatred, the bitterness, the prejudice." Recently, Wantland reflected on the increasing hostility toward Indians since 1983: "I felt I was caught in a time warp this spring in Wisconsin. I thought I saw the 50s and 60s. I thought I saw Selma and Little Rock and Montgomery" (*Masinaigan* 1990f, 7-8). In June of 1989, University of Wisconsin-Eau Claire History Professor James Oberly raised this question for the nation to ponder, "How could a northern state with a progressive tradition {like Wisconsin} become such hospitable ground for flagrant racism?" (Oberly 1989b, 844).

The white backlash of the 1980s in Wisconsin actually had its roots in the 1970s. Concern over the Wisconsin Supreme Court's 1972 ruling in *State* v. *Gurnoe* (see Chapter 7) led some six hundred sportfishers to form an organization known as Concerned Sportsmen for Lake Superior. Fearing the Bad River and Red Cliff Bands would use the Court's recognition of their fishing rights in Lake Superior to deplete the lake's supply of trout, walleye, and whitefish, the members of Concerned Sportsmen argued that Indians had to "be subject to the same tough commercial fishing regulations as white men" (*Milwaukee Journal* 1972a, b). In 1973, Republican Reuben La Fave of Oconto, claiming he was only interested in the "welfare" of the Indians, introduced a resolution in the state senate calling for the Department of Natural Resources to "purchase" the fishing rights of the Chippewas. In response to the resolution, the *Capital Times* of Madison editorialized, "anytime the whites profess interest in the Indians it is time for these native Americans to keep their backs against the white pine and their peace pipes hidden" (1973).

While Indian commercial fishing in Lake Superior was of growing concern to some groups in Wisconsin in the early 1970s, the conflict between state wildlife regulations and treaty-protected hunting and fishing rights of Indian tribes came to a head in the State of Washington. A brief review of what has been referred to as "the opening salvo in this century's 'treaty wars'" (*Christian Science Monitor* 1987), and the public reaction to it will help place the situation in Wisconsin from 1974 to the present in its larger context.[57]

In 1974, Judge George Boldt of the U. S. District Court for the Western District in Washington ruled in *United States* v. *State of Washington* that Indian tribes had the treaty right to up to one-half of the salmon and steelhead trout harvest, both the right to catch the fish and the right as governments to be involved in the actual regulation of the resource. Popularly known as the *Boldt Decision,* the case had taken three and a half years of litigation involving testimony from fourteen Indian tribes, the State of Washington Departments of Fisheries and Game, and various commercial and sportfishing organizations. Judge Boldt based his decision not only on the "facts" existing at the time of the litigation but also on an exhaustive historical examination of events and information going back to the actual treaty negotiations (U. S. District Court 1974). Public reaction to the ruling included the appearance of bumper stickers, buttons, and T-shirts with anti-Boldt slogans and open defiance of the ruling by non-Indian fishers (U. S. Commission on Civil Rights 1981, 71). The State of Washington promptly appealed the decision, but the U. S. Court of Appeals for the Ninth Circuit upheld Boldt (1975) and the U. S. Supreme Court declined to review the case (1976). After spending nearly a decade on costly appeals and countersuits, state officials finally embarked on the path of co-management by which the federally recognized Indian tribes and the state are partners in the management of timber, wildlife, and fish (U. S. Commission on Civil Rights 1981, 70-100; Olson 1984; *Wisconsin State Journal* 1990c, 47; Cooper and Stange 1990, 52).

The *Boldt Decision,* together with a shift in federal Indian policy toward greater self-determination for Indian tribes and the growing Indian militancy of the early 1970s described earlier, alarmed some segments of American society (Olson 1984, 511). Indeed, one account of the treaty rights controversy written in the mid-1970s referred to Indian treaties as an "American nightmare" (Williams and Neubrech 1976). Anti-Indian editorials and articles claiming that federal officials were "obsessed" with providing "goodies" to Indians and other minorities appeared in both the local and national media. "We have found a very significant backlash that by any other name comes out as racism in all its ugly manifestations," Republican Senator Mark Hatfield of Oregon advised his colleagues on the U. S. Senate Select Committee on Indian Affairs in 1977 (U. S. Commission on Civil Rights 1981, 1). In 1978, an article in *Newsweek* magazine spoke of a "Paleface Uprising" spreading from Maine to Washington state as Indians "earned that ultimate badge of minority success—a genuine and threatening white backlash" (Boeth *et al.* 1978, 39).

The leading anti-Indian lobbyist group was the Interstate Congress for Equal Rights and Responsibilities (ICERR). This organization sprang into existence in 1976 arguing that Indian political power and treaty rights were antithetical to the American system of equality. The outgrowth of a meeting in Salt Lake City, Utah, of anti-treaty rights representatives from ten western states, the ICERR attracted considerable attention in other regions as well. Indian interests, ICERR spokespersons argued, must give way to those of the larger society. "We seek just one thing," commented founder Howard Grey, "that is equal rights for all people living under the Constitution of the United States and the 14th amendment . . . the 14th amendment gives equal rights for all people; that's all we're requesting." ICERR lobbyists worked hard to persuade local and national legislators to introduce bills calling for the abrogation of Indian treaties, the removal of tribal jurisdictional powers, the reversal of favorable judicial rulings on Indian treaty rights, the restriction of Indian access to natural resources, and the elimination of eastern Indian land claims (U. S. Commission on Civil Rights 1981, 1, 9-10).

The "equal rights" rhetoric of ICERR and other anti-treaty groups since the 1970s distorts a very important fact. Contrary to the arguments of such organizations, there is no conflict between Indian treaty rights and the guarantee of "equal protection of the laws" under the Fourteenth Amendment to the U. S. Constitution. Congress unilaterally declared *all* native-born American Indians citizens of the United States in 1924. This was done as further recognition of the voluntary contributions of Indian veterans of World War I who had received citizenship in 1919. Indian treaty rights and property rights remained unaffected (U. S. Congress 1919, 1924; Cohen 1982, 639-40, 644-46). "It is no more a denial of my 14th amendment rights that Indians continue to receive the benefits of the agreement they made {in a treaty}," Seattle attorney and Indian law specialist Alvin Ziontz told the U. S. Commission on Civil Rights in 1977, "than it is a denial of my rights that any groups that sold land to the United States Government get paid for their land." The federal courts and the Civil Rights Commission have reached the same conclusion, but anti-treaty rights groups continue to stress the need for "equal rights" for non-Indians and Indians. ICERR members ignore the status of Indians as members of tribes with which the United States has had a long history of government-to-government relationships. Instead, the ICERR and similar groups portray Indians as members of a racial minority receiving ''special'' privileges at the expense of non-minority citizens because of century-old documents that are supposedly no longer relevant (U. S. Commission on Civil Rights 1981, 9-12).

The ICERR and similar organizations of the 1970s were the forerunners of such Wisconsin anti-treaty groups in the 1980s as Equal Rights for Everyone (ERFE, Hayward), Wisconsin Alliance for Rights and Resources (WARR, Superior), Butternut Lake Concerned Citizens (Butternut), Protect Americans' Rights and Resources (PARR, Minocqua-Park Falls), and Stop Treaty Abuse (STA, Minocqua).[58] The primary goals of these organizations are the abrogation of Chippewa treaty rights and the dissolution of reservations. ERFE, led by Paul A. Mullaly of Hayward, appeared shortly after the *Voigt Decision*. Decrying the Chippewa off-reservation deer season as ''a rape,'' Mullaly openly threatened Indian hunters. ERFE was the forerunner of other organizations, including PARR, whose leaders responded to the resumption of Chippewa spring spearfishing in 1985 by protesting the alleged ''rape'' of the fish population in northern Wisconsin by the Chippewas (U. S. Commission on Civil Rights 1981, 180; *PARR Issue* 1987, 1991v; Wisconsin Advisory Committee 1989, 24; *Masinaigan* 1991c, 8).

PARR, which has attempted to become an umbrella organization for many other anti-treaty rights groups, has very actively lobbied state and federal officials for the abrogation of Indian treaties. At PARR's first National Convention in Wausau on March 28th to 29th in 1987, some five hundred people from as many as thirteen states and two Canadian provinces met to call for the abrogation of Indian treaties, the dissolution of Indian reservations, and an end to ''special privileges'' for Indians (*Eau Claire Leader-Telegram* 1987a, b; *Christian Science Monitor* 1987, 6). Former newspaper editor and newly selected executive director Larry Greschner of Woodruff referred to treaty rights as ''a sacred cow'' and warned:

> There isn't enough milk in that sacred cow to go around if it's not handled very carefully. Because the natural wonder of our land and a billion dollar sports-tourism industry can easily be transformed into a tiny fraction of that value once those resources have been killed, cut, wrapped, frozen and processed. And we will have traded our children's birth right for a futile gesture of remorse. (Greschner 1987)

PARR National Executive Director at Large Wayne Powers of Bloomer warns that Wisconsin will become ''the home of the dead seas'' if Indian treaty rights are not curtailed (*PARR Issue* 1991m). When presented with data indicating that, contrary to PARR news releases, Indian spearfishing and hunting is *not* endangering the state's resources or tourism industry, the organization's leaders usually return to the equal rights theme that has been the rallying cry of anti-treaty rights groups since the *Boldt Decision* (*Fig. 36*). ''When you have separate rules for different colors living side by side, you're bound to have conflicts,'' Greschner stated in 1988 (*Racine Journal Times* 1988). ''Our position,'' PARR cofounder Wayne Powers stated in 1990, ''is not a few fish and a few deer—it's equal rights'' (*Eau Claire Leader-Telegram* 1990f, 2A).

The same arguments have been made by other anti-treaty groups. Equal Rights for Everyone President Mullaly claims that the treaty rights issue in Wisconsin ''is

Fig. 36. *A Cartoonist Talks to An Anti-Treaty Protester. Cartoon by Joe Heller, Green Bay Press Gazette,* copyright 1990. Reprinted with permission.

not a natural-resources issue, it is a rights issue.'' He says ''there can be no special treatment of a race in a democratic society.'' In reference to the entire treaty rights issue, Mullaly claims, ''Like cancer this situation would have been much easier to cure if action had been taken in the earlier stages . . . . I am sorry that our elected officials have let this cancer spread to the point that it is almost uncurable {*sic*} and unbearable to those close to the infected area'' (*Eau Claire Leader-Telegram* 1984a; *Wisconsin Counties* 1985). Stop Treaty Abuse (STA) leader Dean Crist, a former Chicagoan who now resides in Minocqua, also argues that the ''real'' issue is ''equality.'' Described by his own attorney as a ''lightening rod'' on northern Wisconsin boat landings, Crist has marketed Treaty Beer (called ''hate and prejudice in a can'' by detractors) and undertaken other efforts to draw people to the boat landings to protest Indian spearfishing and treaty rights. ''Whether you're a Chippewa or a Chinaman,'' he asserts, ''when you're on the water Wisconsin conservation laws pertain and you have to fish by those rules'' (*La Crosse Tribune* 1990). Crist and his organization portray the Chippewas as freeloaders who are benefitting from government largesse while the ''true'' working men—to whom STA's treaty beer is supposedly marketed (see Fig. 34)—are denied equal rights (*Wisconsin State Journal* 1990c, 21).

Supporters of treaty rights disagree with members of PARR, STA, and other opponents who claim that ''the basic point is not fish—it's equal rights.'' As one supporter puts it, ''But, of course, the issue *is* fish and other treaty-protected Indian resources'' (Cornell 1986, 124). A number of prominent non-Indian civic leaders responded to the growing opposition to Chippewa reserved rights in northern Wisconsin after the *Voigt Decision* in 1983 by openly defending those rights. Meanwhile, concerned by the increasing appearance of posters urging people to ''Spear an Indian, Save a Walleye'' and reports of threatened violence and actual acts of violence against Indians, an Ad Hoc Commission on Racism was convened by the Lac Courte Oreilles (LCO) Band in the fall of 1984. The commission held public hearings in the town of Cable near the LCO Reservation to examine evidence and issue findings about alleged acts of discrimination and violence. Chaired by educator Veda Stone from Eau Claire, the commission included the Governor's advisor on Indian affairs, a member of the Governor's Committee on Equal Rights, members of the Catholic and Protestant clergy, a member of the B'nai B'rith Anti-Defamation League, an attorney and Board member of the Wisconsin Civil Liberties Union, and representatives from higher education. The Final Report of the commission, issued in November of 1984, cited numerous examples of growing racism; stressed the roles of churches, schools at all levels, and parents in combating the growth of racism; called for state economic development efforts in the north; urged the creation of state, county, and local forums for Indians and whites to discuss issues of mutual concern; and urged the mass media to play a more responsible role (*Eau Claire Leader-Telegram* 1984b; Ad Hoc Commission on Racism in Wisconsin 1984, 5-30).

As demonstrated by the role of the LCO Band in the creation of the Ad Hoc Commission, the Chippewas have been deeply concerned about the mounting white hostility and have sought to lessen tensions in a variety of ways. Anthropologist Nancy O. Lurie, an authority on Wisconsin Indians, noted in the mid-1980s that most Chippewas living on the six reservations in the state are determined not to abuse their treaty rights and are as devoted as white residents, if not more so, to protecting the resources in the northern third of Wisconsin. The harvest of fish by non-Indians since the *Voigt Decision* has consistently been several times that of Indians. In those lakes where fish production is down, moreover, the culprit has been pollution and habitat degradation by whites, not excessive harvesting by Indians, or for that matter, non-Indians. Since 1984, Chippewa leaders have worked through the Great Lakes Indian Fish and Wildlife Commission (GLIFWC) head-quartered at Odanah to gather natural resources data, to develop legal codes for protecting fish and wildlife, and to implement a system for dealing with those Indians who fail to comply (*Fig. 37*). GLIFWC spokesperson Walter Bresette op-timistically commented in 1984 that "following the {Voigt} decision, what the tribes are responsible for is basically the management of those resources in the region." While there are some non-Indians who believe that Indian participation in the management of the region's natural resources would benefit all Wisconsinites, anti-treaty groups and State officials have resisted such efforts (Lurie 1985, 379; *Wisconsin Sportsman* 1985, 42; Wilkinson 1990, 4; *Milwaukee Journal* 1984a; *Wisconsin State Journal* 1990c, 55; Michetti 1991).

Under LCO VI, the Chippewas were to be free from state regulation of off-reservation harvesting of walleye and muskellunge so long as they enacted "a management plan that provides for the regulation of their members in accordance with biologically sound principles necessary for the conservation of the species being harvested" (U. S. District Court 1989, 1060). There have been charges that the state has attempted to indirectly regulate the Chippewas by restricting bag limits of non-Indian fishers, which in turn has led to an escalation in the hostility of protesters at the boat landings. After Crabb's ruling in LCO VI, DNR officials cut creel limits for non-Indian anglers. The public perception, which critics charge DNR did little to correct, was that Indian spearing depleted the fish and caused the lower limits for anglers (*Wisconsin State Journal* 1990c, 7, 16).

Legal scholars Rennard Strickland of the University of Oklahoma and Stephen J. Herzberg of the University of Wisconsin-Madison are among those who believe that the DNR has attempted to circumvent the court's ruling in LCO VI. In a report prepared at the request of members of the U. S. Senate Select Committee on Indian Affairs in 1990, Strickland, Herzberg, and University of Wisconsin-Madison Juris Doctor candidate Steven Owens concluded that

> . . . Denied the right to *directly* regulate the Chippewa by the courts, {Wisconsin DNR officials} have attempted to *indirectly* regulate the Chippewa by restricting the bag limits placed on non-Indian fishers, which they have done by manipulating fish population estimates (termed "voodoo biology" by several observers). Since the Chippewa have historically been sensitive to the needs of non-Indians, the state uses bag limits to place pressure on the Chippewa to "voluntarily" restrict their treaty rights. Under this approach the state can contend, "But we are not regulating the Chippewa, we're regulating the non-Indians." (Strickland *et al.* 1990, 9 n. 19)

Judge Crabb's findings in LCO VI support these conclusions. Acknowledging that the DNR will impose additional restrictions on fishing in the next few years, following a comprehensive long-term fisheries plan it developed in the late 1970s, Crabb commented:

> These restrictions would have been imposed even if the tribes' treaty rights had not been judicially recognized. It is purely fortuitous that the time of their implementation came shortly after the start up of Indian spring spearing. (U. S. District Court 1989, 1047)

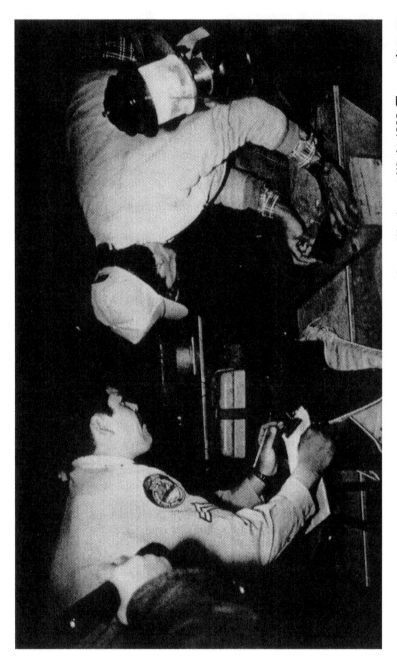

Fig. 37. *Tribal and Great Lakes Indian Fish and Wildlife Commission Game Wardens at Work, 1990.* The wardens are checking the size and sex of fish taken by spearfishers. After state officials prohibited Indians from exercising their usufructuary rights off reservation for most of the twentieth century, the Chippewas resumed harvesting fish on lakes and rivers in ceded territory in northern Wisconsin in 1985 under an interim agreement with state officials pending further resolution of treaty rights in court proceedings. Photograph by Jason Tetzloff. Reprinted with permission.

Citing Crabb's remarks as evidence, LCO Tribal Chair Gaiashkibos charges the DNR with duplicity. "Exercising our rights off-reservation gives the DNR their out. They lower the bag limit for non-Indian people and put the blame on the Chippewa" (Michetti 1991, 7).

Chippewa spearfishers have actually voluntarily limited their harvest every season since the *Voigt Decision* so non-Indians could fish the lakes of northern Wisconsin. The Chippewas have also taken an active role in fish rearing and stocking programs. In fact, the lakes on the Lac du Flambeau reservation are heavily stocked by the Indians, who permit non-Indians to take 90% or more of the *on-reservation* walleye catch. Other Chippewa bands also maintain hatcheries and stock *off-reservation* lakes with fish, many of which are caught by non-Indians (Strickland *et al.* 1990, 10, 10 n. 21; *Masinaigan* 1990g).

The opposition of some non-Indians today to the exercise of Indian hunting and fishing rights in northern Wisconsin must be viewed in the context of the legal and moral obligations of American citizens to uphold Indian treaty rights as the "supreme Law of the Land" as stipulated in Article 6, Clause 2 of the American Constitution:

> This Constitution, and the Laws of the United States which shall be made in Pursuance thereof; and *all Treaties made, or which shall be made, under the Authority of the United States, shall be the supreme Law of the Land; and the Judges in every State shall be bound thereby, any Thing in the Constitution or Laws of any State to the Contrary notwithstanding.* {emphasis added}

Anti-treaty rights groups in Wisconsin, especially PARR, erroneously claim there is no constitutional basis for treaty making with Indian tribes and that existing Indian treaties are no longer valid. Three historical events are often cited as evidence that tribal sovereignty is a fiction: Chief Justice John Marshall's reference to Indian tribes as "domestic dependent nations" in the early 1830s, the ending of treaty making under the 1871 Indian Appropriations Act, and the granting of U. S. citizenship in 1924. PARR Chair Larry Peterson claims that Indian sovereignty is a "fabricated" concept and that Indian treaty rights are merely "court-granted" privileges resulting from "ludicrous court decisions" that cater to Indian "greed." PARR's newspaper editor Jerry Schumacher argues that the courts have erred in basing their decisions on Indians' "oral understanding of treaties" since "the Indians understood them as written." In a manner reminiscent of the Communist-baiting tactics of U. S. Senator Joseph McCarthy in the 1950s, PARR's newsletter prominently displays a list of "Traitors to the Constitution," claiming that U. S. and state legislators, teachers, church leaders, and others who recognize tribal sovereignty deserve the label "traitor" (*PARR Issue* 1991c, d, e, f, g, j, k, l, n, o, p, r, s, t).

In presenting their case against tribal sovereignty, PARR's spokespersons seriously distort the historical record. While Chief Justice Marshall did refer to the Cherokee Nation as a "domestic dependent nation" in 1831, he did not deny the existence of a government-to-government relationship between the Cherokee Nation and the United States. Marshall's characterization of Indian tribes recognized their "peculiar" relationship with the United States—i.e., that of nations existing *within* the borders of states of the Union. Marshall acknowledged that the Cherokee Nation constituted "a distinct political society" that was "capable of managing its own affairs" with "unquestionable" right to its lands (U. S. Supreme Court 1831). The following year, Marshall ruled that Georgia could not intervene in the Cherokee country within its borders because federal—not state—jurisdiction extended over Indian country. According to Marshall, status as a domestic dependent nation did not preclude treaty making by the Indians with the United States nor lessen American obligations to uphold treaty commitments:

> The constitution, by declaring treaties already made, as well as those to be made, to be the supreme law of the land, has adopted and sanctioned the previous treaties with the Indian nations, and consequently admits their rank among those powers who are capable of making treaties. The words "treaty" and "nation" are words of our own language, selected in our diplomatic and legislative proceedings, by ourselves, having each a definite and well understood meaning. We have applied them to Indians, as we have applied them to other nations of the earth. They are applied to all in the same sense. (U. S. Supreme Court 1832, 559-60)

PARR leaders also distort the intent of the Indian Appropriations Act of 1871. The legislation, which abolished future treaty making for domestic political reasons as noted in Chapter 5, unequivocally stated that "nothing herein contained shall be construed to invalidate or impair the obligation of any treaty heretofore lawfully made and ratified with any such Indian nation or tribe" (U. S. Congress 1871). Similarly, while Congress made all Indians U. S. citizens for reasons outlined earlier in this chapter, it specifically stipulated that "the granting of such citizenship shall not in any manner impair or otherwise affect the right of any Indian to tribal or other property" (U. S. Congress 1924).

As demonstrated in Chapters 2-5, there is overwhelming evidence that oral explanations of treaty provisions by U. S. treaty commissioners and interpreters did not always match the written provisions. Chief Justice Marshall's colleague, Associate Justice John McLean, remarked in the 1832 case mentioned above: "how the words of the treaty were understood by this unlettered people, rather than their critical meaning, should form the rule of construction." Believing that treaties with Indian tribes represented "more than an idle pageantry," Justice McLean reminded American citizens of his day of the "binding force" of the agreements and of the "principles of justice," which dictated that the United States uphold its commitments (U. S. Supreme Court 1832, 582-83).

While some Wisconsinites have joined or supported the various backlash groups like PARR and STA mentioned earlier, voices of moderation have appeared. Some non-Indians have attempted to set the record straight on the actual amount of tribal harvesting of fish and game and the impact on tourism. A Minocqua motel owner, for example, urged Wisconsinites to separate fact from fiction: "my biggest concern is that people think the Indians are shooting all the deer . . . . It hasn't happened. The Indians aren't catching and spearing all the fish that swim . . . and they aren't shooting that many deer" (*Milwaukee Journal* 1984c). He was correct on both counts. The Chippewa deer harvest (*Fig. 38*) is minimal compared either to the entire deer population or to the harvest by state-licensed hunters; it is smaller even than the annual road kill in the ceded territories (Busiahn 1989a). Similarly, Chippewa spring spearfishing, which resumed in 1985 under intensely monitored conditions, has never come close to approaching the impact that sportfishing has on

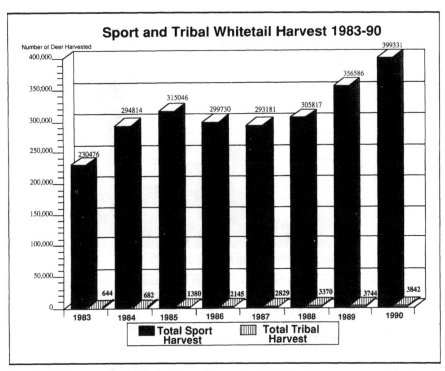

Sport and Tribal Whitetail Harvest 1983-90

Fig. 38. *Chippewa White-Tailed Deer Harvest, 1983–90.* Data courtesy of the Great Lakes Indian Fish and Wildlife Commission (GLIFWC) and of the Bureau of Wildlife Management of the Wisconsin Department of Natural Resources (DNR). The graph compares the DNR's record of the registered sport whitetail harvest and GLIFWC's record of the tribal whitetail harvest. Because the difference between sport and tribal harvests is so great, the tribal harvest barely registers on the graph. Graph courtesy of the University of Wisconsin-Eau Claire Media Development Center.

the fish population in northern Wisconsin (*Figs. 39-40*). Contrary to the information released by anti-treaty rights groups, eighty percent of the fish speared during the 1990 spearfishing season were males (*Masinaigan* 1990h, 11). Considering the small number of fish actually taken annually by tribal spearfishers in comparison to that taken by anglers, former head of the DNR District Office in Spooner Dave Jacobson has observed that "there is virtually no possibility that tribes can destroy the resource" (*Isthmus* 1990, 9).

Attempts have also been made to set the record straight as to the impact of Chippewa off-reservation fish and game harvests on tourism. Director of the Wisconsin Division of Tourism Dick Matty has recently stated that, contrary to the reports issued by anti-treaty groups, there has been "*no real negative impact*" on tourism as a result of Indian spearfishing. Chamber of Commerce officials in northern communities like Minocqua and Boulder Junction report that tourism is thriving. What is having a greater impact on tourism in the north than Indian spearfishing or deer hunting harvests according to tourism experts such as Rollie Cooper of the University of Wisconsin-Extension Recreation Resource Center are (1) the failure of resort owners to market their facilities in response to demographic trends such as the growth of two-income households, an aging population, and an increased

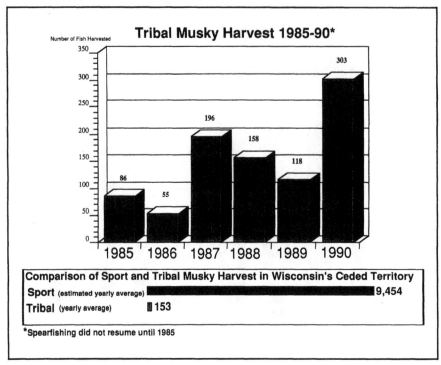

Fig. 39. *Chippewa Muskellunge Harvest, 1985–90.* Data courtesy of the Great Lakes Indian Fish and Wildlife Commission (GLIFWC) and of the Bureau of Fisheries Management of the Wisconsin Department of Natural Resources (DNR). Graph courtesy of the University of Wisconsin-Eau Claire Media Development Center.

number of single-parents families, (2) the declining quality of resorts due to their age or the failure of owners to make improvements, and (3) the poor public image given to Wisconsin by the actions and words of anti-treaty rights demonstrators at the boat landings (Thannum {1990}, 15-17; *Masinaigan* 1990c, and 1990h, 7).

Despite the efforts mentioned above, there is still a great deal of misinformation and many misunderstandings about Chippewa treaty rights issues across Wisconsin. A recent survey conducted by the St. Norbert College Survey Center and Wisconsin Public Radio concluded, for example, that only 30% of the respondents knew that the Chippewa Indians are limited in the number of fish and game they can harvest. The public's lack of accurate information has made it easier for anti-treaty rights leaders to exploit the fears and frustrations of their neighbors, especially during the hard economic times in the north since the *Voigt Decision.* During this period, the adjusted gross income in many northern Wisconsin counties failed to reach the State's 1983 average. In addition to its lower income level, the north suffers from high seasonal unemployment rates. Such conditions create an excellent breeding ground for anti-Indian propaganda. As resource development specialist Jim Thannum has observed, ''ignorance, poor economic conditions, and fear of the unknown'' in the north have helped to create a hostile environment for Indian treaty rights in recent years (Thannum {1990}, 10-13).

In addition to attempting to correct misinformation about Indian fishing and hunting harvests, some residents of the state including the leaders of numerous

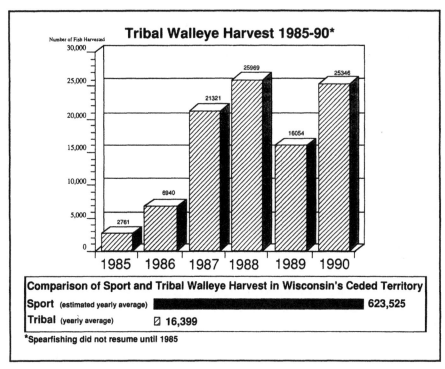

Tribal Walleye Harvest 1985-90*

Number of Fish Harvested

Comparison of Sport and Tribal Walleye Harvest in Wisconsin's Ceded Territory

Sport (estimated yearly average) **623,525**

Tribal (yearly average) **16,399**

*Spearfishing did not resume until 1985

Fig. 40. *Chippewa Walleye Harvest, 1985–90.* Data courtesy of the Great Lakes Indian Fish and Wildlife Commission (GLIFWC) and of the Bureau of Fisheries Management of the Wisconsin Department of Natural Resources (DNR). Graph courtesy of the University of Wisconsin-Eau Claire Media Development Center.

religious organizations have reacted to the violence at boat landings, the marketing of Treaty Beer, and other signs of growing racism by peaceful, non-confrontational observation at the boat landings and by speaking out in support of Indian treaty rights and tribal sovereignty. The purpose of such "witnessing" is to convey calm in the midst of tension and to demonstrate non-Indian support for treaty rights (Midwest Treaty Network {1990}; *USA Today* 1990, 2A; *Wisconsin State Journal* 1990a; *News from Indian Country* 1990g).

Perhaps the most prominent of the treaty support organizations is Honor Our Neighbors' Origins and Rights (HONOR), a coalition of individuals, human rights groups, church organizations, and other groups. The organization began in Wausau, where in February of 1988 a group of Indians and non-Indians responded to the increasing intensity of anti-Indian rhetoric and activity by meeting to affirm the constitutionally recognized government-to-government relationship that has been the cornerstone of American federal Indian policy. Under the coordination of Sharon Metz of the Milwaukee-based Lutheran Human Relations Association of America, HONOR organized itself as a coalition of individuals and groups dedicated to positive actions promoting peace, harmony, and intercultural understanding. Members speak of the Chippewa treaties as a matter of national honor, hence the name of the organization. HONOR's promotional literature quotes the following statement by eighteenth-century English statesman Edmund Burke: "The only thing necessary for evil to prevail, is that good people do nothing" (*Vanguard* 1988; *News from Indian Country* 1988, 1989b; HONOR {1989}).

Although the exact definition of the extent of treaty rights is open to interpretation by the federal courts, efforts to abrogate Indian treaties and thereby redefine the status of Indian people within American society are efforts to undermine the rule of law and to ignore our contractual and moral obligations to the Indian people. As one Lac du Flambeau Band member commented, "if people want to abrogate the treaty, then abrogate it all. Give us back the top third of the state" (*Chicago Tribune* 1987). Legal scholar Charles F. Wilkinson reminds us that "for American Indians, their survival as a people—mark down those words, survival as a people—ultimately depends on 19th-century treaties recognizing a range of special prerogatives, including hunting, fishing, and water rights; a special trust relationship with the United States; and, ultimately, the principal of tribal sovereignty, the right of tribal members to be governed on many key issues by their own tribal governments, not by the states" (1990, 4-5).

The Chippewa Indians of Wisconsin have emerged from the treaty rights controversy of the last two decades "increasingly conscious of the importance of maintaining an identity in the modern world that is not based merely on the white man's categorizations of them . . . but rather emphasizes the continuity of the modern Indian people with a historical tradition that precedes and is independent of whites in America." The Chippewas find this continuity in hunting, fishing, ricing, powwows, and numerous other elements of their traditional culture that "serve not only as structural and cultural supports of the Chippewa entity but also become transformed into symbolic devices for explicit furthering of ethnic distinctiveness" (Paredes 1980, 406-07, 410). As a Lac du Flambeau Chippewa Indian commented in the summer of 1989, "spearing fish in the spring is what got me in touch with my heritage. Part of it meant food. Getting food on the table to eat, to live. But part of it, connected to eating and living, is being Chippewa." Indeed, Chippewas argue that *they* are "the endangered species" in northern Wisconsin. "If we give up our ways," they contend, "we die" (Kenyon 1989, 18, 22, 30).

Despite the important relationship between reserved treaty rights and the ethnic consciousness of the Chippewa people, some influential Wisconsinites including Attorney General Donald J. Hanaway began pursuing efforts in April of 1987 to seek a negotiated out-of-court, long-term settlement between the state and the Chippewa bands. Although some media spokespersons have loosely referred to the Thompson administration's efforts as aimed at securing an outright cash "buy-out" of Chippewa hunting, fishing, and gathering rights, Hanaway sought an agreement by which the Chippewas would curtail or lease their harvesting rights in exchange for economic and other forms of assistance from the state (*Milwaukee Journal* 1987b; Hanaway 1989, 8-10; *Wisconsin State Journal* 1990c, 5).

In order to help Hanaway in bringing the Chippewas to the negotiating table, Republican Congressman Frank James Sensenbrenner, Jr. of Menomonee Falls introduced legislation in the U. S. House of Representatives during July 1987 calling for the abrogation of off-reservation usufructuary rights in Wisconsin (U. S. Congress 1987a, b). Sensenbrenner may have been inspired in part by a comment made by Judge Doyle during the LCO III trial. Doyle, who clearly recognized the "practical dilemma present in the ceded lands" and the emotional dimensions of the treaty-rights issue, stated on February 18, 1987, that a "practical" solution would come not through court action but through negotiations leading to a new treaty or through unilateral congressional action (U. S. District Court 1987a, 1433). Sensenbrenner defended his bill by remarking, "the treaties don't recognize twentieth century life in America." The congressman's timing assisted Hanaway. Armed with a "carrot" from the governor—his willingness to negotiate a multi-million dollar lease of treaty rights—and a "stick" from Representative Sensenbrenner—the threat of "serious efforts" to secure enactment of the Abrogation Bill should negotiations stall in Wisconsin, Hanaway worked hard to secure a settlement (*Milwaukee Sentinel* 1987).

Governor Thompson publicly called Sensenbrenner's bill "counterproductive when negotiations are going on," but Republican Senator Robert Kasten soon provided the state's negotiating team with yet another "stick." Kasten threatened to withhold federal aid if the Chippewas did not negotiate a settlement. Moreover, Democrat State Representative Mark D. Lewis of Eau Claire accused the governor himself of heavy-handedness in the negotiations with the tribes. Lewis, chair of the Trade, Industry, and Small Business Committee of the State Assembly, claimed that the governor was holding legislation creating jobs on Indian reservations hostage until the Chippewas agreed to a negotiated settlement (*Wisconsin State Journal* 1987; *Green Bay Press Gazette* 1987a, b; Lewis 1987).

Negotiations between state officials and the leaders of the Mole Lake reservation, the poorest of the six Chippewa reservations in Wisconsin (*Wisconsin State Journal* 1990c, 10), led to a tentative agreement offering ten million dollars to lease their usufructuary rights over a ten-year period. On January 14, 1989, the Mole Lake Indians overwhelmingly rejected the offer. Frustrated by this turn of events, Attorney General Hanaway acknowledged that the prospect of achieving such a settlement with other bands in the near future was equally gloomy (Hanaway 1989, 8-10).

Several months after the Chippewas of the Mole Lake reservation rejected the state's offer, Representative Sensenbrenner again introduced legislation in the House calling for the abrogation of Chippewa usufructuary rights in Wisconsin. Nevertheless, there were "clear messages" that neither Congress nor the President would abrogate treaties. As a result, the Thompson administration continued to work toward leasing Chippewa usufructuary rights (U. S. Congress 1989a, b; Hanaway 1990, 12).

In 1989 Al Gedicks of La Crosse, Executive Secretary of the Wisconsin Resources Protection Council, charged that Governor Thompson had "a hidden agenda" for continuing to push a "buy-out" arrangement. According to Gedicks, Secretary of Administration James R. Klauser, the governor's top aide and point man on treaty issues, was eager to have the Chippewas lose their legal standing to intervene in any court challenges to proposed mining operations in ceded territory. Claiming that Klauser formerly lobbied for Exxon, which in the early 1980s had proposed a zinc and copper mine near Crandon, Gedicks questioned the governor's motivation and urged the Chippewas not to give up any rights that would weaken their legal clout against environmental threats from mining interests. Gedicks's remarks undoubtedly found a sympathetic audience among Chippewa leaders who have long suspected that anti-treaty rights organizations have "an agenda far broader than just spearfishing." In particular, some Indian leaders have openly asserted that these groups may be associated with or bankrolled by big companies interested in mineral rights in the state. Whatever the validity of such fears, suspicions, and accusations, Governor Thompson continued to seek a negotiated settlement (*Milwaukee Journal* 1989c; Gedicks 1985, 180-89, 1989, 8; *Wisconsin State Journal* 1990c, 9, 17, 37).

When anti-treaty rights protesters broke through police lines during the 1989 spearfishing season, the *Milwaukee Journal* urged Governor Thompson to call in the National Guard (1989a). The rowdy crowds at the landings exceeded that of the previous year by ten times, and State Republican Party Chair Donald K. Stitt of Port Washington urged the Republican governor to "strongly consider" declaring a state of emergency and closing off northern lakes to spearfishers *and* anglers (*Capital Times* 1989c). Thompson took a different approach. He made an unprecedented appearance in Judge Crabb's courtroom to personally request the issuance of an injunction to halt Indian spearfishers (*Capital Times* 1989b).

Crabb refused to grant the Governor's request. Commenting that it was her obligation "to enforce the law and the rights of all people under the law," Crabb addressed the charge made by anti-treaty protesters that the Chippewas had *more* rights than non-Indians:

> Many people in the northern part of the state complain that the tribes are accorded unequal rights because they are permitted to hunt, fish, and gather in ways denied to the non-Indian population. The fact is, however, that the tribes do not have unequal rights. They have the same rights as any other resident of the United States to enter into contractual agreements and to go to court to enforce their rights under those contracts. In previous phases of this litigation, it has been found that the Chippewas gave up the ceded territory but retained rights to hunt, fish, and gather. Those rights are not in question now. As those rights relate to the spearing of walleye, they are circumscribed by the Department of Natural Resources' determination of a biologically safe catch. In addition, and I emphasize this, they have the same rights as any other resident of this state to seek the state's protection in exercising their lawful rights.

The judge argued that "the fact that some {non-Indians} are acting illegally and creating unjustified fears of violence does not justify abridging the rights of those {Indians} who have done nothing illegal or improper." Referring to the "constitutional underpinnings" of American society, Crabb refused to permit "violent and lawless protests" to determine the rights of Indians in Wisconsin. "What kind of country would we have if brave people had not faced down the prejudiced, the violent, and the lawless in the 1960s? What kind will we become if we do not do the same today," she asked in rebuffing the Governor (*Wisconsin State Journal* 1989b).

Judge Crabb's popularity among protesters at the boat landings can be surmised from a slogan on one of their signs—"Save a Walleye, Spear A Crabb" (*Wisconsin State Journal* 1990c, 35). Although Governor Thompson failed in his efforts to obtain a court order ending the spearfishing season, his worst fears went unrealized. Cold weather helped reduce crowds and cool tempers at the boat landings. Thompson aide Klauser remarked, "fortunately, Mother Nature cooperated better than Mother Crabb" (*Capital Times* 1989d).

Meanwhile, Governor Thompson's assertion to Judge Crabb that state law enforcement officers were "unable and in some cases, unwilling, to guarantee the protection of the tribes in the exercise of their lawful rights" especially angered treaty supporters. Some commentators suggested that instead of proposing to spend

Fig. 41. *Stop Putting Your Head Under That Poor Man's Club!* Cartoon by Bill Sanders, *The Milwaukee Journal*. Reprinted with permission.

a million dollars for promoting tourism in the north the Governor should earmark funds for law enforcement to protect Chippewa spearfishers and to arrest, prosecute, and incarcerate those who would deny them their rights (*Wisconsin State Journal* 1989b, c). The administration apparently had other ideas about the best way to handle the Chippewa treaty rights controversy.

In October of 1989, after months of intense bargaining, Wisconsin Attorney General Hanaway and a team of negotiators reached a tentative settlement with the Lac du Flambeau Chippewa Band, the heaviest spearers in northern Wisconsin (*Fig. 41*). If the Indians agreed to give up gill netting, as well as most of their spearfishing rights and reached an agreement with the state on outstanding issues pertaining to hunting, trapping, and gathering, Hanaway offered them annual payments of about 3.5 million dollars and other economic incentives for a ten-year period with a renewal option for five-year periods by mutual agreement. Estimates of the total cost ranged from 42 to 50 million dollars. According to top Thompson aide James Klauser, "the cost would be paid out of surplus revenue and would require no tax increase" (*Green Bay Press Gazette* 1989; *Milwaukee Sentinel* 1989c; Lac du Flambeau Band and State of Wisconsin 1989).

Before the Lac du Flambeau pact with the state came up for a vote on the reservation, Lac Courte Oreilles Tribal Chair Gaiashkibos and Bad River Tribal Chair Donald Moore went on record against the arrangement (*Milwaukee Sentinel* 1989d). "Our rights are not for sale and they're not for lease. What other tribes

Fig. 42. *Thomas Maulson, Walleye Warrior.* Maulson, an active spearer, says of PARR and similar anti-treaty groups, "All these guys are lacking are the white sheets" (*Capital Times* 1986b, 25). Photograph by Mary Beth Berg. Reprinted with permission.

do is their business," Gaiashkibos said (*Capital Times* 1989e). Opposition to the proposed settlement led officials of the Great Lakes Indian Fish and Wildlife Commission (GLIFWC) to replace Lac du Flambeau Tribal Chair Michael W. Allen with Bad River Tribal Chair and "buy out" critic Donald Moore as the GLIFWC chair. At the same time, Lac du Flambeau Tribal Attorney Kathryn Tierney resigned under pressure from the other Chippewa bands as lead counsel for the Chippewa treaty rights trial pending in federal court (*Milwaukee Sentinel* 1989e).

On October 25, 1989, members of the band stunned state officials by rejecting the multimillion-dollar pact by a vote of 439 to 366. Thomas Maulson (*Fig. 42*), a leader of the off-reservation spearfishing group Wa-Swa-Gon, told a jubilant crowd outside the tribal hall after the votes had been counted that "the 'Walleye Warriors' will be back" (Hanaway 1990, 11; *Wisconsin State Journal* 1989d, f).

Governor Thompson, Attorney General Hanaway, Administration Secretary Klauser, and DNR Secretary C. D. "Buzz" Besadny were caught off guard by the news. The vote was obviously a major setback to proponents of a negotiated settlement.

But efforts to secure such an arrangement would continue. Thompson and his aides told a group of editors and publishers two days after the balloting at Lac du Flambeau that Indian treaty rights remain the biggest problem facing the State of Wisconsin (*Wisconsin State Journal* 1989f, 1990c, 2). DNR Secretary Besadny had publicly stated weeks earlier that "we can—and we must—support a negotiated settlement. The treaties will not be abrogated and the Chippewa will never agree to a buyout. There can only be a lease arrangement" (Besadny 1989, 7). Former Dane County District Attorney James E. Doyle, Jr., the son of the late U. S. District Court judge who ruled against the Chippewas in 1978, called for a reopening of efforts to reach a negotiated settlement as he challenged Attorney General Hanaway in the 1990 election (*News from Indian Country* 1990f).

While many politicians support a negotiated settlement of Chippewa reserved rights as a means of ending the annual treaty rights controversy centered around the Indian spearfishing season in northern Wisconsin, there has also been talk about cooperative efforts between state conservation officials and the Chippewa bands in managing natural resources. In particular, attention has focused on the so-called "Washington model." As noted earlier, Washington State was embroiled in its own treaty rights controversy following the *Boldt Decision* in 1974. But while the treaty rights issue has been raging in Wisconsin since 1983, Indian tribes in Washington have worked with state and federal government officials as well as with private recreational and commercial fishing interests to manage fish populations with excellent results. Between 1974 and 1987, for example, salmon harvests increased by nearly thirty percent and steelhead harvests increased by almost seventy percent. Bruce Stewart, a fish pathologist who left Wisconsin's DNR to work in Washington State, claims that "Washington is 10 years ahead of Wisconsin" in terms of cooperation between Indians and state government in managing various resources (*Appleton Post-Crescent* 1989; *News from Indian Country* 1989a, 1990a; Thannum {1990}, 20; *Wisconsin State Journal* 1990c, 54, 56).

Traditional Chippewa culture reinforces cooperation rather than competition in hunting, fishing, and gathering, and the Indians have a long history of sharing resources with non-Indians (Strickland *et al.* 1990, 27). Lac du Flambeau spearfishing organizer Thomas Maulson, an avid opponent of the Thompson administration's abortive negotiated settlement, reminded an Eau Claire audience in 1990 that Indians have willingly shared the natural resources of North America "from the first day white people stepped foot on this continent." Non-Indians, he argued, need to understand the "cultural aspect," the fact that spearfishing is "important to American Indian heritage" (*Eau Claire Leader-Telegram* 1990d, 1A). Recently the national president of Trout Unlimited, Inc., Robert Herbst, a veteran of conflicts involving Indian treaty rights in the states of Washington, Minnesota, and Alaska, observed "there are now global environmental concerns, which demand our united attention. The magnitude of problems we jointly face make it imperative that we act as partners for the good of the resource itself, and not for the selfishness in each of us." For these reasons, Herbst's organization has moved from a position of opposing Indian treaty rights to one of stressing the cooperative management of resources (Kerr 1990a, 14).

Some supporters of cooperative management reacted very positively to the interest shown in 1990 by U. S. Senate Select Committee on Indian Affairs Chair Daniel K. Inouye in helping to resolve the treaty dispute in Wisconsin. Inouye, who had mediated the dispute in Washington State years earlier, indicated that his goal in the Wisconsin controversy was to "resolve this matter, not only amicably and fairly, but with justice to the Native Americans" (*News from Indian Country* 1990b, 13). In an editorial entitled "Inouye Riding to Rescue State from its Rednecks," *Capital Times* associate editor John Patrick Hunter deftly summed up the thinking of many advocates of cooperative management: "if the white establishment, here and in Washington, accepts the Indian nations as equal partners, then perhaps an agreement can be reached on fishing and timber cutting, without the explosive confrontations that have disgraced Wisconsin in recent years" (1990b).

Suggestions that the Chippewa Indians co-manage natural resources with State officials infuriate anti-treaty rights groups (*PARR Issue* 1991u, v). In 1990 when State Assembly Speaker Democrat Thomas Loftus of Sun Prairie, who opposes spearing of spawning fish, endorsed co-management as an answer to the strife over Chippewa treaty rights, Governor Thompson's aide James Klauser and DNR Secretary "Buzz" Besadny ruled out the approach as practiced in the state of Washington. Declaring co-management to be "probably illegal" under the state constitution, Klauser claimed it would take legislative action or a referendum changing the constitution to make the approach legal (*Wisconsin State Journal* 1990b, c, p. 55; *Milwaukee Sentinel* 1990f). "It will be a cold day in hell," Attorney General Hanaway told a legislative committee, before voters would agree to share authority for natural resources management with the Chippewas. In responding to Hanaway's comment, Great Lakes Indian Fish and Wildlife Commission executive director Jim Schlender poignantly observed, "the affect of all the attention on the term co-management has been to divert attention from the need to develop consensus and meaningful cooperation in managing the resources" (*News from Indian Country* 1990e).

Many Wisconsinites remain suspicious of what some continue to call the "special rights" of the Chippewas, and some state and county officials continue to search for ways to "modernize" Indian treaties and to curtail those rights. Between January 18th and 20th of 1990, for example, representatives of the Wisconsin Counties Association (WCA) and Wisconsin Administration Secretary James Klauser met in Salt Lake City, Utah, in closed session with county officials from a dozen states to discuss strategies for dealing with treaty rights issues. WCA Executive Director Mark Rogacki told reporters he was hopeful the meeting would lead to a coalition that would pressure Congress to rewrite nineteenth-century treaties. The organizers of the meeting were widely criticized in the press for refusing entry to several Wisconsin Indian county officials.[59] Indians picketed the meeting, calling the conferees "cockroaches hiding from the sun" (*Capital Times* 1990a; *Eau Claire Leader-Telegram* 1990a; *Milwaukee Sentinel* 1990a; *Wisconsin State Journal* 1990a; *Christian Science Monitor* 1990).

The Salt Lake City meeting took place as Indian law specialist Douglas Endreson of San Francisco addressed the members of the State Bar of Wisconsin at their mid-winter convention in Milwaukee. While Secretary Klauser and Wisconsin county officials discussed ways to circumvent the treaty rights of Indians, Endreson advised Wisconsin attorneys that solutions to treaty rights conflicts would not come about until states officially recognized treaties as "existing, viable, live documents, with live people on both sides" (*Milwaukee Sentinel* 1990b). Endreson's comments received reinforcement a few days later from the U. S. Commission on Civil Rights.

The Commission issued a formal report condemning documented cases of discrimination against Chippewa Indians in northern Wisconsin and reminding Wisconsinites that Indian treaty rights are protected by the U. S. Constitution as part of the "supreme Law of the Land" (*Eau Claire Leader-Telegram* 1990b).

The actions of the Wisconsin Counties Association described above are of particular concern since justice for the Indians depends largely on the willingness of opinion leaders in the majority society to learn about the evolution of treaty rights and to respect the continuation of those rights. Unlike non-Indian Americans, the most cherished civil rights of Indian people are not based on equality of treatment under the Constitution and modern civil rights laws. Rather, treaty rights and tribal sovereignty are of the utmost concern (Wilkinson 1990, 4-6).

Non-Indians in Wisconsin must come to understand that legal and moral considerations recognized by early American leaders are as pertinent today as when the Chippewa treaties were originally negotiated. Upon returning from the ill-received conference in Salt Lake City, Secretary of Administration Klauser claimed that he had gained a stronger appreciation for the Indian position. "I came back and ordered textbooks and started reading them," he said. Klauser's reexamination of the issues led him to remark, "the significance of the treaties is much greater than I understood months ago. I don't see the treaties as being the problem" (*Wisconsin State Journal* 1990c, 4). As the Equal Rights Commission of the Governor of the State of Wisconsin editorialized in the first issue of its newsletter in 1988, "the state, both as a people who live within its border and as a government, must have a conscience" with respect to the reserved rights of the Indians (*ERC Conscience* 1988, 2).

Recent events make it clear that the federal government must also have a conscience if the Wisconsin Chippewa Indians are to receive redress for more than a century of injustices. In her October 11, 1990, ruling denying the Chippewas damages against the State of Wisconsin, Judge Crabb acknowledged, "after more than sixteen years of litigation during which this court and the Court of Appeals for the Seventh Circuit have determined that the State of Wisconsin has violated plaintiffs' treaty rights for over 130 years, plaintiffs are left with no means of recovering monetary damages from the state except in the unlikely event that the United States joins this suit on their behalf." Crabb's ruling, as she herself recognized, "leaves the plaintiff tribes without an adequate remedy for the wrongs they have suffered" (U. S. District Court 1990b, 922-23).

Today, to quote Judge Crabb, the prospect of a federal resolution of the Chippewas' claim against the State of Wisconsin for redress of their grievances remains "as elusive as most of the promises made to them over the years" (*Eau Claire Leader-Telegram* 1990i, 2A). Although spoken by a member of a Southern Indian tribe, the following words of Cherokee Chief John Ross during the removal crisis in Georgia in 1831 seem appropriate for the present controversy over Chippewa hunting and fishing rights and claims against the State of Wisconsin for violating those rights:

> . . . President {George} Washington and his successors well understood the constitutional powers of the General Government, and the rights of the individual states, as well as those belonging to the Indian Nations, and that the treaties made under their respective administrations with the . . . {Indians} were intended to be faithfully & honestly regarded

on the part of the United States; and that the judicial power would extend to all cases of litigation that might arise under those treaties. (Ross 1831, 227)

Chippewa hunting and fishing rights are part of "the supreme Law of the Land." Applying the words of Chief Justice John Marshall in the 1832 Supreme Court case of *Worcester* v. *The State of Georgia* to Chippewa treaty rights in Wisconsin, we must remember that the Lake Superior Chippewa people constitute distinct communities, occupying their own territories, with boundaries accurately described, in which the laws of Wisconsin have no right to enter, but with the assent of the Chippewa people themselves, or in conformity with treaties, and with the acts of Congress.

The Chippewa bands, like the Cherokee people Marshall was speaking about in 1832, constitute distinct political communities having the right to make their own laws and be governed by themselves without the interference of state government except in those areas specifically provided by federal laws or federal court decisions. As "domestic dependent nations," using Marshall's words, the Chippewa bands have lost the sovereign power to treat with nations other than the United States, but they retain the right to have the meaning of treaty clauses resolved in their favor whenever the meaning is in doubt (Cohen 1982 222, 241-42). They also have the right, as Lac Courte Oreilles Tribal Chair Gaiashkibos recently commented, to decide that their reserved rights "are not for sale, not for lease" (*Masinaigan* 1990e).

9 Conclusion: An Agenda for the Future

Since the arrival of whites in Wisconsin, as scholar Gerald Vizenor has poignantly observed, the Chippewa people have been "divided by colonial, national, territorial, and state claims" (1984, 32). Wisconsin Chippewa communities survived several periods of economic exploitation—the fur-trapping period, the timber-cutting period, the copper-mining era, and the resort industry period. The entrepreneurs of each of these periods, with only rare exceptions, were whites (James 1954, 33; Nesbit and Thompson 1989, 516-17).

Through its treaties with the Chippewas, the United States obtained vast resources. According to historian David R. Wrone, these include 19 million acres of land, 100 billion board-feet of timber, and 13.5 billion pounds of copper, in addition to water, ports, power sites, quarries, and a "cornucopic treasure" of fish, fowl, and game. In return, the Chippewas received "only a few thousand dollars, some odds and ends of equipment, and a few thousand acres of reservation lands" (1989, 5). They did, however, reserve their rights of hunting, fishing, and gathering as well as the "other usual privileges of occupancy" on ceded territory (Kappler 2: 492 *App. 1,* and 542 *App. 4*). But, state officials prevented the Chippewas from exercising those rights for *most* of this century. In doing so, the state promoted a pattern of natural resource use that benefitted non-Indians at the expense of the Chippewas. Whites have garnered what several astute economists call an "exploitation premium" from the as yet uncompensated taking of Chippewa usufructuary rights. While supporters of PARR, STA, and other groups adamantly oppose a negotiated lease arrangement with the Chippewas on the basis that it would be too costly to non-Indian taxpayers, these same individuals ignore the fact that the Chippewas have suffered great monetary losses—among other things—in being denied their usufructuary rights through whites' misallocation of resources, which benefitted non-Indians at the expense of Indians (Bromley and Sharpe 1990, 15-16; Evers and Bromley 1989, 30-34).

As we move toward the twenty-first century, officials of the State of Wisconsin must seize every opportunity to redress the wrongs of the past and to work cooperatively with the Chippewa bands for the benefit of *all* Wisconsin residents. The governor and his administration can play a positive role in facilitating cooperation between the Great Lakes Indian Fish and Wildlife Commission and the State Department of Natural Resources, between tribal governments and state/county/local governments, between Indian parents and the public schools, and between aspiring tribal entrepreneurs and private business interests in order to foster economic development and to promote the general welfare of all of the people in the north country.

Several examples of such cooperation point the way. The efforts of the Lac Courte Oreilles Band (LCO) and the Hayward Lakes Association (HLA), an influential group of resort owners, to build a foundation for cooperation over many years have paid dividends. Not only have the LCO Indians spearfished without the rock throwing, vulgar threats, and racial slurs prevalent elsewhere in the north, but these Indians have also received support from the HLA for the construction and operation of a new fish hatchery. Non-Indians have joined the LCO in a variety of activities aimed at promoting better understanding and mutual respect. I have personally participated in workshops at which Indian and non-Indian teachers from the Hayward area have come together to study Indian treaty rights and various aspects of Indian culture. In the Cable area, local sportfishers have cooperated with the tribal fisheries of the Bad River and Red Cliff Bands to collect eggs from speared fish, to incubate the eggs at tribal hatcheries, and, finally, to stock rearing ponds or to restock the lakes. At Long Lake, Chamber of Commerce members not only asked area residents to honor the spearing rights of St. Croix tribal members, but they also manned two boats and accompanied the spearfishers to help promote calm. At least twelve Chambers of Commerce in the north have issued a joint statement recognizing Indian treaty rights. The Department of Natural Resources (DNR) announced on November 12, 1990, that ten wardens from the Great Lakes Indian Fish and Wildlife Commission will receive special credentials to enforce state laws alongside DNR wardens for the remainder of the year and that the DNR expects to authorize some tribal wardens to enforce state law independently of DNR wardens in 1991. The Wisconsin Department of Public Instruction and the governor's American Indian Language and Culture Education Board have taken steps to help today's children understand Indian cultures and appreciate Indian treaties and tribal sovereignty as something more than historical artifacts. These examples of cooperation deserve emulation (Kerr 1990b; *Eau Claire Leader-Telegram* 1990c, e; Thannum {1990}, 18-19; *News from Indian Country* 1990h; Wisconsin Education Association Council 1989, 1-2; *Wisconsin State Journal* 1990c, 20; Solterman 1991).

National economic and demographic trends suggest that success in meeting the challenges of the twenty-first century will require American leaders to understand, appreciate, and accommodate the needs of minority groups in society (Thomas 1990). This includes the needs of the members of the Chippewa bands, who have a unique relationship with state and local governments as a result of treaties made at great sacrifice to the Indians under pressure from the federal government. Wisconsinites—Indian and non-Indian alike—have more to gain by adhering to the constitutional principles upon which this nation was founded, including the recognition of and respect for treaty rights, than by disrespecting the law and disregarding human rights.

Wisconsin has deep progressive roots. There is an underlying reservoir of good will toward cultural, ethnic, religious, and political diversity in the state. Yet, one must not forget: the state that produced Senator Robert M. La Follette also produced Senator Joseph McCarthy, the state that enacted laws to prevent southern slaveowners from retrieving fugitive slaves and from molesting free blacks in the 1850s was the scene of violent race riots against blacks a hundred years later, and the state that poignantly argued against the removal of the Chippewas in the 1850s flagrantly violated the treaty rights of those Indians during most of this century.[60]

Much of our state's past treatment of the Chippewas is shameful (*Fig. 43*). The future, however, presents Wisconsinites an opportunity to redress the wrongs of the past and the present. As we approach the next Chippewa spearfishing season, let us uphold the constitutional principles that have governed this nation for more

Fig. 43. *Centuries-Old Indian Tradition/Centuries-Old White Tradition.* Cartoon by Steve Sack, *Star Tribune,* Minneapolis, MN. Reprinted with permission.

than two hundred years and honor the treaty rights of the Indians. Let us encourage our political and community leaders to build strong, positive relationships with tribal communities. Efforts to establish "committees of understanding" to improve cooperation at the local level between the Chippewa bands and neighboring communities are a step in the right direction. (*Wisconsin State Journal* 1990c, 4).

Northern Wisconsin must be transformed from a battle zone over treaty rights issues each spring and summer to a sanctuary of peace and beauty for Indians and non-Indians. False data and malicious rumors about Indian utilization of natural resources must be replaced with accurate information. On April 3, 1991, Senator Daniel Inouye came to Wisconsin to receive the results of a year-long study on the impact of spearfishing. Inouye, chair of the Senate Select Committee on Indian Affairs, had secured a congressional appropriation enabling representatives of the six Wisconsin Chippewa bands, the U. S. Bureau of Indian Affairs, the U. S. Fish and Wildlife Service, the Wisconsin Department of Natural Resources, and the Great Lakes Indian Fish and Wildlife Commission to conduct the fishery assessment. The committee's final report, *Casting Light Upon the Waters,* concludes that "fear and uncertainty generated by biased perceptions" have fueled the controversy over Indian fishing rights and have obscured the fact that "Chippewa spearing has not harmed the resource" (U. S. Department of the Interior 1991, 13).

The time and energy expended by those protesting the treaty rights of Indians (to say nothing of the taxpayers' funds spent in providing emergency police services at the boat landings to protect Indians from physical abuse as they engage in legal pursuits) need to be redirected toward resolving the serious environmental and societal issues facing our communities. If Indians and non-Indians cooperatively manage the resources of northern Wisconsin, perhaps we will be able to create what Red Cliff Band member Walter Bresette has called "a unique environmental zone" that will be recognized throughout the world as "the jewel of the planet" (*Isthmus* 1990, 9). Lac Courte Oreilles Tribal Chair Gaiashkibos refers to the Chippewas as "keepers" of the Earth placed here to preserve, not to destroy and abuse the resources. He tells the following traditional story:

> Each day the creator sends an eagle out, and he looks down and sees if the Indian people are still practicing the teachings. One day, when he doesn't see the smoke from the Indian people, then he will destroy the Earth. (*Wisconsin State Journal* 1990c, 52)

"Successful co-management," Biological Services Director Thomas R. Busiahn of the Great Lakes Indian Fish and Wildlife Commission asserts, "requires building bridges between cultures and world views, and recognizing the worth in each of them" (1989b, 5).

All Wisconsin residents have something to gain by the preservation of the world view that led nineteenth-century Chippewa leaders to stubbornly resist efforts to evict them from this state and its resources. Efforts to nourish that world view continue to lead the Chippewas to resist all attempts to curtail their treaty rights.

Our treatment of the Chippewas today, like our treatment of them during the dark days of the Wisconsin Death March in the mid-nineteenth century, serves as an index to our commitment to the rule of law and our democratic faith. Legal scholar Felix Cohen asserted nearly forty years ago that "like the miner's canary, the Indian marks the shift from fresh air to poison air in our political atmosphere; and our treatment of Indians, even more than our treatment of other minorities, reflects the rise and fall of our democratic faith" (1953, 390). For, as President George Bush noted in his 1989 inaugural address, "Great nations like great men must keep their word." As the last decade of the twentieth century unfolds before their eyes, Wisconsin's Chippewa Indians have new reasons to be hopeful that—as President Bush asserted in his inaugural address—"when America says something, America means it, whether a treaty or an agreement or a vow made on marble steps" (Bush 1989, 349).

Appendices

Introduction

Appendices 1, 3, and 5 describe the proceedings of the 1837, 1842, and 1854 Chippewa treaties from the perspective of federal treaty negotiators. Appendices 2, 4, and 6 reproduce the treaties as ratified by the U. S. Senate and proclaimed by the President. For photographs of the first pages of the original handwritten treaties, see Figures 10, 12, and 22. Figure 14 reproduces the first page of President John Tyler's proclamation of the 1842 treaty.

Accuracy has been stressed in the reproduction of the documents, which have been transcribed in the Appendices without changes in capitalization, grammar, punctuation, or spelling. The authors' inconsistancies and errors are also retained. Quotation marks that originally appeared at the beginning on each line of a direct quotation have been deleted, leaving quotation marks only at beginnings and endings of paragraph quotations—if the marks were used. These writers also repeated the last word of a page at the beginning of the following page; we did not repeat these words. Notes written in the margins of the documents are included here as footnotes. Asterisks * were used by the authors to indicate placement of marginal notes; numbers in braces { } were added to show sequence. Frame numbers are provided in braces for Appendices 1, 3, and 5 so that readers may easily locate pertinent pages in the microfilm edition available from the National Archives and Records Service. Page numbers from volume 2 of Kappler's *Indian Affairs* are provided in braces for Appendices 2, 4, and 6. Editorial additions and clarifications, which have been kept to a minimum, are also in braces. Corrections have not been added in braces where the meaning of a misspelled word is obvious.

Appendix 1

Negotiations for the "Chippewa Treaty of July 29, 1837"

Proceedings of a Council held by Governor Henry Dodge, with the Chiefs and principal men, of the Chippewa Nation of Indians near Fort Snelling, at the confluence of the S͏ͭ. Peters and Missisippi Rivers, commencing on the 20͏ͭʰ day of July 1837.

The Head Men of the nation, having by direction of Governor Dodge, been advised of his desire to meet them in council, their different bands assembled together near Fort Snelling between the first and 20͏ͭʰ of July, to the number of upwards of a thousand individuals, men, women, & children, and on the last mentioned day, met the Governor at the Council House.

Gen͏ͤ. William R. Smith of Pennsylvania, appointed by the President of the United States, the colleague of Governor Dodge in the commission, did not arrive to be present at the council.

The following named Chiefs were present, and recognized as such, by the Governor.

Bands	Chiefs
From Leech Lake,	Aish-ke-boge-kozho, or Flat Mouth and The Elder Brother
" Gull Lake & Swan River,	Pa-goona-kee-zhig, or The Hole in the day, and Songa-Komig or, The Strong Ground
" Mille Lac,	Wa-shask-ko-koue, or Rats Liver
" Sandy Lake	Ka-nam-dawa-winro, or Le Brocheux
" Snake River,	Naudin, or The Wind, Sha-go-bai, or The Little Six, Pay-a-jik, & Na-qua-na-bie, or The Feather.
" Fond-du-Lac,	Mang-go-sit, or Loons Foot, and Shing-gobe, or The Spruce
" S͏ͭ. Croix River,	Pe-zhe-ke, or The Buffalo

Ver Planck Van Antwerp of Indiana, appointed by the President, Secretary to the Commission, was also present at the meeting of the Council.

The usual ceremonies for opening a council with the Indians, having been first duly observed, Governor Dodge addressed them as follows:{0548} "Chiefs, Head Men, and Wariors of the Chippewa Nation of Indians."

"Your Great Father The President of the United States, has sent me to see you in Council, to propose to you the purchase of a small part of your country East of the Missisippi River.

"This country, as I am informed, is not valuable to you for its game, and not suited to the culture of corn, and other Agricultural purposes.

"Your Great Father wishes to purchase your country on the Chippewa and S͏ͭ. Croix Rivers, for the advantage of its Pine Timber, with which it is said to abound.

"A Map of the Country which your Great Father wishes to buy from you, will be shewn you, where on which the Rivers and Water courses are laid down; and such explanations given through your Interpreter, as will fully explain to you, the particular part of your country East of the Missisippi River, which Your Great Father proposes to purchase, for the use of his White Children.

Your Great Father knows you are poor; and this Pine region of Country, is not valuable to you for hunting purposes. His wish is, to make you a full compensation for it, the country, by giving you its full value, payable in such manner, as will be most serviceable to your people.

"An estimate will be made of the probable value of your country which it is proposed to purchase, of which you will be informed. I will request you, after fully deliberating upon the subject, to tell me your price for the country, with as little delay as possible.

"Your Great Father The President was desirous that the Chippewas should be fully represented in this council, that all might know what had been done; and that equal justice should be done to all. I wish you to be prepared with your answer to the proposition made you, at our meeting in Council tomorrow."

Governor Dodge having confided his remarks and intimated his readiness to hear any thing which the Chiefs or principle men might have to say to him, Aish-ke-boge-kozhe, (Flat Mouth, or La Guelle Plat) advanced and spoke as follows: "My Father, I have but little to say to you now. Living in a different part of the country from that which you propose to buy from us, I will be among the last of those who will speak to you upon that subject.

"After those shall have spoken who live in and nearer to that country, I will talk more to you.

"My Father, My people have all the same opinion with me, and will abide by what I say to you. I have come to listen first, to all you have to say to us, and will afterwards speak to you. My heart is with you. I have nothing more to say now.

Naudin (The Wind) then came forward and said "My Father, I once shook hands with our Great Father The President of the United States, as I do with you now. I have not much to say at present; and my brother-in-law who stands near me wishes to speak to you. On tomorrow I expect that some more people will be here from the country that you wish to buy from us. I was present when they began to run the boundary line between our country and that of the Sioux at the "Red Devils Riverss {See Note A}." When you are ready to examine that line I will say more to you."

Pe-zhe-ke (The Buffalo) "My Father. I am taken by surprise by what you have said to us, and will speak but few words to you now. We are waiting for more of our people who are coming from the country which you wish to buy from us.

"We will think of what you have said to us, and when they {0549} come, will tell you our minds about it. Men will then be chosen by us, to speak to you. I have nothing more to say now."

{Note A: Red Devils Riverss is the interpretation decided upon after much analysis of the penmanship, context, and historical possibilities in consultation with Richard St. Germaine. It fits the context because an Indian named Red Devil did sign the 1825 treaty to which the speaker here refers. In an earlier transcript of this document (Iowa News 1837, 410-11), this phrase was transcribed as Red Deer's Rump, but this has no historical meaning with which I am familiar.}

Pa-goona-kee-zhig (The Hole in the Day) "My Father, what Aish-ke-boge-ko-zhe (Flat Mouth) & the others who have spoken have told you, is the opinion of us all."

Na-ca-ne-ga-be (The Man that Stands Foremost) "My Father. The people will come from the country where my fathers have lived before me. When they arrive here, they will speak to you. Until then I have nothing more to say."

Governor Dodge, then, after urgently impressing upon the Indians, the great importance and necessity of their remaining quiet among each other and at peace with the Sioux, during the time that they were at S⁻t. Peter's attending the Council, adjourned it to meet again at 10 O'Clock Tomorrow Morning.

Friday July 21ˢᵗ 1837

The Governor was advised this morning by Mr. {M.M.} Vineyard their Agent, that the Indians did not wish to meet in council to day, as the people whom they expected, had not yet arrived, and they wanted more time to council among themselves.

Saturday July 22ᵈ

The Morning being cloudy with a threatening appearance of rain, the Council did not meet until 3 O'Clock P.M. when Governor Dodge directed the Interpreter to say to the Indians, that when he had parted with them two days ago, they had told him that they expected to meet more of their friends here, and were desirous before taking any further steps about what he had spoken to them, of councilling among each other—that he had now met them to hear what they might have to say about their absent friends, and to listen to any communications which they might wish to make to him, in regard to the councils which they had held, or the conclusions resulting from them, at which they had arrived.

After an interval of some 15 or 20 minutes, during which time the Intrepreter by direction of The Governor, repeated the expressions of his readiness to hear any remarks, which the Indians might wish to make to him. Flat Mouth advanced and said

"My Father. I shall say but little to you at this time. I am called a Chief. I am not the Chief of the whole nation, but only of my people or tribe. I speak to you now only because I see nobody else ready to do so. I do not wish to take any further steps about what you have proposed to us, until the other people arrive, who have been expected here. They have not yet come; and to do so before their arrival, might be considered an improper interference, and unfair towards them.

"The residence of my band is outside of the country which you wish to buy from us. After the people who live in that country shall have told you their minds, I will speak.

"If the lands which you wish to buy, were occupied by my band, I would immediately have given you my opinion. After listening to the people who we are expecting, and who will speak to you, I will abide by what they say, and say more to you myself.

"My Father, on getting up to speak to you, I hardly knew what to say. If I say no more, it is not because I am afraid or ashamed to speak my mind before my people, & those of the whole nation, and all others present, but because I have nothing more to say.''

The Buffalo remarked, that he was quite deaf, and could not hear distinctly what was said; that he had seen the Governors lips move, and turned each ear to him to listen, but could not hear well, his words; that there was another {0550} man here, who with himself had the confidence of their people, but that they did not wish to say more until the rest of them who they were expecting, should arrive.

Pay-á-jik ''My Father. Your children are not displeased with what you have said to them—but they wish you to give them four times more tobacco than you have yet given them. My Father, what has happened to you? Have you cut off your breasts that you can not suckle your children? If you did so *[1], it would render them more pliant and ready to yield to your wishes. This was the case at the the Treaty of Prairie du Chien in 1825. I was there, and know what was done. The boundary line between our country and that of the Sioux, was then established; & my people wish now to have it explained to them. I have been told by the other Chiefs and Wariors to say what I have said to you. I do not say it of my own accord. My people have chosen me and another, to talk with you about the proposition that you have made to them, to buy a part of our country.

''I am ready to proceed whenever the others are ready. Other men of power and authority are behind, and are expected here. They will soon come, when we will give you our answer.''

The Wind ''My Father''—turning round to the Indians—''I shake by the hand all the people of the different tribes of my nation who are around you,''—and then turning to Governor Dodge—''My Father, What I said to you two days ago, I would say to the President of The United States if I saw him. My forefathers were a great and powerful people, which gives me confidence to speak. All your Children here heard what you said when you spoke to them about the lands which you wish to buy from us. I understood that it was the country upon the S^t. Croix and Chippewa Rivers, and towards the East; and when I slept, I had a dream, and a little bird passed by and told me what was meant.

I will listen to what others have to say, and will then speak my mind to you plainly and fully. My Father I attended a council at Prairie-du-Chien which lasted ten days. Some of those now here, were then present. This will last longer; as it is one of greater importance. It is now late in the day. When the Council meets again we will begin earlier in the morning, that we may have more time to speak.''

Rats Liver (Wa-shask-ko-koue) ''My Father I have nothing to say to you different from what has been said by those who have already spoken. We are all of the same mind.''

Governor Dodge then directed the Intrepeter to ask the Chiefs, whether their people who were here, were troubled by the Sioux; that he had seen the Sioux dancing in their Encampment yesterday, and was glad to witness the friendly feeling, which seemed to exist among them; that he had been informed by the Agent for the Sioux, Major Taliaferro, that he had told them, they must not visit the Chippewa encampment during their stay here, but upon the most friendly terms; & that if the Sioux had given them any trouble he wanted to know it, and wished some one of the Chiefs would now mention it to him.

---

*[1] meaning, that if he would give them whiskey

The Wind replied to the Governor that there was no trouble; that they were all satisfied; that all his children around him both Chippewa and Sioux wished to be friendly together, and wanted to carry on a little trade and bartering among themselves; but that he was directed by his people to tell the Governor that the Soldiers and White people troubled them in their Encampment.

Governor Dodge "I am glad to hear that you are on friendly terms with the Sioux, & hope you will continue to be. I wish you to take each other strong by the hand; and you must conduct yourselves well while you remain here

"I will speak to the officer commanding the Garrison & request him to forbid his soldiers disturbing you for the future.{0551} He will prevent it".

The Wind. "My Father, I wish you would give the same advice to the Sioux that you have given us; but do not wish thereby, to prevent them from coming in a friendly way to visit us". And then the Gov. adjourned the Council.

Monday July 24ᵗʰ 1837.
The Council met at 11. O'Clock A.M.

Governor Dodge directed the Interpreter to inform the Indians, that he had just been advised, that four of their friends (Indians) who they had been expecting, had arrived at their encampment; and that fifty others, were said to be near here, who had come from La Pointe with Messrs. {Lyman M.} Warren and {Daniel P.} Bushnell, & who it was believed would arrive here this evening; that as they were all of the same nation, & brethren of each other, he wished those present to consult with them; that he did not wish to hurry their deliberations among themselves, but to give them full time to consult their friends who had arrived, and those who were coming in; & that he would now hear any thing that they might have to say to him upon the subject.

The Wind "My Father. I am very sorry to keep you so long, in a painful state of suspense upon the matter which you have proposed to us. My people are glad to see you, and they are gratified at the proposition which you have made to them. My Father, I speak to you now through the lips of "The Buffalo." (the latter had advanced to the Governors table with "The Wind", shaking him by the hand, & remarking that he would do the same with all those present, but his arm was too short— & then stepping back, to allow the latter to speak for him). He has been to see our Great Father the President of the United States, and came back safe. When I look at you it frightens me. I cannot sufficiently estimate your importance, and it confuses me. I have seen a great many Americans, but never one whose appearance struck me as yours does. You have heard of the coming of those, whose absence has prevented our proceeding, in what you have proposed to us. This is the case with all our people here. My Father. Listen to what I am going to say to you. I listened to our Great Father the President of the {0552} United States, & have never forgotten what he said to me. Others will speak after me, whose language will please you, and set all things right

"My Father. We are a distracted people, and have no regular system of acting together. We cast a firm look on the people who are coming; and all think alike, about this matter. What we are going to say to you, will not dissatisfy—but please you".

Pay-a-jik, "My Father. What I am going to say to you is not my own language, but the words of Chiefs and others around you. They all look at you, who are so different from them You are all white, while they are half red *[2]. How can we possibly forget the traders in this matter? You have come to dispense charity to us, and we must think of the traders. I think well of them. They have used me well, and supported me, and I wish to do them justice. We should certainly all be benighted if they did not do for us, what they have done heretofore; & if we do wrong to them, how can we expect it.

"My Father. Look around on all your red children here. The trader has raised them; and it is through his means that they are, as they are; We wish you to do him justice. They will, by this means go on and support us as heretofore. I refered, in commencing to speak, to the half breeds. Many of them have been brought up among us, and we wish to provide for them. We want justice done to them".

Ma-je'-ga-bo. "My Father. I shall not say much to you. You are not a man to be spoken to in a light manner. I am not a Pillager*[3], but went among them when small, which gives me the right to speak as one of them. My brother (The Wind) stands beside me, and we are descended from those, who in former days, were the greatest orators of our nation".

"My Father. I am not backward in saying what I wish to. I am not going to do any thing, to make your heart lean; am not going to tell you what will be said by the Chiefs. I will answer you, when you make us an offer for our lands. As soon as our friends arrive, & I hear their decision, I will say all that I have to say. I conclude upon that subject for the present, and will speak upon another.

"My Father. Listen closely to me. I will hide nothing from you that has passed. But for the Traders, you would not {illegible} see all your children sitting around you, as they do, to day. It is not the Chiefs, but the traders who have supported them to the present time. Our Great Father has told us that An Agent would be sent to us—but he has not yet been among us. The Traders are in our country, to trade for the skins of animals, which we take to them. Half of what they bring into the country and sell to your children is lost to them. I am glad to see the Agent here, who is to go into our country, & support our young men, women, & children.

"We wish to do justice to the half breeds, who have been brought up among us, by having them provided for.

Sha-go-bai (The Little Six). "My Father, I heard of you, when I was yet a young man, a long time ago; & now I see you. I am frightened when you look at me. I am startled when the wind comes rustling by; and the thunder cloud, tho' I know it will pass along without harming, alarms me.

"So it is, my father, when you talk to your children around you, of their lands; which you wish to buy from them.

"But I have great confidence in the Chiefs who are here, and others who are coming. When they come to treat fully with you, we (pointing to the two men standing beside him, & himself) will sit far off and listen. I spring from the same stock with the people who stand behind you (white men—Sha-go-bai is a half breed) and am related to all the half breeds in the country where I live.

"My Father. Look at the man who is standing near me. His, {0553} and my ancestors, were the Chief Men of the Country, that you want to buy from us. The Traders have raised our children, and we like them. I owe my life to the Traders,

---

*[2] alluding to the half-breeds
*[3] The common name of the Leech Lake Band

who have supported us. I am glad to see the Agent here who will live among us, & give us tobacco when we want it".

The Little Buffalo ''My Father. Listen to what I am going to say to you. Let it enter deeply into your ear, & upon your heart. Tho' I may appear contemptible in your sight; when I address the wariors of my tribe, they listen to me.

Nobody—no trader—has instructed me what to say to you. Those who have spoken before me, have told you the truth; & I shall speak on the same subject. I have been supported by the Trader; & without his aid, could not get through the winter, with my naked skin. The grounds where your children have to hunt, are as bare as that on which I now stand, & have no game upon them.

''My Father, I am glad to see you here, to embrace the Earth We are at a loss to give anything to the Traders, as our lands and hunting grounds are so destitute— do us a kindness, by paying our old debts. I have nothing more to say. You are our Father, and we look up to, and respect you. I have come here and seen you, and my heart is at peace. I have talked with my wariors & heard their words, & my mind is tranquil''.

Flat Mouth, ''My Father. Your eyes are upon me, & mine upon you. Wherever I have been, the prints of the white mans hand's have been left upon my own. Yours are not the first that I have shaken. It is I and those men (pointing to The Elder Brother, The Strong Ground and The Hole in the Day) that have brought many of your children here. Their opinions are mine.

''My Ancestors were chiefs of their tribes and villages while they lived: I do not however hold my title from them, but have derived it from my own acts and merits

''My Father. When I came here this morning, I supposed you wanted to talk to us about the lands, you wish to get from us, and not about the Traders.

''After the question about selling the land shall be settled—it will then be time enough to talk about these Traders''.

''My Father. I shall not be backward in speaking of what you propose to us at the proper time. Many of my people have told me to say so. But we can do nothing until the other people arrive. We must listen to them. As I have told you before after they shall speak I will say more.

The Hole in the day ''My Father. He who is the Master of all hears me speak. I know the Traders, & what has been their conduct. I know which of them are good men, and those who are bad, and act like drunken men. When the other people come I will speak again.

Rats Liver. ''My Father I am but little accustomed to speaking, and am generally, one of those who listen. Our Father here (the Agent) knows me, and is acquainted with my character. If I wished to speak much, I should feel no shame for my personal appearance—but this you may not wish to hear.

''We are talking about the land which you have come for—I have tread all over it, with my war club in my hand. My ancestors and those of Pa-goona-kee-zhig (The Hole in the Day) were the Chiefs and protectors of that country, and drove the bad Indians (The Sioux) away from it.

''My Father It is only to you that I look and listen, & not to the bad birds that are flying through the air. My own merit has brought me to the place which I occupy to day; and I do not wish any body to push me forward as a speaker

''I have nothing to add now, but will say more when the business about the land has been settled.''

Que-me-shan-shee or <u>Big Mouth</u>, "My Father, What I am going to say to you; is of not much consequence. I have smoked with some of my friends & have come to tell you the result. After reflecting upon the subject we came to no definite conclusion—but wish to do like those who have already spoken. We do not wish to do any thing to injure the white people. My Father, all that has prevented us from doing {0554} what you came here to have us do, is, that we have been waiting for others of our people who we have expected here, and who we are afraid to dissatisfy. I never before have spoken to Americans at any length; and fear My Father, that you will think that I am drunk—but I have here (putting his hand to his breast) a great deal of sense (intelligence) which I have obtained from the white people. As soon the other people come, we will unfold our minds to you.

Sha-we-niq-wa-nabe. _____ "My Father, What I have to say to you, place it strongly to your heart. The Master of life, and The Spirit of the Earth listen to us. The Master of life made the Earth, the grass and the trees that grow upon it, and the animals that roam over it. When the Great spirit made the Earth, he placed the Red Men upon it; & when the Chiefs were put upon it, it became very strong. Some of these chiefs are now here, and others are coming. They do not wish to act precipitately".

<u>Shing-go-be</u> (The Spruce) "My Father, I shall speak but few words to you. It is only I who can tell you the truth about the lands where I live. If you speak of the lands yonder (pointing towards the country proposed to be purchased) I will not talk foolishly about them here, in the midst of so many Indians. Altho' only a child, I speak at once into the middle of a subject, and you shall hear straight about my lands, because I am the Master of them. After you shall have spoken to me further about them, the Master of life will hear me answer you.

"My Father I could speak all day long in a loud tone of voice—but have nothing further to say to you now

<u>Mang-go-sit</u>, (The Loons Foot) "My Father, I do not wish to say much to you. You do not know who I am, & from whence I have sprung. I never speak at any length; but it is not because I can not speak strong. I only wish to tell you now who my Ancestors were. I am the son of Le Brocheux—one of the greatest chiefs of our nation. I have given my thoughts before to your children who have spoken to you—and I think before I speak.

"My Father, I will speak to you more when you know who I am. When I speak to the Chiefs, I do not speak long, but to the point.

<u>Ma-ge-go-be</u>—after a long speech to the Indians & urging upon them to sell the land; but before doing so, to press upon the Governor to give them presents, and furnish them with more provisions—said

"My Father This is all your children have to say to you now, about the lands. They are going to take a rest, and will then say more to you about them. Listen My Father, to what I have said to your children & what they have answered. What I am going to say to you now is to the purpose. The provisions that you have given us, are not enough for us. We want those of another kind—some of the cattle on the prairie. Our people do not cook properly what you have given them to eat. It has made them sick, and they want you to give them something else that will cure them.

<u>The Wind</u>, "My Father When I saw our Great Father, the President of the United States he gave me sense. Listen to me, & let me tell you the truth. I listen to you,

and accede to your purposes. You must not suppose that things will not be as you wish. We are now arrangeing them to your liking. The Station of Chief is a very difficult one to hold, but when I was made one by the President I thought I never should be refused anything that I asked for. It is hard to hear our children crying here for something to eat. When I have heard their cries in the dead of winter, I have put on my belt and started off to look for it. Your look is so firm that I think it would not be possible for you not to do what you wished to. You and I both speak from what the President of the United States has told us. You have plenty of every thing to eat around you, & can give us some of the cattle that are {0555} upon the Prairie. At the treaty at Prairie du Chien, the case was as difficult as this. The Great Chief then fed us well and gave us ninety head of cattle.

The Spruce. "My Father, I am not one who has asked for cattle to eat. You have come too far to bring them with you. If you wish to give meat; give it to those who want it—I do not. Continue to give me what you have furnished to us before".

Governor Dodge, then directed the Interpreter to say to them that their father (the Agent) would tell them whether he could get any cattle for them; that he wished to see them again in council early tomorrow morning; that he was glad to hear their friends would be here this evening; that the weather was now good, & they must make up their minds as soon as they could; that he hoped the Chiefs & principal men would see that their people kept on friendly terms, with the Sioux, & if any difficulty occurred inform their Agent; that the Sioux & themselves had met here as friends, & he wanted them to part so—And then Adj^d. the Council until tomorrow.

Tuesday, July 25<u>th</u>

Governor Dodge was advised at 10 O' Clock this morning, that seventy Five or Eighty Indians belonging to four or five different Bands, from Lakes, De Flambeau and De Courtereille, and La Pointe &, accompanied by M^r. Bushnell the Sub-Agent and a M^r. Warren a trader from La Pointe, had just arrived. These Gentlemen waited upon Governor Dodge, immediately on their arrival & informed him, that the Indians who had come with them would not be ready or willing to go into council with him to day. At their suggestion therefore, and the solicitation of M^r. Warren, The Governor postponed the meeting of the Council until 9 O' Clock tomorrow morning.

Wednesday July 26<u>th</u>

On meeting in Council this morning, in addition to the Indians who have been present heretofore, a large number of others appeared. The following are the bands, to which they principally belong; and the names of their Chiefs.

Bands	Chiefs
From Lake De Flambeau.	Na-wa-ghe-wa, or "The Knee".
	O-ge-ma-ga, or "The Dandy"
	Pa-se-quam-jis, or "The Commissioner", and Wa-be-ne-me-ke, or "The White Thunder"
" Lake Coutereille,	We-non-ga-be or "The Wounded Man", and Ke-wat-se, or The Old Man

139

"   La Pointe (on Lake Superior).   Ghe-bish-ghe-e-kow, or "The
                                        Buffalo and Ta-qua-ga-na or
                                        "Joining Lodges"".

Governor Dodge directed that in the future proceedings in the Treaty, Stephen
Bouga, and Patrick Quin, should intrepret from the English language into Chippewa,
and Scott Campbell and Jean Batiste Dubé, from Chippewa into English.

He then addressed the Indians thus:

"My Children of the Chippewa Nation assembled here.

"I have been informed, that since I last met you, your people, whose absence
had prevented the proceeding with our Councils, have arrived here.

"I wish now to learn from you, if this is the case, & whether you are ready to
proceed. I have before made a proposition to you—which those then present, have,
I presume, communicated to the others who have recently arrived, for the purchase
of a portion of your territory. You have defered giving me an answer until your
friends should arrive, and as I believe they are now all here, I will renew my
proposition to you; and will show you a map, explaining which part of your country
it is, that I wish to buy.

"I will now place the map before me, and wish the Chiefs and {0556} Principal
Men, and particularly those from that part of the country which I wish to purchase,
towit: Lakes De Flambeau, and Coutereille, and the Chippewa, S^{t}. Croix, & Rum
Rivers &^{c}, to come forward and examine it with me, as I direct it to be explained
to them. And after this examination, I wish you to inform me whether or not you
will sell the country to me.

Ghe-bish-ghe-e-kow, or "The Buffalo", (from La Pointe), replied, "My Father.
We have come from a distance, and but lately arrived here, and what you have
proposed to us, we want more time to think about. The notice that you have given
us is rather too short. Let us wait another day, and tomorrow we will be able to
give you our answer".

The Governor, directed it to be said to them, that they could examine the map
now & have it explained to them—consult among each other between this &
tomorrow morning, & be prepared then, to give him an answer; that he did not
wish to hurry them, but that he had already waited patiently for them during several
days, and was anxious to bring the business to a close as soon as possible; that he
would now be glad to hear any thing from any of the other Chiefs who might wish
to speak to him; & that if they desired it, he would remain there until sundown for
that purpose.

He then explained the map fully, to the Chiefs and principal men, and repeated
to them, that he had been informed, that the country which he wished to get from
them, was barren of game, and of little value for Agricultural purposes; but that it
abounded in Pine timber, for which, their Great Father the President of the United
States wished to buy it from them, for the use of his white children, & that he
would give them a fair price for it; that he wished them to understand the Map, &
to enable them to do so, had mentioned & pointed out to them natural boundaries
comencing at the mouth of Crow Wing River; thence to Lake S^{t}. Croix, thence to
the head waters of the Ouisconsin River, & down said river to the Plover portage
where the line dividing their Territory from the other Indians comenced; while on
the west the tract would be bounded by the Missisippi River; that he wished them

140

to be prepared to morrow morning, to tell him not only, whether or not they would sell him the land, but their price for it; that he wished them all—but more particularly those from that part of the country which he wished to buy, to go home satisfied; so that when they met their people there, they might not be ashamed to tell them what they had done; that so many bands of their nation, & from such remote parts of it, had never before, he believed, met together, & that he wished them now to advise with each other, and unite and act together, as one people; that he wished the Chiefs and Wariors to consult together this evening, and select, out of their number two Chiefs in whom they had confidence to speak for them; that he wished to meet them all in council, but that not more than two of them should speak; that this was done merely to save time, & that they could all consult together, and tell the two speakers what to say to him; that altho' they were of different bands, they belonged to the same great nation, and their interests were in common; that he wished them all to be satisfied with what should be done; that their Great Father The President of the United States would be just towards them, & that they must be just towards each other; that in their consultations he did not wish them to forget their Half breed relatives and their traders, but to do them justice, also; and that he would be glad now to hear whatever any of the Chiefs might have to say to him''.

Pay-a-jik, replied that those of the S.ᵗ. Croix River band who had come in yesterday had chosen him to speak for them, tho' it had always been his custom to sit quiet, and say but little; that he and his friends had talked together, and agreed what to do.

After waiting half an hour or more & none of the other Chiefs or Wariors rising to speak, The Governor again took occasion to urge upon the Indians how important {0557} it was that during their stay here, they should keep quiet among each other, and at perfect peace with the Sioux; that for one of them to strike a Sioux, or a Sioux to strike one of them, might be productive of the greatest harm; that he wished to impress this upon those who had lately arrived, as well as the others; and that he hoped his views and wishes were now fully understood by them; that if they were not, as they were now about to part until tomorrow morning, if they would ask him any questions, he would give such further explanations, as might be necessary.

Several of the chiefs came forward to ask some questions in regard to the map, after which seeming to understand, & to be satisfied with it, and having nothing further to say, The Governor adj.ᵈ the Council until Tomorrow Morning

Thursday Morning July 27.ᵗʰ

The Council met at 11. O'Clock A.M. and the map with the boundaries of the country proposed to be purchased, was again fully explained to the Indians; when Gov.ʳ Dodge inquired of them, through the Intrepeter, whether they were all satisfied upon that point; whether the bands assembled here, were now, all represented in council, by their Chiefs; whether they had selected speakers to speak for them, as had been suggested to them yesterday—and if so, that they would designate them; & that these speakers would now communicate their sentiments to him.

They answered each of these questions, in the affirmative, & replied that they had chosen Ma-ghe-ga-bo *[4] or Latrappe, and Pa-goo-na-kee-zhig (The Hole-in-The Day) to speak for them on this occasion.

Ma-ghe-ga-bo then came forward in true Indian costume towit; naked, except as to his leggings, breech cloth and flap; his full head of hair hanging loosely upon his shoulders; a sort of crown upon his head, made for the occasion, & filled with feathers of the Bald Eagle, placed there by the chiefs; and the medals of several of the Chiefs hung round his neck. He advanced to the Governors table with his War Flag, and planted it there, & then turned round and addressed the Indians at considerable length. Pa-goo-na-kee-zhig followed him in an address to the Indians.

Ma-ghe-ga-bo, then, with the map before him and his finger pointing to it, said to the Governor

"My Father. This is the country which is the home of many of your children. I have covered it with a paper (he had done so) and so soon as I remove that paper, the land shall be yours. But should the Wind blow it off, that shall not make it so. I have listened closely to the words that the Chiefs have told me to say to you.

"My Father, when we first met here, we smoked and shook hands and talked together. Four times we have gone through the same ceremony, and now on the fifth, we have come to give you our answer. I stand here to represent the Chiefs of the different bands of my nation assembled here, & to tell you of their detirmination, to sell to you the lands that you want of them.

"My Father, Listen to me. Of all the country that we grant you we wish to hold on to a tree where we get our living, & to reserve the streams where we drink the waters that give us life *[5]. I have but few words to say, but they are those of the Chiefs, and very important. What I am now going to say to you, is a kind of history of our Chiefs. The Being that created us, made us naked, He created you and your people with knowledge and power to get a living. Not so with us; we had to cover ourselves with moss and rotten wood; & you must be merciful to us. The Chiefs will now show you the tree we want to reserve. This is it (placing an oak sprig upon the Table near the map). It is a different kind of tree from the one you wish to get from us. Every time the leaves fall from it, we will count it as one winter past." {0558}

"My Father, In regard to the lands that you have spoken to us about, you have told us what you want, & I answer you in the name of the Chiefs. I am no Chief, but a Warior; & the badge that I wear, is not a mark of my bad conduct, but to make myself respected by my people.

"We have understood you will pay us in goods and money for our lands, and we want to know now, what amount, you will give us for them".

Gov.ʳ Dodge—through the Intrepeter—"As the land belongs to them, I want them to say, what they wish me to pay them, for it. If they can not come to a conclusion upon this point among themselves, I would recommend to them, to ask the aid of Their Father's (the Sub Agents, Messrs. Vineyard and Bushnell) to assist them. But if they can determine among themselves, let them do so.

---

*[4] A War Chief the same who killed Gov.ʳ {Robert} Semple

*[5] This of course is nonsense—but is given literally as rendered by the Intrepeters, who are unfit to act in that capacity. I presume it to mean that the Indians wish to reserve the privilege of hunting & fishing on the lands and making sugar from the Maple

Ma-ghe-ga-bo "My Father. If you offer us money and goods we will take both. You see me count upon my fingers (counting six) Every finger counts ten. For so many years we wish you to secure to us the payment of an anuity. At the end of that time our grand children who will have grown up, can speak to you for themselves.

"We will consult with our Fathers (The Sub-Agents) and ask them what will be the value of the land, and what we ought to ask for it, for sixty years*[6]. My Father, Take the lands that you want from us. Our Chiefs have good hearts. Our women have brought the half breeds among us. They are poor, and we wish them to be provided for {illegible}. Some of them are here, and they have left many of their children behind them. We wish to divide with them all. This is the decision of the Chiefs.

"Since we have met here this morning we have fully made up our minds. We have talked it over and over again among ourselves—and we accept your proposition.

"My Father, we will not look back at what has transpired heretofore, but will commence our business anew with you, from this day*[7]. What you propose to give us, we wish to share only with the half breeds, that our people may enjoy the benefit of it. We will hold firmly in our Arms what you give us, that no body may get it from us".

"My Father. We once more recomend our half breeds to your kindness. They are very numerous. We wish you to select a place for them on this River, where they may live and raise their children, and have their joys of life. If I have rightly understood you, we can remain on the lands and hunt there. We have heretofore got our living on them. We hope that your people will not act towards ours, as your forefathers did towards our own—but that you will always treat us kindly, as you do now.

"My Father. We understand you, that you have been told our country is not good to cultivate. It is false. There is no better soil to cultivate than it, until you get up, to where the Pine region commences.

"My Father. You will now see All your Children in whose behalf I speak. All the Chiefs who agree to selling you the land will now rise" [They did so to the number of Thirty, and upwards]

Ma-ghe-ga-bo then raised the paper that he had placed over the Map, took Governor Dodge by the hand and continued

"My Father, I will not let go your hand 'till I count the number of our villages. The Great Spirit first made the Earth thin, but now it is much heavier*[8]. We do not wish to disappoint you and our Great Father (The President of The United States) in the object you had in coming here. We therefore grant you the country, which you want from us; and your Children, the Chiefs that represent all the villages within its limits, are now present. The number of villages (Nineteen) is marked on this paper, and I present it to you in acknowledgement that we grant you the land. This piece (retaining in his hand another piece of paper,) we will keep, because we wish to say something more, on it. At the Conclusion of this Treaty you will ask us to touch the quill*[9]; but no doubt you will grant what we ask, before we

---

*[6] What anuity
*[7] forgetting what has been said before. and alluding to the Traders
*[8] meaning, it was of little value,—but has now become much more so.
*[9] sign the Treaty

do so. At the End of the Treaty, I will respect what the Chiefs have to say to you, & keep this paper for that purpose. {0559} My Father The Great Spirit has given us a clear sky to talk together today. We must now rest awhile, and when we meet again, we will speak further".

Governor Dodge. "Do you wish to give me your answer this evening, or to wait until tomorrow morning".

Answer. "Tomorrow morning, and we will consult this evening with our two Fathers (Messrs Vineyard & Bushnell)

Governor Dodge. "It is proper for me to explain to you that your Great Father, never buys land for a term of years. I will agree on the part of the President, that you shall have the free use of the rivers, and the privilege of hunting upon the lands you are to sell to the United States, during his pleasure. If you sell these lands, you must sell them as all the other nations of Indians have done; & I tell you this now, that you may not, hereafter, say I have deceived you. Your Great Father has sent me to treat you as his children; to pay you the value of your land; & not to deceive you in any thing I may do with you, or say to you. If you had determined upon asking the assistance of your two Fathers (The Sub-Agents) of arriving at a conclusion in regard to the value of your lands, it is my wish, as well as that of your Great Father at Washington, that they shall do you justice. You have spoken frequently of your half breed relations. It is a good principle in you, to wish to provide for them. But you must do so in money, and can not give them land. You have mentioned your wishes to receive one half of the consideration that I may agree to give you for your lands, in goods, & the other half in money.

I do not object to this, but have a proposition to make to you now, which I wish you to consider. Your Great Father recomends to you, that you take from year to year the following items in part payment for your lands, towit: certain sums of money, to provide for Teachers to educate your children, & make them wise like those of the white people; for Farmers, and Instructors in Agricultural pursuits; for Agricultural implements. and seeds to plant in the Earth; for Provisions, and salt; for tobacco; for Blacksmiths, Iron and Steele &c; and for Mills and Millers to grind your corn, and other grain that you may raise. You will determine, whether you will accede to this proposition, and after consulting with your Fathers (The Sub-Agents) let me know what amount you wish me to pay you, for your lands; and I will be glad to meet you in council at an early hour tomorrow Morning".

The Governor then Adj<u>d</u>. the Council.

Friday Morning July 28<u>th</u>

The Council met at 12 O'Clock N.

Governor Dodge said to the Indians "My Friends, I have met you in council this morning to hear your answer to the proposition I made to you yesterday. I now wish to know if you have made up your minds; and who will speak for you to day. I am ready to hear you"

Aish-ke-bo-gi-ko-zhe (Flat Mouth) with many of the Chiefs came forward, and all shook hands with the Governor, the Secretary, & the Agents; after which Flat Mouth spoke thus—

''My Father. What I am going to say, is not the expression of my own will, but that of the Chiefs present. I did not know when I started to come here this morning, that they wished me to speak for them; but I have learned their wishes, since I came here. It is hard for me to say—but it is the wish of the Chiefs, that I should speak to you; & they have appointed me to do so.''

''My Father. Your children are willing to let you have their lands, but they wish to reserve the privilege of making sugar from the trees, and getting their living from the Lakes and Rivers, {0560} as they have done heretofore, and of remaining in this Country. It is hard to give up the lands. They will remain, and can not be destroyed—but you may cut down the Trees, and others will grow up. You know we can not live, deprived of our Lakes and Rivers; There is some game on the lands yet; & for that reason also, we wish to remain upon them, to get a living. Sometimes we scrape the Trees and eat of the bark. The Great Spirit above, made the Earth, and causes it to produce, which enables us to live.

''My Father. We would have detirmined long ago to let you have these lands; but when we have agreed upon any point, there have been people to whisper in our ears, and trouble and distract us. What the Chiefs said yesterday they abide by. They can not look back and change.

''My Father. The Great Spirit above, placed us on this land; and we want some benefit from the sale of it. If we could derive none, we would not sell it; and we want that benefit ourselves. I did not intend to speak. What I say is the language of the Chiefs. They came to me, and asked me to speak for them. I will soon be through. I was not in council yesterday because I was not well. I have heard many things said—That we were going to put out the fires of the white people in our country, that we were going to send the Traders out of it, & so forth. But I know nothing of it; and when I speak it is not with sugar in my mouth.

''My Father. Your Children are rejoiced to day to see the Agents here, one of whom is to live on Lake Superior, and the other on the Missisippi, to keep peace in the country. We are pleased too that our Agents are here, that they may estimate the value of our lands, that our Young men, women, & children, may go home, with their hearts at ease. We will wait to hear what you offer to give us for the lands, & will then make you our answer.

We will depend upon our two Fathers (Agents) to interest themselves for us; and will submit it to them, whether, what you offer us is enough. Yesterday when I came down after the Council, to see you, & told you I was going home, you asked me to wait; but I did not then know that I should be asked to speak to day— and I never wish to hide any thing, when I do so''.

''This is all I have to say now; but I may have omitted something—and some one else may wish to speak to you. Wait a few moments, to afford them an opportunity to do this; & then we will wait for your offer. I have spoken my sentiments openly to the Americans now here, as I would do to all of them, and to the English, the French, and the people of all other nations.

''My Father. The reason of my telling you yesterday that I was going home, arose from the many reports going back & forth, which I was tired of hearing—and not from any desire to mortify your feelings, or out of disrespect to you. I now give way, as some of your other Children may wish to speak to you''.

After an interval of a few minutes Flat Mouth again advanced, and said

"My Father. I came forward again to speak to you. There are many of your children here from a distance, and among them, one of my relations, who I have just seen. They wish me to speak to you, for them. Three of them, are Chiefs from the Chippewa River; & what they say, is the opinion & wish of the people living there. So, they tell me, to say to you. They have granted a privilege to some men, of cutting timber on some of their lands; for which they are paid in Tobacco, & ammunition, for hunting. They wish you not to break their word with these people— but to allow them to continue to cut Timber. They have granted you all you asked of them—& they wish you now to grant their request".

Governor Dodge "My Friends. I have listened with great attention, to your Chief, from Leech Lake. I will make known to your Great Father, your request to be permitted to make sugar, on the lands; and you will be allowed, during his pleasure, to hunt and fish on them. It will probably be many years, before your Great Father will want all these lands for the use of his white Children. As you have asked me what I will give you for the country, I will now tell you; & will recommend to you, the manner in which I think it ought to be paid to you. {0561} In full consideration for that part of your country which I wish to buy from you, I offer you the sum of Eight hundred Thousand Dollars ($800,000). I propose to give you an annuity for Twenty years, of $20,000 (Twenty thousand dollars) a year, in goods and money, one half in each—or all in goods, if you choose; To apply $3000 dollars a year for the same length of time, for providing you with Three Blacksmiths with their shops & implements, of labor, to be placed at different points in your country—for Provisions and Cattle $4000 dolls a year—for building Mills, and paying Millers to attend them 2000 dollars a year—For Agricultural Implements— hoes, ploughs &ᶜ & Farmers to teach you how to cultivate your lands 1000 dolls a year—for schools, in which your Children may be taught to read and write like the whites, 1000 a year—& for Tobacco 500 dolls a year for 20 years.

"These are the provisions I propose to make for you. The matter will be submitted to your Fathers (The Sub-Agents) who you have chosen, to consult with, in regard to it. As you have spoken of your half breed relatives, I wish each band of your nation assembled here, to name to me, all the half breeds connected with it; and I will recommend to you, as an act of benevolence, to donate to them, the sum of $100,000. I will also recomend that you pay your creditors, such amounts, as, upon examination, may be found justly due to them—& that the sum of $70,000 be applied to that purpose. These different sums will make up the amount of 800,000 dolls. This paper will now be submitted to your Agents for their consideration, & if you detirmine that your Creditors shall be paid, you had better let them take their accounts also, and let them be settled up to this date.

Aish-ke-bo-ge-ko-zhe (Flat Mouth) "My Father. I rise once more to speak to you. We have listened to what you have said to us, & I am requested by the Chiefs to reply. You have mentioned the different sums you will pay us, and have spoken of our creditors. My Father. I wish the lands we are selling to day were mine! If the accounts of the Traders ought to be paid, why will not our Great Father help us to do it? Many of those of our people who owed them, are perhaps long since dead. Your children are rejoiced at the amounts which you have mentioned you would pay them; But wish you to appropriate the sums, that you have proposed to apply for them in Cattle and schools, to the purchase of goods also.

"My Father. Your Children wish that all the different sums be paid to themselves, and they will hold closely onto them. As to the payments to the Traders, we will look to our Great Father for his assistance. My Father. If it was my land you was buying, I would, instead of an annuity for only 20 years— demand one from you, as long as the ground lasted. You know that without the lands, and the Rivers & Lakes, we could not live. We hunt, and make Sugar, & dig roots upon the former, while we fish, and obtain Rice, and drink from the latter

"My Father. Those in whose behalf I speak, wish you to supply them with goods also, instead of the Mills, that you have proposed to provide for them. They now understand the different sums as you have set them apart".

Governor Dodge. "I only make the recomendation to you, in regards to your half breed relatives, and The Traders, as an act of kindness to the former, and of justice to the latter. But it is for you to say how it shall be. The whole amount, including the 100,000 dollars proposed to be given to the half breeds, & the 70,000 to be paid to the Traders, will be yours, to dispose of, as you shall direct, on consulting among each other—& with your Agents.

Flat Mouth. "My Father. Had I known that such matters would occur as have take place here, I should never have come. If I had thought that these old accounts were to be brought up against us, I would have stayed away.

"My Father. Where are our young men, that have hunted {0562} for these Traders—and supplied them with their Furs? They have, when upon their hunting excursions for them, been killed off by the Sioux—and swept away. Where have they got the Fish that they have eaten, and the wood that they have burned? They were caught from our Lakes, & Rivers, and taken from our Land—And they talk to us about paying them our debts!

"My Father. If I were to repeat all that has occurred for many years back, since the Traders have been among us, I should have a long story to tell. What I now say to you, expresses the wishes and sentiments of my friends and relations, who are here. The lands to be sold are not mine. I have no claim to them. I live here like a beggar on charity. They divide with me, what they have to eat.

"My Father. I never look back, and will hold to what I have said to you.

Gov.ʳ. Dodge. "My Friends If you have nothing further to say now, we will adjourn to meet again early tomorrow, when I shall be fully prepared, & I wish you to be so, to finish our business—And then the Govʳ. Adj.ᵈ. the Council.

Saturday Morning July 29ᵗʰ

The Council met at 12 O'Clock N.

Govʳ. Dodge said to the Indians

"My Friends. When the council adjourned yesterday you had selected your two Fathers (The Sub-Agents) to examine for you into the amount, which I have offered

147

to give you for your country, and the manner of its payment. I have confered with these two gentlemen, and they agree that the amount offered is a fair price for the lands, and approve of the arrangement which I propose in relation to the payments.

"There is one subject which it is necessary for you now to detirmine upon. It is, whether you will make any donation to your half breed relatives; & if so, how it shall be paid to them.

"I submit that matter to you for your consideration, and will wait until you decide upon it".

The Chiefs sat down to council together, and a few minutes there-after, a large number of Braves, or Wariors, approached the council Lodge, singing and dancing, with their war flag flying, & in their war costume—but without arms. They were accompanied by two or three chiefs, and on entering the Council*[10], Sha-go-bai (The Little Six) advanced to Governor Dodge and spoke thus.

"My Father. I address myself to you, and wish you to repeat my words to our Great Father at Washington.

"We are the Braves of our different bands assembled here, and we wish to say something to you. It is your desire, as we have understood you, and from our fathers here (the Sub-Agents) that the people here should all go home satisfied. The Braves of the different bands have smoked and talked together. You now see them all before you. They have not come here to undo what our Chiefs have done—but to ask a favor of you. They take you by the hand, and would like to see your wish accomplished, that all should return home in peace. But they are afraid to return home, if their traders are not paid. They fear they should not survive during the winter without their aid. It is the wish of the Braves that you should pay the Traders; but they do not want to undo what the Chiefs have done.

"My Father. You see your children that are here. They are many. But they are only a small portion of their whole nation.

"They wish you to give them something more, than you have offered them for their lands. They think it is not quite enough. You have established two agencies, one here, and the other at the Sault de S^t. Mary. It is now more than Twenty years since you have assisted your children at these places. But those {0563} now before you, have never gone to either of them to beg. My Father. You come now to buy our lands from us; & why do you offer us so little for them. The speaker who told you that we ought ought to be paid for them for sixty years, expressed our opinions. This is the wish of all the Braves here. If you will accede to what has been mentioned in regard to the Traders, they will come forward and "touch the pen" (sign the Treaty). We have told you what we want, and after hearing what is to be granted to us, we will go, & prepare to return home.

"My Father. What I have spoken to you, is the wish of the Braves before you. If you agree to what they propose they will be ready to take you by the hand and close the bargain. If not, they will retire and go home peaceably. They will now wait your answer".

Governor Dodge, to Shag-o-bai. "Would the sum of Seventy Thousand Dollars, applied to paying all the demands of the Traders against you, satisfy you all"?

---

*[10] Sha-go-bai is a petty chief, and placed himself at the head of the Braves as a peace maker; to conciliate both them and the Chiefs

Shag-o-ba, after consulting with the Braves, and several of the Chiefs, answered that it would satisfy them.

Governor Dodge to the Intrepeter "Say to the Chiefs that I have listened to the words of the Braves, and it is to them (the Chiefs) that I now speak. It is the wish of the Braves it appears, that their Traders should be paid. The sum of 70.000 dollars, it is believed will cover all their just demands; & they ask that that amount shall be paid to them. I want them to be satisfied. I wish all to be satisfied, that they may take each other strongly by the hand. To reconcile all, I will agree to pay the seventy Thousand Dollars, in addition to what I have already offered them for their lands—and that is all I will give them. I want now to hear what they have to say upon that subject".

The Hole-in-The Day—evidently under high excitement first addressing himself to the Chiefs said! "Chiefs what we agreed and determined upon yesterday; shall consent to undo, when my head is severed from my body and my life no more— We must abide by it, firmly".

"Braves! There are many of you—but none of you have done what I have— nor are any of you my equals!!—Our Father wishes us to go home in peace." Then turning 'round and addressing the Governor, he proceeded,

"My Father, Listen to me—my words shall be few. What the braves have come and told you must be true, & should be listened to. The Great Spirit who placed us on this Earth hears both you and me. He put us upon it to live. Yesterday in council The Chiefs told you what they would do. They are perfectly content with that arrangement, & they abide by it to day.

"Death alone shall prevent the fulfilment of it on my part; And I call the Great Being to witness what I say. We agree to what has just been done, & are satisfied with it"

"My Father. The country that we are selling to you is not land that we have borrowed, but that has descended to us from our forefather. The Chiefs now before you are the descendants of those who occupied it many years ago; and some of them live upon the lands we are selling you. They are now all satisfied with what you proposed to them, to day as well yesterday—and the Great Spirit hears it".

Governor Dodge "Chiefs and Braves, I am much pleased to hear that you are all satisfied. You are brethren of the same great Nation. I met you at peace, and want you to be so, when I part from you. I hope the most friendly understanding will continue to exist between the Chiefs and Braves, as well as between them both and their Traders.

"It is the duty of the Braves to be obedient to their Chiefs (applause from the Indians). They should listen to them in peace, and obey them in War. Both Chiefs & Braves should respect the Traders and treat them justly and kindly, that harmony and good feeling {0564} may exist among you all; & that you may be serviceable to each other."

Sha-go-ba (The Little Six) "My Father. Your children have listened to you. You have done what is good for us. We know you came here to do what was right, and to keep peace. It is our duty to encourage others to be upright and act justly. I speak to you the sentiments of both the chiefs and the Braves.

"My Father Listen now to what they have told me to say to you. It has reference to one of our traders. You came here to do good, and allay bad feelings. I came here this morning with my Braves, and asked a favor for the Traders, which has been granted. Let them now give us, our friend who they have in Jail*[11]. (a loud response of assent from the Indians)

Governor Dodge, to the Intrepeter, "Say to them that their friend is in the hands of our Laws, and of their Great Father The President of the United States—That neither I or the Traders have any power over him—That he will be judged by the Laws, & his case then submitted to the President, who will do him justice.

Shag-o-bai. "My Father. I speak to you again at the request of the Chiefs and Braves. We do not know whether you have a control over all the Traders; but we wish you to aid us, by speaking to them in our favor, as you have done to us, in theirs. There are some of them who have dealt severely with us".

Governor Dodge. "It is my duty in the relation in which I stand to you, to see justice done to you, and so far as it is in my power, I will do it in all things.

I hope the Traders will have a proper respect for your rights & that you will respect those of the Traders. We are now done with that subject, & I wish to know your decision with regard to the half breeds.

Son-ga-ko-mik (The Strong Ground. "My Father. We are now bringing to a close what we have been so long talking about. In regard to the Half Breeds you will be answered by some other Chief. I speak upon another subject. Look at your Children My Father, & notice their clothing. At the end of the year we wish you to bring such articles for us. We do not know the value or use of money, & don't want it. See our women too, & the Articles they wear, & bring such for them. Kettles are very useful to our people and you must not forget them. With guns we get our living, & them you must remember".

It was intimated by some of the other Chiefs that they would prefer to receive, a part of their annuity in money.

Pe-The-ke (The Buffalo from La Pointe) "My Father, you have come here and got all your children together as if you wished to embrace and treat them kindly. We approve of what was said and done yesterday, in regard to the half breeds. I am an Indian and do not know the value of money, but the half breeds do, for which reason we wish you to pay them their share in money. You have good judgment in whatever you do, and if you do not act yourself, you will appoint some one else to didide it between the half breeds.

"We wish you to do this; for if they were to divide it themselves they might cheat each other. But if you appoint some one to do it, it will be fairly done. It will be as you please. You will either direct it to be done by our two fathers (the sub-agents) or whoever else you may choose. I have good reasons for saying to you, what I have just said; for at a certain Treaty held heretofore, there were some got rich, while others received nothing".

Governor Dodge. "My Friends What you have said shall be considered; and your wishes attended to. It will now take some two or three hours to prepare the Treaty & have copies made of it, when I wish you to meet me here again, {0565} will read it by articles, so that every word may be clearly conveyed and understood by you. Three copies of the Treaty are prepared, of which one will be sent to your Great Father The President of the United States, for him to keep, one delivered to yourselves, and the other kept by me".

---

*[11] A son of one of the Traders was killed a short time since by an Indian, who is now in confinement at Prarie-du-Chien awaiting his trial

The Secretary then read The Treaty in the following words:

"Articles of a Treaty made and concluded at S̲ᵗ. Peters (the confluence of the S̲ᵗ. Peters and Missisippi Rivers) in the Territory of Wisconsin, between the United States of America, by their Comissionor Henry Dodge, Governor of said Territory, and The Chippewa Nation of Indians, by their Chiefs and Head Men."

"Article 1. The Chippewa Nation cede to the United States all that Tract of country included within the following boundaries: Beginning at the junction of the Crow Wing and Missisippi Rivers betwenty and Thirty miles above where the Missisippi is crossed by the Forty Sixth parallel of North Latitude, and running thence to the North point of Lake S̲ᵗ. Croix one of the sources of the S̲ᵗ. Croix River; thence to and along the dividing Ridge between the Waters of Lake Superior & those of the Missisippi to the sourcess of the Ocha, Sua Sepe, a tributary of the Chippewa River; thence to a point on the Chippewa River Twenty miles below the out-let of Lake De Flambeau; thence to the junction of the Wisconsin and the Pelican Rivers; thence on an East course Twenty Five Miles; thence Southerly, on a course parallel with that of the Wisconsin River, to the line dividing the Territories of the Chippewas and Menomines; thence to the Plover Portage; thence along the southern boundary of the Chippewa Country, to the comencement of the boundary line dividing it from that of the Sioux half a days march below the Falls on the Chippewa River; thence with said boundary line to the mouth of Wah-tap River at its junction with the Missisippi; & thence up the Missisippi to the place of beginning."

"Article 2. In consideration of the cession aforesaid the United States agree to make to the Chippewa Nation annually for the term of Twenty years, from the date of the ratification of this Treaty, the following payments. 1. Nine Thousand Five Hundred Dollars to be paid in Money.

2. Nineteen thousand dollars, to be delivered in goods.

3. Three Thousand dollars for establishing three Black Smiths shops, supporting the Black Smiths, & furnishing them with Iron and Steel. 4. One Thousand Dollars for Farmers, and for supplying them and the Indians, with Implements of labor, with grain or seed; & whatever else may be necessary to enable them to carry on their Agricultural pursuits."

5. "Two Thousand Dollars in Provisions."

6. "Five Hundred Dollars in Tobacco."

"The Provisions and Tobacco to be delivered at the same time with the goods and money to be paid, which time or times, as well as the place or places where they are to be delivered, shall be fixed upon under the direction of the President of the United States."

"The Black Smiths Shops to be placed at such points in the Chippewa Country as shall be designated by the Superintendant of Indian Affairs, or under his direction.

"If at the expiration of one or more years, the Indians should prefer to receive goods, instead of the Nine Thousand Dollars, agreed to paid to them in money, they shall be at liberty to do so. Or, should they conclude to appropriate a portion of that Annuity to the establishment of a school, or schools among them, this shall be granted them".

Article 3. The Sum of One hundred thousand dollars shall be paid by the United States to the Half Breeds of the Chippewa Nation under the direction of the President. It is the wish of the Indians that their two Sub-Agents Daniel P. Bushnell and Miles

M. Vineyard super- {0567}intend the distribution of this money among their half breed relations'':

Article 4. The sum of Seventy Thousand Dollars shall be applied to the payment, by the United States of certain claims against the Indians; of which amount Twenty Eight Thousand Dollars shall at their request be paid to William A. Ailkin; Twenty Five Thousand to Lyman M. Warren, & the ballance applied to the liquidation of other just demands against them—which they acknowledge to be the case with regard to that presented by Hercules L. Dousman, & they request that it be paid''

Article 5. The privilege of hunting, fishing, & gathering the wild rice, upon the Lands, The Rivers and The Lakes included in the territory ceded, is guarantied to the Indians, during the pleasure of the President of the United States.

Article 6. This Treaty shall be obligatory from and after its ratification by the President and Senate of the United States''

''Done at S⁺. Peters in the Territory of Wisconsin the Twenty Ninth day of July, Eighteen hundred and Thirty seven.''{0566—Note: frames 0566 and 0567 are transposed on the microfilm.}

The Treaty was then signed by Governor Dodge (and great eagerness was evinced by the Indians to see him do so—some of them declining to sign it, until he had, to satisfy them, run the pen a second time over his name) when it received the signatures of between Forty and Fifty of The Chiefs, Head Men, & Wariors present, with the names of some Twenty witnesses appended, and was concluded.

The Indians having declined to name a Chief to whom their copy of the Treaty should be delivered for safe keeping, Governor Dodge addressed them as follows:

''Chiefs and Wariors: I have asked you to name one of the number of your Chiefs, who should take your copy of the Treaty which we have just signed, & keep it safely as a sacred instrument. You decline to do so, & it becomes necessary and proper, for me to name one. I will hand it to the man who was the first among you to give it his signature'. Note ['Many of the other and older Chiefs, evincing a reluctance, & hesitating to step forward, Pa-goona-kee-zhig, or The Hole in The Day, did so promptly, with his characteristic intrepidity, offered his signature to the Treaty.] He is to keep it for all your people to look at, and know what it is; and each of your Agents will be supplied also with copies.

''My Friends I regret that on parting with you after our long conference, I have not Medals to give to all of your Chiefs, and Flags to all of your Bands. Your conduct on this occasion, marked throughout by the utmost decorum propiety, and good sense, well merits something of the kind. But you shall have them when your first annuity is paid to you. These Medals & Flags have to come from your Great Father at Washington.

''I will see him soon, and he will furnish me with them for you. I am very sorry too, that I have not more presents to make you. All the ammunition that I have is 10 Kegs of Powder; and 900 lbs. of Lead to be given to the Chiefs, to distribute among the Braves & Wariors of the different Bands. The small amount of goods, which I have, will be fairly distributed through the different Bands. & I wish there were many more of them. Supplies of provisions to take you home, will be immediately procured, and apportioned equitably among you by your Agents. I will remain here a day or two longer, to see that all that can be done for you now, is properly arranged.

"We are now about to part my friends, and it may be some time before we meet again. I expect however to make an excursion through your country next summer when I hope I shall meet many of you. I will recomend you to your Great Father the President, as a good people, who deserve the confidence and friendship of Our Government. And although you are far away from him, and scattered over a great extent of country, he will often think of you, and never forget you. I trust you will now return peaceably to your homes, and not shed the blood of any man. I hope to hear that you have made no attack upon others, unless first attacked yourselves, & in self defence. I repeat to you, that if any of the Sioux strike you, or you them, the blow will fall upon me and your Great Father the President, at the same time. They have been told not to molest you, and you have shaken hands with them in friendship.

"I trust that on parting from each other, you will strengthen the grasp, and let it be a pledge of perpetual peace among you.

"Your Great Father will see the Sioux, in a short time, at Washington, & will tell them, from his own mouth, that they must live in peace. He is determined that the hands of his Red Children shall no longer be stained with the blood of each other.

"I recommend to you, to listen closely to the words, and to be governed in your conduct by the advice, of your two Fathers (The (Sub Agents). They have been selected by your Great Father to be your friends, & I know they will tell you the truth, & advise you for your own good.

"The Treaty which we have now made will bring us oftener together hereafter, and I hope always, as friends"—And then the Governor adj^d. the Council Sine Die.{0568}

Appendix 2

Treaty With the Chippewa, 1837

Articles of a treaty made and concluded at St. Peters (the confluence of the St. Peters and Mississippi rivers) in the Territory of Wisconsin, between the United States of America, by their commissioner, Henry Dodge, Governor of said Territory, and the Chippewa nation of Indians, by their chiefs and headmen.

ARTICLE 1. The said Chippewa nation cede to the United States all that tract of country included within the following boundaries:

Beginning at the junction of the Crow Wing and Mississippi rivers, between twenty and thirty miles above where the Mississippi is crossed by the forty-sixth parallel of north latitude, and running thence to the north point of Lake St. Croix, one of the sources of the St. Croix river; thence to and along the dividing ridge between the waters of Lake Superior and those of the Mississippi, to the sources of the Ocha-sua-sepe a tributary of the Chippewa river; thence to a point on the Chippewa river, twenty miles below the outlet of Lake De Flambeau; thence to the junction of the Wisconsin and Pelican rivers; thence on an east course twenty-five miles; thence southerly, on a course parallel with that of the Wisconsin river, to the line dividing the territories of the Chippewas and Menomonies; thence to the Plover Portage; thence along the southern boundary of the Chippewa country, to the commencement of the boundary line dividing it from that of the Sioux, half a days march below the falls on the Chippewa river; thence with said boundary line to the mouth of Wah-tap river, at its junction with the Mississippi; and thence up the Mississippi to the place of beginning. {491}

ARTICLE 2. In consideration of the cession aforesaid, the United States agree to make to the Chippewa nation, annually, for the term of twenty years, from the date of the ratification of this treaty, the following payments.

1. Nine thousand five hundred dollars, to be paid in money.

2. Nineteen thousand dollars, to be delivered in goods.

3. Three thousand dollars for establishing three blacksmiths shops, supporting the blacksmiths, and furnishing them with iron and steel.

4. One thousand dollars for farmers, and for supplying them and the Indians, with implements of labor, with grain or seed; and whatever else may be necessary to enable them to carry on their agricultural pursuits.

5. Two thousand dollars in provisions.

6. Five hundred dollars in tobacco.

The provisions and tobacco to be delivered at the same time with the goods, and the money to be paid; which time or times, as well as the place or places where they are to be delivered, shall be fixed upon under the direction of the President of the United States.

The blacksmiths shops to be placed at such points in the Chippewa country as shall be designated by the Superintendent of Indian Affairs, or under his direction.

If at the expiration of one or more years the Indians should prefer to receive goods, instead of the nine thousand dollars agreed to be paid to them in money, they shall be at liberty to do so. Or, should they conclude to appropriate a portion of that annuity to the establishment and support of a school or schools among them, this shall be granted them.

ARTICLE 3. The sum of one hundred thousand dollars shall be paid by the United States, to the half-breeds of the Chippewa nation, under the direction of the President. It is the wish of the Indians that their two sub-agents Daniel P. Bushnell, and Miles M. Vineyard, superintend the distribution of this money among their half-breed relations.

ARTICLE 4. The sum of seventy thousand dollars shall be applied to the payment, by the United States, of certain claims against the Indians; of which amount twenty-eight thousand dollars shall, at their request, be paid to William A. Aitkin, twenty-five thousand to Lyman M. Warren, and the balance applied to the liquidation of other just demands against them-which they acknowledge to be the case with regard to that presented by Hercules L. Dousman, for the sum of five thousand dollars; and they request that it be paid.

ARTICLE 5. The privilege of hunting, fishing, and gathering the wild rice, upon the lands, the rivers and the lakes included in the territory ceded, is guaranteed to the Indians, during the pleasure of the President of the United States.

ARTICLE 6. This treaty shall be obligatory from and after its ratification by the President and Senate of the United States.

Done at St. Peters in the Territory of Wisconsin the twenty-ninth day of July eighteen hundred and thirty-seven.

Henry Dodge, Commissioner.

From Leech lake:
Aish-ke-bo-ge-koshe, or Flat Mouth,
R-che-o-sau-ya, or the Elder Brother.
Chiefs.
Pe-zhe-kins, the Young Buffalo,
Ma-ghe-ga-bo, or La Trappe,
O-be-gwa-dans, the Chief of the Earth,
Wa-bose, or the Rabbit,
Che-a-na-quod, or the Big Cloud.
Warriors.
From Gull lake and Swan river:
Pa-goo-na-kee-zhig, or the Hole in the Day,
Songa-ko-mig, or the Strong Ground.
Chiefs.
Wa-boo-jig, or the White Fisher,
Ma-cou-da, or the Bear's Heart.
Warriors.
From St. Croix river:
Pe-zhe-ke, or the Buffalo,
Ka-be-ma-be, or the Wet Month.
Chiefs.

Pa-ga-we-we-wetung, Coming Home Hollowing,
Ya-banse, or the Young Buck,
Kis-ke-ta-wak, or the Cut Ear.
Warriors.{492}
From Lake Courteoville:
Pa-qua-a-mo, or the Wood Pecker.
Chief.
From Lac De Flambeau:
Pish-ka-ga-ghe, or the White Crow,
Na-wa-ge-wa, or the Knee,
O-ge-ma-ga, or the Dandy,
Pa-se-quam-jis, or the Commissioner,
Wa-be-ne-me, or the White Thunder.
Chiefs.
From La Pointe, (on Lake Superior):
Pe-zhe-ke, or the Buffalo,
Ta-qua-ga-na, or Two Lodges Meeting,
Cha-che-que-o.
Chiefs.

From Mille Lac:
Wa-shask-ko-kone, or Rats Liver,
Wen-ghe-ge-she-guk, or the First Day.
                                    Chiefs.
Ada-we-ge-shik, or Both Ends of the
    Sky,
Ka-ka-quap, or the Sparrow.
                                    Warriors.
From Sandy Lake:
Ka-nan-da-wa-win-zo, or Le
    Brocheux,
We-we-shan-shis, the Bad Boy, or Big
    Mouth,
Ke-che-wa-me-te-go, or the Big
    Frenchman.
                                    Chiefs.
Na-ta-me-ga-bo, the Man that stands
    First,
Sa-ga-ta-gun, or Spunk.
                                    Warriors.
From Snake river:
Naudin, or the Wind,
Sha-go-bai, or the Little Six,

Pay-ajik, or the Lone Man,
Na-qua-na-bie, or the Feather.
                                    Chiefs.
Ha-tau-wa,
Wa-me-te-go-zhins, the Little
    Frenchman,
Sho-ne-a, or Silver.
                                    Warriors.
From Fond du Lac, (on Lake
    Superior):
Mang-go-sit, or the Loons Foot,
Shing-go-be, or the Spruce.
                                    Chiefs.
From Red Cedar lake:
Mont-so-mo, or the Murdering Yell.
From Red lake:
Francois Goumean (a half breed).
From Leech lake:
Sha-wa-ghe-zhig, or the Sounding Sky,
Wa-zau-ko-ni-a, or Yellow Robe.
                                    Warriors.

Signed in presence of—

Verplanck Van Antwerp, Secretary to the
    Commissioner.
M. M. Vineyard, U. S. Sub-Indian Agent.
Daniel P. Bushnell.
Law. Taliaferro, Indian Agent at St.
    Peters.
Martin Scott, Captain, Fifth Regiment
    Infantry.
J. Emerson, Assistant Surgeon, U. S.
    Army
H. H. Sibley.

H. L. Dousman.
S. C. Stambaugh.
E. Lockwood.
Lyman M. Warren.
J. N. Nicollet.
Harmen Van Antwerp.
Wm. H. Forbes.
Jean Baptiste Dubay, Interpreter.
Peter Quinn, Interpreter.
S. Campbell, U. S. Interpreter.
Stephen Bonga, Interpreter.
Wm. W Coriell.

(To the Indian names are subjoined a mark and seal.)   {493}

Appendix 3A

Extract of Annual Report

Michigan Superintendency
Detroit October 28th 1842—

Hon: T. Hartley Crawford
  Com: Ind: Affairs

    Sir:

        In compliance with your instructions, and the regulations of the Department, I have the honor to submit the following statement, embracing the general matters relating to this Superintendency, as also to a portion of Wiskonsin Territory — My unavoidable detention in the Lake Superior country, has alone caused so long delay in the performance of this duty — {146}

. . . .

In pursuance of my appointment as Com^r. to treat with the Chippewas, at La Pointe, on Lake Superior, I proceeded thither, after a few days delay at this place, on my return from Washington in August last: but owing to the difficulties of notifying the distant and scattered bands, we had arrived some time before they could be all assembled; the interim however was well employed in dividing the goods for their annuity payments, and enlighting the minds of such as had arrived, in relation to the objects of our mission — After the views {147} and intentions of the Govt. had been explained to them in general council, they agreed to sell all their lands between Lake Superior, and the Mississippi, including the islands belonging to them in said Lake, amounting in the aggregate to about 15.000.000 of acres — from the best information we have been able to obtain, the mineral district is extensive and valuable; the copper ore is said to be of the purest quality — Silver ore has been found between Lake Vieux deserts, and Trout Lake, but as no scientific person has examined it, both its quality and extent must for the present remain uncertain. The fisheries for trout, whitefish & sisquet {siscowets} along the shore and Islands of Lake Superior, may be carried on to almost any extent, and must at no distant period, become a considerable source of revenue to our citizens — much of the soil now purchased, is reported both by the geologists and surveyors, to be of excellent quality: but the mineral region bordering on Lake Superior, is rather barren and rugged —

Serious feuds and difficulties have for some years past, existed between the Bands on Lake Superior, and those on the Mississippi; these troubles principally arose in consequence of the annuity payments, under the Treaty of 1837; but every irritating cause has happily been done away by the provisions of the Treaty now made; which provides that all shall share equally in the annuities of both Treaties — thus their jealousies and hostile feelings both among themselves, and toward the U. S., have been entirely allayed, which, (had they been neglected,) were likely to break into open hostility, and call for the interposition of the Govt: at great expense and hazard of our present amicable relations. — The Chiefs and head men consulted much with me, relative to their long and cruel wars with the Sioux, and before we parted, they unanimously expressed their earnest desire, that the Government would interfere and effect a reconciliation between them; they pledge themselves to abide strictly by any terms which the President may in his wisdom prescribe. Even the Flat Mouth, Chief of the Pillagers, of Leech Lake, visited La Pointe, to aid in these deliberations, they have of late suffered so severely in these barbarous hostilities, that they seem appalled — they are also kept in perpetual agitation and alarm, which hinders them from pursuing their usual avocations; even the Missionaries and Schools, as well as our own Mechanics and Farmers who are among them, are kept in constant uneasiness — I promised to represent their condition and wishes to the Department, and gave it as my opinion, that their appeal would not be disregarded, as I thought you could rely upon their sincerity — I wrote to M^r. Bruce, the Agent at S^t. Peters, on the subject, and requested him to use his influence with the Sioux, to suspend hostilities for the winter, and urge upon them their obligations to agree to a general peace — I trust Sir, that you will not only approve of the project, but use your influence to bring about so desirable an end — there is no doubt in my mind of its feasibility, provided the proper men be appointed on the Commission; and to ensure the durability of peace, it is only necessary, to make one or two examples, should any aggression occur — Both the dignity and honor of our country are involved in this matter; and every dictate of humanity calls for speedy and decided action. Most of these Bands express great desire for Missionaries, and especially for schools, also Blacksmiths, Carpenters, and Farmers, to teach and aid them in the arts of civilized life — After much consultation with the Chiefs, Missionaries and Traders; I venture to recommend the following, as the most favorable stations, viz: L'Ance {L'Anse} on {148} Quiwinon {Keweenaw} Bay, for a Blacksmith's shop, Farmer and Carpenter, part of the time, (for they should itinerate) — La Pointe for a Blacksmith's shop, and Carpenter, part of the time — Fond du Lac, for a Blacksmiths shop, Farmer, and Carpenter part of the time — the Sandy Lake region, probably near Crow wing River, for a Blacksmiths shop, Farmer, and Carpenter part of the time — Pokegamo, or Snake River, where the Blacksmiths shop and Farmer now are, is a good station, provided peace be established with the Sioux, but if not, the station should be removed to some place near LaPointe — The station now on Chippewa River, should be abandoned in any event; the Indians are led by it into too close contact with the whites; the facility of getting whiskey there is runious, and they are often accused of committing depredations on the settlers — I would suggest whether it would not be well to have the places named for stations, visited by some judicious person, before they are determined upon; if you think so, permit me to recommend for that duty, Jeremiah Russell, the present Farmer, at Pokegamo, he is a very intelligent and judicious man; the expense of his tour would be trifling, for he would only require an Indian or half breed, acquainted with the country, to accompany him, and it is of much importance that such points be selected as will enable the Missionaries and Schools, as well as the Government Farmers, & Blacksmiths to settle together.

The Indians complain much that their wishes have not been attended to in regard to the assortment of their goods, they annually receive a number of articles which are of little use to them — They earnestly beg that in the future, the following articles only, shall be sent, viz: — 3.2 1/2.2 & 1 1/2 point white Mackinac Blankets

— Blue strouds — grey List blue cloth — Fine blue cloth (fancy list) to cost $2.50 @ $3. — common sattinette — domestic plaids — Linsey — Red Flannel — Red Flannel and Callico shirts — 400 N.W. Guns — $2000 worth ammunition i.e. 1 1/2 lbs: of Balls & 1 1/2 lbs: Duck shot, to our lb: of Powder — the Powder to be put up in water tight casks, of 25 lbs: each — 10.000 Indian gun flints — 100 Brass Kettles, none very large — 100 Nests Tin Kettles, of 8 each, none very small; such quality and kind as the Am: Fur C^o. procure — 50 yd^s: of Callico, (high colors) not to cost over 12 1/2^{cts}. per yard — Their own Blacksmiths will hereafter make their axes, besides those sent heretofore were not suitable — the small and fancy articles they prefer purchasing from the Traders, with their money. —

I am respectfully Sir,
Your obt: Servant
Robert Stuart
Actg: S̄up: In^d. Affairs {149}

Appendix 3B

Treaty Commissioner Robert Stuart's Remarks
of November 19, 1842

Detroit November 19th 1842

Hon: T. Hartley Crawford

  Com: Indian Affairs

    Sir:

        My anxiety to transmit to you the Supt.^{cy} a/c.^{s} and annual report in due season, must plead my apology for the delay in forwarding the Treaty concluded with the Chippewa Indians of the Mississippi and Lake Superior at La Pointe, on 4th October last; the claims are now adjusted and I have the honor to enclose herewith the Treaty complete; which I trust will be satisfactory to the Department. The whole amt. of claims laid in, amounted to $244.331 21/100 — and for a time, it was doubtful whether at least $100.000 for debts, and $50.000 for half breeds, would not be insisted upon; but ultimately $75.000 for debts only, was agreed to, and the Indian annuities were somewhat increased, so as to enable them annually, to aid their poor half breed relatives. It is unnecessary to trouble you with further details, as you understand the advantages of the Treaty as regards both our country and the Indians; besides, the whole subject was discussed pretty fully in my late Report.—

These Indians are through our late efforts, entirely reconciled among themselves, and highly delighted with the kind and generous dealing of the Government toward them; and if the impression made this summer, should be followed up next season, by the benevolent effort on the part of the Government, to mediate a Treaty of peace between the Chippewas {0196} and Sioux, it would promote the cause of humanity, and greatly advance the civilization and happiness of these hapless beings. There will not in my opinion, be much difficulty in accomplishing this object, if you appoint men who have influence with the Indians. Both Tribes should be made fully to understand, that the very first aggressor shall be severely punished; and full faith should be kept in this as well as in every other respect; for at present, both the threats and promises of the Government, are treated with <u>incredulity</u>, at least— If the Government, (as <u>many</u> think,) is in honor and duty bound to use its best endeavors, to put a stop to the horrible carnage which these Tribes are continually committing upon each other; permit me to suggest, that it might be well, soon to issue orders to the Agent of St. Peters, to notify <u>all</u> his bands of Sioux, to assemble there, about the 1st of July next.— And the <u>Sub</u> Agent at La Pointe, should have similar instructions, as relates to <u>all</u> his Chippewas; so that they also may be at Fort Snelling on 1st July. The Chiefs, Head Men and Braves only, need be called, and $6000 might defray the whole expenses.—

The Flat Mouth, Chief of the Chippewas of the Leech Lake Country, with about 60 of his Warriors, came to visit me at La Pointe — his main object was to complain, that his people are not protected from the incursions of the British Half breeds, of Red River, who every summer hunt and drive the Buffalo away from his lands—

I promised to represent the case to you, but need not enlarge, as the subject was fully brought before the Sect^y. of War in my communications last winter, at Washington— I was then sorry that M^r. Nicollets views seemed to prevail, for I know that a serious injury is thereby inflicted on our frontier Indians, and our influence over them in consequence, greatly diminished — if you deem it advisable, please to urge the subject once more on the notice of the Sect^y. of War.—

I have not yet received the funds for the 3rd and 4th qrs. of this year; if not sent before this reaches you, please to procure these in N. York, if practicable, for our navigation of the Upper Lakes is now nearly closed, and it would cost too much to send by land, either to Chicago, or Milwaukie.—

Have the goodness also to remit me $1500, contingent fund, as we are considerably in arrears under this head.

Enclosed herewith, are two diagrams of the country treated for &c:— that on wrapping paper, was made by a Half Breed at La Pointe, and is the more accurate of the two — with the boundary of the Treaty, is also traced on it, the boundary of the country reserved as the common property and home of the Indians party to the treaty, whenever they may be required to remove from their present residence.———

> I am respectfully Sir
> Your Obt: servant
> <u>Robert Stuart</u> {0197}

Appendix 3C

I am happy to shake hands with so many of my old friends, and very glad to find them all well— Last winter I visited your Great Father at Washington, and talked with him about your circumstances — he knows that you are poor, that your lands are not good, and that you have very little game left, to feed and clothe your women & children— He therefore pities your condition, and has sent me here to see what can be done to benefit you — some of you now get a little money, goods & provisions — others get none at all, because the Govt: did not think your lands worth buying, at former Treaties— By the treaty you made with Gov: Cass at Fond du Lac in 1826, you granted the right to carry away any minerals which might be found on your lands, so that they are now no longer yours: and the whites have been asking your Great Father to give them permission to take away all they can find — but your Great Father wishes first to make a new treaty, and pay you well for these lands and minerals; he knows you are poor and needy, and that you could be made comfortable by getting a little money, Goods, provisions, & tobacco — also farmers to shew you how to cultivate the earth — carpenters to aid you to build your houses; and some more blacksmiths, to mend your Guns, Traps, Axes, & other things you need — and something for schools, that your {0061} children may be taught to read and write, like the whites — I understand that you have been displeased about your present Blacksmiths and farmers, but if any thing has been wrong, and that you will let me know it, I will write to your Great Father, and he will be glad to try and put all right, so that hereafter they may be valuable to you. From what I learn, I fear that you do not esteem your teachers & schools as you should — some of you seem to think that you may always live as you have done heretofore; but do you not see that the Great Spirit is changing things all around you — Formerly all the country down to Washington, and the Great Salt Lake, was owned and inhabited by the Red men— But now the whites fill that whole country, they are numerous as the pigeons in the Spring, this all of you who have been at Washington know: whereas many of the poor Indians have died of poverty and drinking whiskey, and others have been sent west of the Mississippi, to make room for the whites— The reason of this is not that the Great Spirit loves the whites more the he does the Indians: but that the whites have listened to their religious teachers & sent their children to school, so that they learned a great deal more than the Indians, and have become wise and rich, while the Indians remain ignorant and poor. If you will give education to your children they will by & by become wise, rich & comfortable as the whites— I hope you will open your ears and hearts to receive this advice, and that you may soon receive great light— But I am afraid for you; I see very few go to hear religious {0062} instruction from the Missionaries, altho' they are preaching every evening in the church, and very anxious that you should learn to become wise, from the good Book of the Great Spirit — If you do this, you shall live happy and have no quarrels among yourselves, as at present, nor with the whites — you would commit no depredations, nor have persons coming to me, or writing to your Great Father, that you kill their cattle, and take from them things which are not yours; and asking us to pay them out of your annuites. These things are very displeasing to your Great Father, and when he writes me about them, I always feel very much ashamed of my Red children— These bad and wicked things, your Great Father is determined to have a stop put to; and he looks to your Chiefs and Braves, to set others a good example, and also to aid him, and the Govt: officers, in bringing to justice every wicked person among you— Then you & I can hold up our heads, and look our Great Father in the face, and he will be able to feel proud of you, and tell other Indians to take an example from his Chippewa Children — Can I tell him on my return, that you will do all this? Before we part, we must have all your jealousies and quarrels about the Treaty of S^t. Peters, made up — a stop must be put to your decoying persons from each others bands, you should and must live all united, as brethren. The greatest evil among you, and that which makes you most miserable, is drinking whiskey, this you must give up, or become poor and miserable; but I will speak more to you on this subject hereafter. When in N.Y. about 3 months since, I found about 800 of your Blankets, which were left there last year, your great Father was very angry about it, and asked me to send them up with your goods of this year — they are now here & shall be delivered to you with the other goods, all together— This shows that your Great Father wishes every Agent to so you justice, and whenever he finds out one who does not, he will dismiss him and send you another — does not this show you the Govt: is not to blame when wrong is done to you?— The President would despise to do any wrong to his Red Children, and is determined to punish every one who will.— You find that I came here to talk to you about more things than the purchase of your lands; and whither you sell them or not, I hope we shall take much pleasant counsel together, which may be the means of improving your condition and rendering you comfortable and happy— But in order not to be too tedious in this first talk — I now propose to buy all the lands within the following boundaries— Beginning at the mouth of Chocolate River, running across the Lake to the British line, and up that line to the Grand Portage, or Pigeon River, thence along the Lake Shore, to the mouth of the Fond du Lac, or S^t. Louis River, thence up said River about 22 miles to the Am: Fur C^o. trading post, near the most southerly bend of said river —thence south to the line of the treaty you made with Gov: Dodge at S^t. Peters — thence along said line to its southeastwardly boundary— thence northeastwardly along the boundary line between the Chippewas and the Menomonees, to its eastern termination — thence {0063} northwardly, along the eastern fork of the Skonaby River, to the mouth of Chocolate River, or the place of beginning — I mean all the lands south and east of Lake Superior, with all the Islands in said Lake— These boundaries you see traced on this map, which I have had made, to help us to have a clear understanding — you must not expect that your great Father is very anxious to buy your lands & will give you a great price for them— I understand that some <u>fools</u> have been telling you <u>Squaw</u> stories about this; but you are not childish enough to believe them— The principal benefit your great Father expects from you lands at present is, the removal of the minerals which are said to be on them; and not that the whites intend to settle on them at present; but as these lands may at some future day be required, your great Father does not wish to leave you without a home, & I therefore propose, that all the Lands, north & west of the Am: Fur C^{os}. trading post on the Fond du Lac River, and from the Shore of the Lake to the British Line, including all the unceded lands yet belonging to the Sandy Lake Bands, shall be reserved as a home in common for you all, unless your great father and yourselves shall hereafter agree upon some other place for you to go to— Go now my friends and consult among yourselves — think well of this important subject, take advice from your wise and good freinds, but be careful not to allow <u>bad Birds</u> to trouble you— Your great Father now offers to do you good, be therefore wise and improve the opportunity — if not you must expect to suffer the consequences— Remember that you have already given {0064} permission by the Treaty of Fond du Lac, to have the minerals taken from your lands, which shall be done, whether you sell your lands or not; and this is all the whites now want of your lands; still, you must be ready to leave them whenever the President shall require you to do so. Tomorrow morning when the gun fires, I wish you to come again into Council, and state whether the proposal now made you in behalf of your great Father, is agreeable to you, if so, I will do all for you that I can with propriety — you know that we have been friends for many years, and I tell you all, before the great Spirit, that I would be very sorry to wrong you even if I could — my earnest desire is to befriend you, if you will allow me to be so; but if you refuse, it may be a long time before your great father will again make you any offer whatever — meet me again tomorrow after the firing of the Gun.—

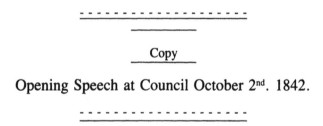

Copy

Opening Speech at Council October 2ⁿᵈ. 1842.

My friends we have met once more in council before the Great Spirit, and let us remember that he witnesses whatever we do or say— It gave me pleasure to learn from a delegation of your Chiefs, that you are now disposed to sell all your lands within the limits pointed out to you in our former Council, and which you now see bounded by a yellow line on this map — it is all your lands between the Mississippi & Lake Superior, south & east of the Am: Cᵒˢ. trading post, on the Fond du Lac River, and all the Islands in the Lake, to the British line— I am thus particular with you, as Indians sometimes say, that the Commissioners often cheat them, just as you thought about Gov: Cass, who made the treaty of Fond du Lac with you in 1826, until I read your names in the Book, then you were satisfied you had signed it—

Most of you know me to be your friend, and a man of truth — the offer now to be made for your lands will I trust be pleasing to you all— I have not come here to make a hard bargain, but to tell you at once all I shall give: this may save us much talk, for if you will not accept my proposals, there can be no treaty— I offer you more now than I intended to give before we opened these councils; partly because I find you are very poor, and the President wishes to make you happy & comfortable, and partly because you are so friendly to the whites, and will always no doubt be ready to comply with the wishes of your Great Father— Now listen to my proposals — you shall be paid annually for 25 years $12.500 in specie — $10.500 worth of Goods, & $2000 worth of Provisions & Tobacco; to be paid so that the money, Goods, Provisions & Tobacco, both of this treaty and the Treaty you made with Gov: Dodge at Sᵗ. Peters in 1837, shall be equally distributed to every person, whether of the Mississippi, or Lake Superior Chippewas, as far up as the Sandy Lake Band, which is included — this will prevent future jealousies and allay the bad feelings which now exist among you, and make you like a band of Brothers; besides, it is just and honorable, and no good man will object to what is right — you see the trouble we are willing to take to make you all happy and bring you once {0065} more under a clear sky, and hope none of you has such a bad heart as to oppose these efforts— The President, with the Great Council at Washington, and all the good people among the whites, are very anxious for you to improve your condition, and become more like the whites, that you may be prosperous and happy — you shall therefore be allowed, besides what I have already stated, (for the 25 years,) 2 Blacksmiths' shops, the cost of annual support, including striker, Iron, steel &c: to be $1000 each — 2 farmers $500 each — 2 Carpenters $600 each — $2000 for the support of schools among you; and a fund of $5000 to be set apart for agricultural and other such purposes, and be expended as your Great Father and Agent will direct, from time to time— To pay your Traders debts, so that you shall owe them nothing, $75.000 will be set apart, for your traders claims, to be apportioned by me, as I shall find their claims just; the money to be paid within three years — but no debt contracted before 1822, (when the British traders were excluded,) can be allowed— I hope as you will now have a great deal of both money and goods every year, that you will get no more in debt to the Traders, and never kill or take any thing belonging to the whites, so that your annuities may always be your own entirely— I am glad that you feel so much friendship for your half breeds, and that you wish to make some provision for them; but your Great Father knows and is angry at the way they have always heretofore foolishly spent their money and allowed themselves to be cheated, and forbids money hereafter to be squandered on them: still, as {0066} I wish to do yourselves and half breeds all the good I can, $15.000 besides all that has already been named, shall be paid to you next year, as a present, which you may give if you please, to your half breeds, and as your annuities will be very large every year, you can make them a present from time to time, so as to make them comfortable, and I hope you will always do so, when they merit it—

I have now make you an offer which will be very beneficial to you if you accept it — do not for a moment entertain the idea that I will increase a single item of the above, nor give any thing more — you have said that other Commissioners offer first, less than they expect to give, so as to buy the land as cheap as they can, but that is not my way at all— I offer you at once all I intend to give, and hope you are satisfied— Some of you have expressed a wish to treat by bands, & others to keep reservations, but I cannot sanction either — your Great Father will not treat with you as Bands, but as a Nation — you, who know any thing of your own history, are aware that when your fathers first came from the east, they drove their enemies before them and took possession of the whole country; afterwards they separated into Bands, & for convenience took up such hunting grounds as suited them; but this gave the separate Bands no other right to the lands than merely to occupy them for the time being — the whole country is your common property — you may easily see how unjust it would be to recognize the right of property by Bands, for several of your small Bands are scattered over a much larger and better country, than some of your large Bands, and why should this secure them the sole ownership, for are you not at all children of the same great Nation? you are; and it pleased me much to hear from most of your Chiefs, that this is your own general view of the subject: altho' a few of those who thought they would gain by it, wished to have it otherwise; — you know that treaties are often made when whole Bands are absent, which could not be but on the principle that all your lands are common property, and the majority of the Nation can sell or not as they please, the absentees being entitled to their share of the annuities &c: — It is all right for you however to live apart as you do, in Bands, each choosing their own hunting grounds, this will prevent many disagreements, and make it easier for you to find game and food in small bands, than if you were all to live together— The payments cannot, as some of you wish, be made at different points, you must all be paid at one place, and this is well, for your Agent and the Missionaries will then see you all together once a year, to give you good advice, and you will thus also keep acquainted with each other—. On monday I will expect your final answer; it is now getting late in the season, and I feel anxious that you get home in good time to your hunts—{0067}

Appendix 4

Treaty With the Chippewa, 1842.

Articles of a treaty made and concluded at La Pointe of Lake Superior, in the Territory of Wisconsin, between Robert Stuart commissioner on the part of the United States, and the Chippewa Indians of the Mississippi, and Lake Superior, by their chiefs and headmen.

ARTICLE I.

The Chippewa Indians of the Mississippi and Lake Superior, cede to the United States all the country within the following bounderies; viz: beginning at the mouth of Chocolate river of Lake Superior; thence northwardly across said lake to intersect the boundery line between the United States and the Province of Canada; thence up said Lake Superior, to the mouth of the St. Louis, or Fond du Lac river (including all the islands in said lake); thence up said river to the American Fur Company's trading post, at the southwardly bend thereof, about 22 miles from its mouth; thence south to intersect the line of the treaty of 29th July 1837, with the Chippewas of the Mississippi; thence along said line to its southeastwardly extremity, near the Plover portage on the Wisconsin river; thence northeastwardly, along the boundery line, between the Chippewas and Menomonees, to its eastern termination, (established by the treaty held with the Chippewas, Menomonees, and Winnebagoes, at Butte des Morts, August 11th 1827) on the Skonawby River of Green Bay; thence northwardly to the source of Chocolate river; thence down said river to its mouth, the place of beginning; it being the intention of the parties to this treaty, to include in this cession, all the Chippewa lands eastwardly of the aforesaid line running from the American Fur Company's trading post on the Fond du Lac river to the intersection of the line of the treaty made with the Chippewas of the Mississippi July 29th 1837.

ARTICLE II.

The Indians stipulate for the right of hunting on the ceded territory, with the other usual privileges of occupancy, until required to remove by the President of the United {542} States, and that the laws of the United States shall be continued in force, in respect to their trade and inter course with the whites, until otherwise ordered by Congress.

ARTICLE III.

It is agreed by the parties to this treaty, that whenever the Indians shall be required to remove from the ceded district, all the unceded lands belonging to the Indians of Fond du Lac, Sandy Lake, and Mississippi bands, shall be the common property and home of all the Indians, party to this treaty.

ARTICLE IV.

In consideration of the foregoing cession, the United States, engage to pay to the Chippewa Indians of the Mississippi, and Lake Superior, annually, for twenty-five years, twelve thousand five hundred (12,500) dollars, in specie, ten thousand five hundred (10,500) dollars in goods, two thousand (2,000) dollars in provisions and tobacco, two thousand (2,000) dollars for the support of two blacksmiths shops, (including pay of smiths and assistants, and iron steel &c.) one thousand (1,000) dollars for pay of two farmers, twelve hundred (1,200) for pay of two carpenters, and two thousand (2,000) dollars for the support of schools for the Indians party to this treaty; and further the United States engage to pay the sum of five thousand (5,000) dollars as an agricultural fund, to be expended under the direction of the Secretary of War. And also the sum of seventy-five thousand (75,000) dollars, shall be allowed for the full satisfaction of their debts within the ceded district, which shall be examined by the commissioner to this treaty, and the amount to be allowed decided upon by him, which shall appear in a schedule hereunto annexed. The United States shall pay the amount so allowed within three years.

Whereas the Indians have expressed a strong desire to have some provision made for their half breed relatives, therefore it is agreed, that fifteen thousand (15,000) dollars shall be paid to said Indians, next year, as a present, to be disposed of, as they, together with their agent, shall determine in council.

ARTICLE V.

Whereas the whole country between Lake Superior and the Mississippi, has always been understood as belonging in common to the Chippewas, party to this treaty; and whereas the bands bordering on Lake Superior, have not been allowed to participate in the annuity payments of the treaty made with the Chippewas of the Mississippi, at St. Peters July 29th 1837, and whereas all the unceded lands belonging to the aforesaid Indians, are hereafter to be held in common, therefore, to remove all occasion for jealousy and discontent, it is agreed that all the annuity due by the said treaty, as also the annuity due by the present treaty, shall henceforth be equally divided among the Chippewas of the Mississippi and Lake Superior, party to this treaty, so that every person shall receive an equal share.

ARTICLE VI.

The Indians residing on the Mineral district, shall be subject to removal therefrom at the pleasure of the President of the United States.

ARTICLE VII.

This treaty shall be obligatory upon the contracting parties when ratified by the President and Senate of the United States. {543}

In testimony whereof the said Robert Stuart commissioner, on the part of the United States, and the chiefs and headmen of the Chippewa Indians of the Mississippi and Lake Superior, have hereunto set their hands, at La Pointe of Lake Superior, Wisconsin Territory this fourth day of October in the year of our Lord one thousand eight hundred and forty-two.

Robert Stuart, Commissioner.
Jno. Hulbert, Secretary.

Crow wing River,	Po go ne gi shik,	1st chief.
Do.	Son go com ick,	2d do.
Sandy Lake,	Ka non do ur uin zo,	1st do.
Do.	Na tum e gaw bon,	2d do.
Gull Lake,	Ua bo jig,	1st do.
Do.	Pay pe si gon de bay,	2d do.
Red Ceder Lake,	Kui ui sen shis,	1st do.
Do.	Ott taw wance,	2d do.
Po ke gom maw,	Bai ie jig,	1st do.
Do.	Show ne aw,	2d do.
Wisconsin River,	Ki uen zi,	1st do.
Do.	Wi aw bis ke kut te way,	2d do.
Lac de Flambeau,	A pish ka go gi,	1st do.
Do.	May tock cus e quay,	2d do.
Do.	She maw gon e,	2d do.
Lake Bands,	Ki ji ua be she shi,	1st do.
Do.	Ke kon o tum,	2d do.
Fon du Lac,	Shin goob,	1st do.
Do.	Na gan nab,	2d do.
Do.	Mong o zet,	2d do.
La Pointe,	Gitchi waisky,	1st do.
Do.	Mi zi,	2d do.
Do.	Ta qua gone e,	2d do.
Onlonagan,	O kon di kan,	1st do.
Do.	Kis ke taw wac,	2d do.
Ance,	Pe na shi,	1st do.
Do.	Guck we san sish,	2d do.
Vieux Desert,	Ka she osh e,	1st do.
Do.	Medge waw gwaw wot,	2d do.
Mille Lac,	Ne qua ne be,	1st do.
Do.	Ua shash ko kum,	2d do.
Do.	No din,	2d do.
St. Croix,	Be zhi ki,	1st do.
Do.	Ka bi na be,	2d do.
Do.	Ai aw bens,	2d do.
Snake River,	Sha go bi,	1st do.
Chippewa River,	Ua be she shi,	1st do.
	Que way zhan sis,	2d do.
Lac Courtulle,	Ne na nang eb,	1st do.
Do.	Be bo kon uen,	2d do.
Do.	Ki uen zi,	2d do.

In presence of—

Henry Blanchford, interpreter.
Samuel Ashmun, interpreter.
Justin Rice.
Charles H. Oakes.
William A. Aitkin.
William Brewster.
Charles M. Borup.

Z. Platt.
C. H. Beaulieau.
L. T. Jamison.
James P. Scott.
Cyrus Mendenhall.
L. M. Warren.

(To the Indian names are subjoined marks.) {544}

173

Schedule of claims examined and allowed by Robert Stuart, commissioner, under the treaty with the Chippewa Indians of the Mississippi and Lake Superior, concluded at La Pointe, October 4th 1842, setting forth the names of claimants, and their proportion of allowance of the seventy-five thousand dollars provided in the fourth article of the aforesaid treaty, for the full satisfaction of their debts, as follows:

No. of claim.	Name of claimant.	Proportion of $75,000, set apart in 4th article of treaty.
1	Edward F. Ely	$50 80
2	Z.Platt, esq., attorney for George Berkett	484 67
3	Cleveland North Lake Co.	1,485 67
4	Abraham W. Williams	75 03
5	William Brewster	2,052 67
	This claim to be paid as follows, viz:	
	William Brewster, or order................. $1,929 77	
	Charles W. Borup, or order 122 90	
	———	
	$2,052 67	
6	George Copway	61 67
7	John Kahbege	57 55
8	Alixes Carpantier	28 58
9	John W. Bell	186 16
10	Antoine Picard	6 46
11	Michael Brisette	182 42
12	Francois Dejaddon	301 48
13	Pierre C. Duvernay	1,101 00
14	Jean Bts. Bazinet	325 46
15	John Hotley	69 00
16	Francois Charette	234 92
17	Clement H. Beaulieu, agent for the estate	
	of Bazil Beaulieu, dec'd	596 84
18	Francois St. Jean and George Bonga	366 84
19	Louis Ladebauche	322 52
20	Peter Crebassa	499 27
21	B.T. Kavanaugh	516 82
22	Augustin Goslin	169 05
23	American Fur Company	13,365 30
	This claim to be paid as follows, viz:	
	American Fur Company 12,565 10	

No. of claim.	Name of claimant.	Proportion of $75,000, set apart in 4th article of treaty.
	Charles W. Borup 800 20	
	$13,365 30	
24	William A. Aitken	935 67
25	James P. Scott	73 41
26	Augustin Bellanger	192 35
27	Louis Corbin	12 57
28	Alexes Corbin	596 03
29	George Johnston	35 24
30	Z. Platt, esq., attorney for Sam'l Ashman	1,771 63
31	Z. Platt, esq., attorney for Wm. Johnson	390 27
32	Z. Platt, esq., attorney for estate of	
	Dan'l Dingley	1,991 62
33	Lyman M. Warren	1,566 65
34	Estate of Michael Cadotte, *disallowed.*	
35	Z. Platt, esq., attorney for estate of	
	E. Roussain	959 13
36	Joseph Dufault	144 32
37	Z. Platt, esq., attorney for Antoine Mace	170 35
38	Michael Cadotte	205 60
39	Z. Platt, esq., att'y for Francois Gauthier	167 05
40	Z. Platt, esq., att'y for Joseph Gauthier	614 30
41	Z. Platt, esq., attorney for J.B. Uoulle	64 78
42	Jean Bts. Corbin	531 50
43	John Hulbert	209 18
44	Jean Bts. Couvellion	18 80
45	Nicholas Da Couteau, *withdrawn.*	
46	Pierre Cotté	732 50
47	W. H. Brockway and Henry Holt, executors to	
	the estate of John Holliday, dec'd	3,157 10
48	John Jacob Astor	37,994 98
	This claim to be paid as follows, viz:	
	Charles W. Borup 1,676 90	
	Z. Platt, esq. 2,621 80	
	John Jacob Astor 23,696 28	
	$27,994 98	
49	Z. Platt, esq., attorney for Thos. Connor	1,118 60
50	Charles H. Oakes	4,309 21
51	Z. Platt, esq., attorney for Wm. Morrison	1,074 70

No. of claim.	Name of claimant.	Proportion of $75,000, set apart in 4th article of treaty.
52	Z. Platt, esq., att'y for Isaac Butterfield	1,275 56
53	J. B. Van Rensselaer	62 00
54	William Brewster and James W. Abbot	2,067 10
	The parties to this claim request no payment be made to either without their joint consent, or until a decision of the case be had, in a court of justice.	
55	William Bell	17 62
		$75,000 00

Robert Stuart, Commissioner.
Jno. Hulbert, Secretary. {545}

Appendix 5

Treaty Commissioner Henry C. Gilbert's Explanation of the Treaty
Concluded in 1854 with the Assistance of David B. Herriman

Office Michigan Indian Agency

Detroit October 17th. 1854

Sir

I transmit herewith a treaty concluded at LaPointe on the 30th Ultimo between Mr. Herriman and myself as Commissioners on the part of the United States and the Chippewas of Lake Superior and the Mississippi.

On receiving your letters of August 10th, 12th, and 14th, relative to this treaty, I immediately dispatched a special messenger from this place by way of Chicago, Galena and St. Paul to Mr. Herriman at the Crow wing Chippewa Agency transmitting to him your letter requesting him to meet me at LaPointe with the Chiefs and Headmen of his Agency at as early a day as possible. I adopted this course in preference to sending a messenger from La Pointe on my arrival there for the purpose of saving time and I was thus enabled to secure the attendance of Mr Herriman and the Mississippi Chiefs some 10 or 12 days earlier than I could otherwise have done.

I left for LaPointe on the 26th. of August last and arrived there the 1st. day of September — Mr Herriman meeting me there the 14th. of the same Month.

By this time a large number of Indians had assembled — including not only those entitled to payment but all those from the Interior who live about Lakes de Flambeau and Lake Courteilles. The Chiefs who were notified to attend brought with them in every instance their entire bands. We made a careful estimate of the number present {0135} and found that there were about 4.000. They all had to be fed and taken care of, thus adding greatly to the expenses attending the negotiations.

A great number of traders and claim agents were also present as well as some persons from St. Paul's who I had reason to believe attended for the purpose of preventing if possible the consummation of the treaty. The utmost precautions were taken by me to prevent a knowledge of the fact that negotiations were to take place from becoming public. The Messenger sent by me to Mr Herriman was not only trust worthy but was himself totally ignorant of the purport of the dispatches to Major Herriman. Information however of the fact was communicated from some source and the persons present in consequence greatly embarrassed our proceedings.

After Major Herriman's arrival we soon found that the Mississippi Indians could not be induced to sell their land on any terms. Much jealousy and ill feeling existed between them and the Lake Superior Indians and they could not even be prevailed upon to meet each other in council. They were all however anxious that a division should be made of the payments to become due under former existing treaties and a specific apportionment made betweeen the Mississippi and the Lake Superior Indians and places of payment designated.

Taking advantage of this feeling we proposed to them a division of the country between them and the establishment of a boundary line, on one side of {0136} which the country should belong exclusively to the Lake Superior and on the other side to the Mississippi Indians. We had but little difficulty in inducing them to agree to this proposition and after much negotiation the line designated in the treaty was agreed upon.

We then obtained from the Lake Indians a cession of their portion of the Country on the terms stated in the treaty. The district ceded embraces all the mineral region bordering on Lake Superior and Pigeon river & is supposed to be by far the most valuable portion of their country. But a small portion of the amount agreed to be paid in annuities is payable in coin. The manner of payment is such as in our judgment would most tend to promote the permanent welfare and hasten the civilization of the Indians.

We found that the points most strenuously insisted upon by them were first the privilege of remaining in the country where they reside and next the appropriation of land for their future homes. Without yielding these points, it was idle for us to talk about a treaty. We therefore agreed to the selection of lands for them in territory heretofore ceded.

The tract for the Ance {L'Ance} and Vieux Desert bands is at the head of Ke, wa, we naw {Keweenaw} Bay Michigan and is at present occupied by them. I estimate the quantity at about 60.000 acres.

These reservations are located in Wisconsin, the principal of which is for the LaPointe Band on Bad river— A large number of Indians now reside there and I presume it will ultimately become the home {0137} of most of the Chippewas residing in that state. It is a tract of land well adapted for Agricultural purposes and includes the present Missionary Station under the care of the American Board of Commissioners for Foreign Missions. About one third of the land however lying on the Lake Shore is swamp & valueless, except as it gives them access to the Lake for fishing purposes.

The other Wisconsin reservations lie on Lac de Flambeau and Lac Courteirelle in the Interior and the whole amount of land reserved in that state I estimate at about 200.000 acres exclusive of the Swamp land included in the LaPointe reservation. In the ceded Country there are two tracts set apart for the Indians — one on St Louis river of 100.000 acres for the Fond DuLac bands and one embracing the point bounded by the Lake and Pigeon river and containing about 120.000 acres.

There are two or three other small reservations to be hereafter selected under the direction of the President. The whole quantity of land embraced within all the tracts set apart we estimate at about 486.000 acres— No portion of the reserved lands are occupied by whites except the Missionary establishment on Bad river.

The provision going to each Half Breed family 80 acres of land was most strenuously insisted upon by the Indians. There are about 200 such families on my pay roll and allowing as many more to the Interior Indians which is a very liberal estimate,{0138} the amount of land required will be about 32.000. acres.

A principal source of embarrassment was the provision setting aside a portion of the consideration to be paid as the Chiefs might direct &c. In other words to pay their debts with. We had much difficulty in reducing the amount insisted upon to the sum stated in the treaty. I have no doubt that there are many just claims upon these Indians. The regular payment of their annuities was so long withheld that they were forced to depend to a great extent upon their traders. There claims they were all disposed to acknowledge and insisted upon providing for their payment and without the insertion of the provision referred to, we could not have concluded the treaty.

I regret very much that we could not have purchased the whole country and made the treaty in every particular within the limit of your instructions. But this was absolutely impossible and we were forced to the alternative of abandoning the attempt to treat or of making the concessions detailed in the treaty.

There are many points respecting which I should like much to make explanations, and for that purpose and in order to make a satisfactory settlement of the accounts for treaty expenses I respectfully request the privilege of attending at Washington at such time after making my other annuity payments as you may think proper.

Hon. Geo. W. Manypenny		Very Respectfully
Com. Ind. Affˢ.		Your Obt. Servt.
Washington D.C.		Henry C. Gilbert
		Commissioner

{0139}

Appendix 6

Treaty With the Chippewa, 1854.

Articles of a treaty made and concluded at La Pointe, in the State of Wisconsin, between Henry C. Gilbert and David B. Herriman, commissioners on the part of the United States, and the Chippewa Indians of Lake Superior and the Mississippi, by their chiefs and head-men.

ARTICLE 1. The Chippewas of Lake Superior hereby cede to the United States all the lands heretofore owned by them in common with the Chippewas of the Mississippi, lying east of the following boundary-line, to wit: Beginning at a point, where the east branch of Snake River crosses the southern boundary-line of the Chippewa country, running thence up the said branch to its source, thence nearly north, in a straight line, to the mouth of East Savannah River, thence up the St. Louis River to the mouth of East Swan River, thence up the East Swan River to its source, thence in a straight line to the most westerly bend of Vermillion River, and thence down the Vermillion River to its mouth.

The Chippewas of the Mississippi hereby assent and agree to the foregoing cession, and consent that the whole amount of the consideration money for the country ceded above, shall be paid to the Chippewas of Lake Superior, and in consideration thereof the Chippewas of Lake Superior hereby relinquish to the Chippewas of the Mississippi, all their interest in and claim to the lands heretofore owned by them in common, lying west of the above boundary-line.

ARTICLE 2. The United States agree to set apart and withhold from sale, for the use of the Chippewas of Lake Superior, the following described tracts of land, viz:

1st. For the L'Anse and Vieux De Sert bands, all the unsold lands in the following townships in the State of Michigan: Township fifty-one north range thirty-three west; township fifty-one north range thirty-two west; the east half of township fifty north range thirty-three west; the west half of township fifty north range thirty-two west, and all of township fifty-one north range thirty-one west, lying west of Huron Bay.

2d. For the La Pointe band, and such other Indians as may see fit to settle with them, a tract of land bounded as follows: Beginning on the south shore of Lake Superior, a few miles west of Montreal River, at the mouth of a creek called by the Indians Ke-che-se-be-we-she, running thence south to a line drawn east and west through the centre of township forty-seven north, thence west to the west line of said township, thence south to the southeast corner of township forty-six north, range thirty-two west, thence west the width of two townships, thence north the width of two townships, thence west one mile, thence north to the lake shore, and thence along the lake shore, crossing Shag-waw-me-quon Point, to the place of beginning. Also two hundred acres on the northern extremity of Madeline Island, for a fishing ground.

3d. For the other Wisconsin bands, a tract of land lying about Lac De Flambeau, and another tract on Lac Court Orielles, each equal in extent to three townships, the boundaries of which shall be hereafter agreed upon or fixed under the direction of the President.

4th. For the Fond Du Lac bands, a tract of land bounded as follows: Beginning at an island in the St. Louis River, above Knife Portage, called by the Indians Pawpaw-sco-me-me-tig, running thence west to the boundary-line heretofore described, thence north along said boundary-line to the mouth of Savannah River, thence down the St. Louis River to the place of beginning. And if said tract shall contain {648} less than one hundred thousand acres, a strip of land shall be added on the south side thereof, large enough to equal such deficiency.

5th. For the Grand Portage band, a tract of land bounded as follows: Beginning at a rock a little east of the eastern extremity of Grand Portage Bay, running thence along the lake shore to the mouth of a small stream called by the Indians Mawske-gwaw-caw-maw-se-be, or Cranberry Marsh River, thence up said stream, across the point to Pigeon River, thence down Pigeon River to a point opposite the starting-point, and thence across to the place of beginning.

6th. The Ontonagon band and that subdivision of the La Pointe band of which Buffalo is chief, may each select, on or near the lake shore, four sections of land, under the direction of the President, the boundaries of which shall be defined hereafter. And being desirous to provide for some of his connections who have rendered his people important services, it is agreed that the chief Buffalo may select one section of land, at such place in the ceded territory as he may see fit, which shall be reserved for that purpose, and conveyed by the United States to such person or persons as he may direct.

7th. Each head of a family, or single person over twenty-one years of age at the present time of the mixed bloods, belonging to the Chippewas of Lake Superior, shall be entitled to eighty acres of land, to be selected by them under the direction of the President, and which shall be secured to them by patent in the usual form.

ARTICLE 3. The United States will define the boundaries of the reserved tracts, whenever it may be necessary, by actual survey, and the President may, from time to time, at his discretion, cause the whole to be surveyed, and may assign to each head of a family or single person over twenty-one years of age, eighty acres of land for his or their separate use; and he may, at his discretion, as fast as the occupants become capable of transacting their own affairs, issue patents therefor to such occupants, with such restrictions of the power of alienation as he may see fit to impose. And he may also, at his discretion, make rules and regulations, respecting the disposition of the lands in case of the death of the head of a family, or single person occupying the same, or in case of its abandonment by them. And he may also assign other lands in exchange for mineral lands, if any such are found in the tracts herein set apart. And he may also make such changes in the boundaries of such reserved tracts or otherwise, as shall be necessary to prevent interference with any vested rights. All necessary roads, highways, and railroads, the lines of which may run through any of the reserved tracts, shall have the right of way through the same, compensation being made therefor as in other cases.

ARTICLE 4. In consideration of and payment for the country hereby ceded, the United States agree to pay to the Chippewas of Lake Superior, annually, for the term of twenty years, the following sums, to wit: five thousand dollars in coin; eight thousand dollars in goods, household furniture and cooking utensils; three thousand dollars in agricultural implements and cattle, carpenter's and other tools and building materials, and three thousand dollars for moral and educational purposes, of which last sum, three hundred dollars per annum shall be paid to the Grand Portage band, to enable them to maintain a school at their village. The United States will also pay the further sum of ninety thousand dollars, as the chiefs in open council may direct, to enable them to meet their present just engagements. Also the further sum of six thousand dollars, in agricultural implements, household furniture, and cooking utensils, to be distributed at the next annuity payment, among the mixed bloods of said nation. The United States will also furnish two hundred guns, one hundred rifles, five hundred beaver-traps, three hundred dollars' worth of ammuni {649} tion, and one thousand dollars' worth of ready-made clothing, to be distributed among the young men of the nation, at the next annuity payment.

ARTICLE 5. The United States will also furnish a blacksmith and assistant, with the usual amount of stock, during the continuance of the annuity payments, and as much longer as the President may think proper, at each of the points herein set apart for the residence of the Indians, the same to be in lieu of all the employees to which the Chippewas of Lake Superior may be entitled under previous existing treaties.

ARTICLE 6. The annuities of the Indians shall not be taken to pay the debts of individuals, but satisfaction for depredations committed by them shall be made by them in such manner as the President may direct.

ARTICLE 7. No spirituous liquors shall be made, sold, or used on any of the lands herein set apart for the residence of the Indians, and the sale of the same shall be prohibited in the Territory hereby ceded, until otherwise ordered by the President.

ARTICLE 8. It is agreed, between the Chippewas of Lake Superior and the Chippewas of the Mississippi, that the former shall be entitled of two-thirds, and the latter to one-third, of all benefits to be derived from former treaties existing prior to the year 1847.

ARTICLE 9. The United States agree that an examination shall be made, and all sums that may be found equitably due to the Indians, for arrearages of annuity or other thing, under the provisions of former treaties, shall be paid as the chiefs may direct.

ARTICLE 10. All missionaries, and teachers, and other persons of full age, residing in the territory hereby ceded, or upon any of the reservations hereby made by authority of law, shall be allowed to enter the land occupied by them at the minimum price whenever the surveys shall be completed to the amount of one quarter-section each.

ARTICLE 11. All annuity payments to the Chippewas of Lake Superior, shall hereafter be make at L'Anse, La Pointe, Grand Portage, and on the St. Louis River; and the Indians shall not be required to remove from the homes hereby set apart for them. And such of them as reside in the territory hereby ceded, shall have the right to hunt and fish therein, until otherwise ordered by the President.

ARTICLE 12. In consideration of the poverty of the Bois Forte Indians who are parties to this treaty, they having never received any annuity payments, and of the great extent of that part of the ceded country owned exclusively by them, the following additional stipulations are made for their benefit. The United States will pay the sum of ten thousand dollars, as their chiefs in open council may direct, to enable them to meet their present just engagements. Also the further sum of ten thousand dollars, in five equal annual payments, in blankets, cloth, nets, guns, ammunition, and such other articles of necessity as they may require.

They shall have the right to select their reservation at any time hereafter, under the direction of the President; and the same may be equal in extent, in proportion to their numbers, to those allowed the other bands, and be subject to the same provisions.

They shall be allowed a blacksmith, and the usual smithshop supplies, and also two persons to instruct them in farming, whenever in the opinion of the President it shall be proper, and for such length of time as he shall direct.

It is understood that all Indians who are parties to this treaty, except the Chippewas of the Mississippi, shall hereafter be known as the Chippewas of Lake Superior. *Provided,* That the stipulation by which the Chippewas of Lake Superior relinquishing their right to land west {650} of the boundary-line shall not apply to the Bois Forte band who are parties to this treaty.

ARTICLE 13. This treaty shall be obligatory on the contracting parties, as soon as the same shall be ratified by the President and Senate of the United States.

In testimony whereof, the said Henry C. Gilbert, and the said David B. Herriman, commissioners as aforesaid, and the undersigned chiefs and headmen of the Chippewas of Lake Superior and the Mississippi, have hereunto set their hands and seals, at the place aforesaid, this thirtieth day of September, one thousand eight hundred and fifty-four.

Henry C. Gilbert,
David B. Herriman,
Commissioners.

Richard M. Smith, Secretary.

La Pointe Band:

Ke-che-waish-ke, or the Buffalo, 1st chief, his X mark.

Chay-che-que-oh, 2d chief, his X mark.

A-daw-we-ge-zhick, or Each Side of the sky, 2d chief, his X mark.

O-ske-naw-way, or the Youth, 2d chief, his X mark.

Maw-caw-day-pe-nay-se, or the Black Bird, 2d chief, his X mark.

Naw-waw-naw-quot, headman, his X mark.

Ke-wain-zeence, headman, his X mark.

Waw-baw-ne-me-ke, or the White Thunder, 2d chief, his X mark.

Pay-baw-me-say, or the Soarer, 2d chief, his X mark.

Naw-waw-ge-waw-nose, or the Little Current, 2d chief, his X mark.

Maw-caw-day-waw-quot, or the Black Cloud, 2d chief, his X mark.

Me-she-naw-way, or the Disciple, 2d chief, his X mark.

Key-me-waw-naw-um, headman, his X mark.

She-gog headman, his X mark.

Ontonagon Band:

O-cun-de-cun, or the Buoy 1st chief, his X mark.

Waw-say-ge-zhick, or the Clear Sky, 2d chief, his X mark.

Keesh-ke-taw-wug, headman, his X mark.

L'Anse Band:

David King, 1st chief, his X mark.

John Southwind, headman, his X mark.

Peter Marksman, headman, his X mark.

Naw-taw-me-ge-zhick, or the First Sky, 2d chief, his X mark.

Aw-se-neece, headman, his X mark.

Vieux De Sert Band:

May-dway-aw-she, 1st chief, his X mark.

Posh-quay-gin, or the Leather, 2d chief, his X mark.

Grand Portage Band:

Shaw-gaw-naw-sheence, or the Little Englishman, 1st chief, his X mark.

May-mosh-caw-wosh, headman, his X mark.

Aw-de-konse, or the Little Reindeer, 2d chief, his X mark.

Way-we-ge-wam, headman, his X mark.

Fond Du Lac Band:

Shing-goope, or the Balsom, 1st chief, his X mark.

Mawn-go-sit, or the Loon's Foot, 2d chief, his X mark.

May-quaw-me-we-ge-zhick, headman, his X mark.

Keesh-kawk, headman, his X mark.

Caw-taw-waw-be-day, headman, his X mark.

O-saw-gee, headman, his X mark.

Ke-che-aw-ke-wain-ze, headman, his X mark.

Naw-gaw-nub, or the Foremost Sitter, 2d chief, his X mark.

Ain-ne-maw-sung, 2d chief, his X mark.

Naw-aw-bun-way, headman, his X mark.

Wain-ge-maw-tub, headman, his X mark.

Aw-ke-wain-zeence, headman, his X mark.

Shay-way-be-nay-se, headman, his X mark.

Paw-pe-oh, headman, his X mark.

Lac Court Oreille Band:

Aw-ke-wain-ze, or the Old Man, 1st chief, his X mark.

Key-no-zhance, or the Little Jack Fish, 1st chief, his X mark.

Key-che-pe-nay-se, or the Big Bird, 2d chief, his X mark.

Ke-che-waw-be-shay-she, or the Big Martin, 2d chief, his X mark.

Waw-be-shay-sheence, headman, his X mark.

Quay-quay-cub, headman, his X mark.

Shaw-waw-no-me-tay, headman, his X mark.

Nay-naw-ong-gay-be, or the Dressing Bird, 1st chief, his X mark.

O-zhaw-waw-sco-ge-zhick, or the Blue Sky, 2d chief, his X mark.

I-yaw-banse, or the Little Buck, 2d chief, his X mark. {651}

Ke-che-e-nin-ne, headman, his X mark.

Haw-daw-gaw-me, headman, his X mark.

Way-me-te-go-she, headman, his X mark.

Pay-me-ge-wung, headman, his X mark.

Lac Du Flambeau Band:

Aw-mo-se or the Wasp, 1st chief, his X mark.

Ke-nish-te-no, 2d chief, his X mark.

Me-gee-see, or the Eagle, 2d chief, his X mark.

Kay-kay-co-gwaw-nay-aw-she, headman, his X mark.

O-che-chog, headman, his X mark.

Nay-she-kay-gwaw-nay-be, headman, his X mark.

O-scaw-bay-wis, or the Waiter, 1st chief, his X mark.

Que-we-zance, or the White Fish, 2d chief, his X mark.

Ne-gig, or the Otter, 2d chief, his X mark.

Nay-waw-che-ge-ghick-may-be, headman, his X mark.

Quay-quay-ke-cah, headman, his X mark.

Bois Forte Band:

Kay-baish-caw-daw-way, or Clear Round the Prairie, 1st chief, his X mark.

Way-zaw-we-ge-zhick-way-sking, headman, his X mark.

O-saw-we-pe-nay-she, headman, his X mark.

The Mississippi Bands:

Que-we-san-se, or Hole in the Day, head chief, his X mark.

Caw-nawn-daw-waw-win-zo, or the Berry Hunter, 1st chief, his X mark.

Waw-bow-jieg, or the White Fisher, 2d chief, his X mark.

Ot-taw-waw, 2d chief, his X mark.

Que-we-zhan-cis, or the Bad Boy, 2d chief, his X mark.

Bye-a-jick, or the Lone Man, 2d chief, his X mark.

I-yaw-shaw-way-ge-zhick, or the Crossing Sky, 2d chief, his X mark.

May-caw-day, or the Bear's Heart, 2d chief, his X mark.

Ke-way-de-no-go-nay-be, or the Northern Feather, 2d chief, his X mark.

Me-squaw-dace, headman, his X mark.

Naw-gaw-ne-gaw-bo, headman, his X mark.

Wawm-be-de-yea, headman, his X mark.

Waish-key, headman, his X mark.

Caw-way-caw-me-ge-skung, headman, his X mark.

My-yaw-ge-way-we-dunk, or the One who carries the Voice, 2d chief, his X mark.

John F. Godfroy,
Geo. Johnston,
S.A. Marvin,
Louis Codot,   } — Interpreters.
Paul H. Beaulieu,
Henry Blatchford,
Peter Floy,

Executed in the presence of—

Henry M. Rice,
J.W. Lynde,
G.D. Williams,
B.H. Connor,
E.W. Muldough,
Richard Godfroy,

D.S. Cash,
H.H. McCullough,
E. Smith Lee,
Wm. E. Vantassel,
L.H. Wheeler.

{652}

Appendix 7

Final Judgment of Judge Barbara Crabb in *Lac Courte Oreilles Band of Lake Superior Indians et al.* v. *State of Wisconsin et al.*, March 19, 1991*

IN THE UNITED STATES DISTRICT COURT
FOR THE WESTERN DISTRICT OF WISCONSIN

- -

LAC COURTE OREILLES BAND OF
LAKE SUPERIOR CHIPPEWA INDIANS;
RED CLIFF BAND OF LAKE SUPERIOR
CHIPPEWA INDIANS; SOKAOGON
CHIPPEWA INDIAN COMMUNITY;
MOLE LAKE BAND OF WISCONSIN;
ST. CROIX CHIPPEWA INDIANS OF
WISCONSIN; BAD RIVER BAND OF
THE LAKE SUPERIOR CHIPPEWA INDIANS;
LAC DU FLAMBEAU BAND OF LAKE
SUPERIOR CHIPPEWA INDIANS,

     Plaintiffs,   FINAL JUDGMENT

  v.   74-C-313-C

STATE OF WISCONSIN, WISCONSIN NATURAL
RESOURCES BOARD, CARROLL D. BESADNY,
JAMES HUNTOON, and GEORGE MEYER

    Defendants,

  and

ASHLAND COUNTY, BURNETT COUNTY,
FLORENCE COUNTY, LANGLADE COUNTY,
LINCOLN COUNTY, MARINETTE COUNTY,
WASHBURN COUNTY, and THE WISCONSIN
COUNTY FORESTS ASSOCIATION, INC.,
  Intervening Defendants.

- -

_____

*As amended on March 22, 1991, to correct a spelling error.

Judgment is entered as follows:

The usufructuary rights retained by plaintiffs as a consequence of the treaties they entered into with the United States of America in 1837 and 1842 include rights to those forms of animal life, fish, vegetation and so on that they utilized at treaty time, set forth in the facts sections of the opinions entered herein on February 18, 1987 and February 21, 1991. Also, plaintiffs have the right to use all of the methods of harvesting employed in treaty times and those developed since. Plaintiffs' retained usufructuary rights do not include the right to harvest commercial timber. They do include the right to gather miscellaneous forest products, namely, such items as firewood, tree bark, maple sap, lodge poles, boughs and marsh hay.

The fruits of the plaintiffs' exercise of their usufructuary rights may be traded and sold to non-Indians, employing modern methods of distribution and sale, as set forth in the opinion entered on February 18, 1987.

The usufructuary rights reserved by the plaintiffs in 1837 and 1842 have been terminated as to all portions of the ceded territory that are privately owned as of the times of the contemplated or actual attempted exercise of those rights.

Plaintiffs' modest living needs cannot be met from the present available harvest even if plaintiffs were physically capable of harvesting, gathering and processing it. The standard of a modest living does not provide a practical way to determine the plaintiffs' share of the harvest potential of the ceded territory.

The state defendants will continue to bear the responsibility and authority for the management of all of the natural resources of the state except as provided herein.

Defendants are enjoined from interfering in the regulation of plaintiffs' off-reservation usufructuary rights to harvest walleye and muskellunge within the ceded territory in Wisconsin, except insofar as plaintiffs have agreed to such regulation by stipulation. Regulation of plaintiffs' off-reservation usufructuary rights to harvest walleye and muskellunge within the ceded territory is reserved to plaintiffs on the condition that they enact and keep in force a management plan that provides for the regulation of their members in accordance with biologically sound principles necessary for the conservation of the species being harvested, as set out in the opinion entered herein on March 3, 1989, as amended on April 28, 1989. The efficient gear safe harvest level shall be determined by the methods described in the opinion and order of this court of March 3, 1989, as supplemented and amended by proceedings in court on March 28, 1989, the court's order of March 30, 1989 (R. 996) and the court's order of April 28, 1989. In the event of a dispute in determining the safe harvest level for any lake that cannot be resolved by the parties, the determination shall be made by the Department of Natural Resources.

Defendants are enjoined from interfering in the regulation of plaintiffs' hunting and trapping on public lands within the ceded territory in Wisconsin, except insofar as plaintiffs have agreed to such regulation by stipulation, on the condition that plaintiffs enact and keep in force an effective plan of self-regulation that conforms to the orders of the court.

All of the harvestable natural resources to which plaintiffs retain a usufructuary right are declared to be apportioned equally between the plaintiffs and all other persons, with such apportionment applying to each species and to each harvesting unit with limited exceptions as set forth in the order entered herein on May 9, 1990; and upon the condition that no portion of the harvestable resources may be exempted from the apportionable harvest. With respect to miscellaneous forest products, the total estimated harvest is to be apportioned equally between the plaintiffs and all other persons, with such apportionment applying to each type of miscellaneous forest product and to each state or county forest unit or state property on which the gathering of miscellaneous forest products is permitted.

The defendants and intervening defendants may regulate the plaintiffs' gathering of miscellaneous forest products through the application of Wis. Admin. Code Section NR 13.54 and Proposed County Regulation Section 5.

Defendants are enjoined from enforcing those portions of Section NR 13.32(2)(f) and Section NR 13.32(r)(2)(b) that include a percentage of "public land" as an element of the formulas for determining the maximum tribal antlerless deer quota (in Section NR 13.32(2)(f)) or the maximum tribal fisher quota (in Section NR 13.32(r)(2)(b)).

Plaintiffs may not exercise their usufructuary rights of hunting and fishing on private lands, that is, those lands that are held privately and are not enrolled in the forest cropland or open managed forest lands program under Wis. Stat. ch. 77 at the time of the contemplated or actual attempted exercise of such rights. Plaintiffs may not exercise their usufructuary rights of trapping on private lands or those lands that are enrolled in the forest cropland or open managed forest lands program under Wis. Stat. ch. 77. Plaintiffs are subject to state hunting and trapping regulations when hunting or trapping on private lands. For purposes of plaintiffs' trapping activities, privately owned stream beds, river bottoms and overflowed lands are private lands unless and until state law having state-wide effect is changed to allow such activities.

Defendants may enforce the prohibition on summer deer hunting contained in Section NR 13.32(2)(e) until such time as plaintiffs adopt a regulation prohibiting all deer hunting before Labor Day.

Defendants are prohibited from enforcing that portion of Section NR 13.32(2)(e) that bars tribal deer hunting during the twenty-four hour period immediately preceding the opening of the state deer gun period established in Section NR 10.01(3)(e).

Defendants may enforce the prohibition on shining of deer contained in Section NR 13.30(1)(q) until such time as plaintiffs adopt regulations identical in scope and content to Section NR 13.30(1)(q).

With respect to the exercise of any of plaintiffs' off-reservation usufructuary rights not expressly referred to in this judgment, the state may regulate only in the interest of conservation and in the interest of public health and safety, in accordance with the applicable standards set forth in the opinion entered herein on August 21, 1987.

The following stipulations by the plaintiffs and defendants and consent decrees are incorporated into this judgment as though fully set forth herein:

Docket Number	Subject
Joint Exhibit p-54 from 12/85 Trial	Stipulation as to the Boundaries of the Territory Ceded by the Treaties of 1837 and 1842 (Incorporated into Order of Feb. 23, 1987, R. 452)
R. 330	Stipulation that the issue of the use of Lake Superior under the Treaty of 1842 shall not be adjudicated in this case, but is reserved for litigation at later time

Docket Number	Subject
R. 911	Stipulation on Biological and Certain Remaining Issues in Regard to the Tribal Harvest of Walleye and Muskellunge (Incorporated into Order of March 3, 1989, R. 991)
R. 912	Stipulation on Fish Processing in Regard to the Tribal Harvest of Walleye and Muskellunge (Incorporated into Order of March 3, 1989, R. 991)
R. 913	Stipulation on Gear Identification and Safety Marking in regard to the Tribal Harvest of Walleye and Muskellunge (Incorporated into Order of March 3, 1989, R. 991)
R. 914	Stipulation on Enforcement and Tribal Court Issues in regard to the Tribal Harvest of Walleye and Muskellunge (Incorporated into Order of March 3, 1989, R. 991)
R. 1167	Stipulation in regard to the Tribal Harvest of the White-tailed Deer on issues related to the (1) Biology of Deer Management, (2) Tribal Enforcement and Preemption of State Law, (3) Sale of Deer, (4) Wild Game Processing, (5) Management Authority and (6) Ceremonial Use (Incorporated into Order of May 9, 1990, R. 1558)
R. 1222	Stipulation and Consent Decree in regard to the Tribal Harvest of Wild Rice on issues related to the (1) Biology of Wild Rice, (2) Tribal Enforcement and Preemption of State Law, and (3) Management of Wild Rice
R. 1271	Stipulation of Uncontested Facts relevant to Contested Issues of Law in regard to the Tribal Harvest of Furbearers and Small Game (Incorporated into Order of May 9, 1990, R. 1558)
R. 1289	Stipulation and Consent Decree (R. 1296) in regard to the Tribal Harvest of Fisher, Furbearers and Small Game (Incorporated into Order of May 9, 1990, R. 1558)
R. 1568	Stipulation and Consent Decree (R. 1570) in regard to the Tribal Harvest of Fish Species Other than Walleye and Muskellunge
R. 1607	Stipulation and Consent Decree in regard to the Tribal Harvest of (1) Black Bear, Migratory Birds, Wild Plants, and (2) Miscellaneous Species and Other Regulatory Matters

Except as otherwise specifically provided by the parties' stipulation (R. 1607), defendants may enforce and prosecute in state courts violations of the state boating laws in Wis. Stat. Ch. 30 and Wis. Admin. Code Ch. 5 committed by members of the plaintiff tribes engaged in treaty activities even if the plaintiff tribes have adopted identical boating regulations for the off-reservation treaty activities of their members.

Plaintiffs' failure to enact an effective plan of self-regulation that conforms with the orders of the court, or their withdrawal from such a plan after enactment, or their failure to comply with the provisions of the plan, if established in this court, will subject them or any one of them to regulation by defendants.

This judgment is binding on the members of the plaintiff tribes as well as on the plaintiff tribes.

Defendants are immune from liability for money damages for their violations of plaintiffs' treaty rights.

Plaintiff Lac Courte Oreilles Band of Lake Superior Chippewa Indians is entitled to actual attorneys' fees and costs for work performed in phase one of this litigation in the amount of $166,722.24, which amount has been paid.

Costs are awarded to plaintiffs and to the defendants and intervening defendants to the extent they are prevailing parties within the meaning of Fed. R. Civ. P. 54(d).

This judgment is without prejudice to applications for additional attorneys' fees for work performed in phase two of the litigation.

The third-party complaint against the third-party defendants United States of America, William Clark, Secretary of the United States Department of the Interior and John Fritz, deputy assistant secretary of Indian Affairs, Bureau of Indian Affairs, is dismissed.

The motion of plaintiff Lac Courte Oreille{s} Band of Lake Superior Chippewa Indians to join the United States of America as an involuntary party plaintiff is denied as untimely.

Approved as to form this 19th day of March, 1991,

Barbara B. Crabb
District Judge

Entered this 19th day of March, 1991,
Joseph W. Skupniewitz, Clerk of Court

Appendix 8

Chippewa Acceptance of Judge Barbara Crabb's Final Judgment

May 20, 1991

TO THE PEOPLE OF WISCONSIN:

The six bands of Lake Superior Chippewa, allied for many years in litigation against the State of Wisconsin in order to confirm and uphold their treaty right to hunt, fish and gather, and now secure in the conviction that they have preserved these rights for the generations to come, have this day foregone their right to further appeal and dispute adverse rulings in this case, including a district court ruling barring them from damages. They do this, knowing that the subject of the latter ruling is currently before the United States Supreme Court, and has been decided in favor of Indian tribes in the Ninth Circuit Court of Appeals and other federal courts. They do this as a gesture of peace and friendship towards the people of Wisconsin, in a spirit they hope may someday be reciprocated on the part of the general citizenry and officials of this state.

GAIASHKIBOS, CHAIRMAN
LAC COURTE OREILLES BAND
OF LAKE SUPERIOR CHIPPEWAS

EUGENE TAYLOR, CHAIRMAN
ST. CROIX CHIPPEWA INDIANS
OF WISCONSIN

PATRICIA R. DePERRY,
CHAIRMAN
RED CLIFF BAND OF LAKE
SUPERIOR CHIPPEWAS

DONALD MOORE, CHAIRMAN
BAD RIVER BAND OF THE LAKE
SUPERIOR TRIBE OF CHIPPEWA
INDIANS

RAYMOND McGESHICK,
CHAIRMAN
SOKAOGON CHIPPEWA INDIAN
COMMUNITY; MOLE LAKE BAND
OF WISCONSIN

MICHAEL W. ALLEN, CHAIRMAN
LAC DU FLAMBEAU BAND OF
LAKE SUPERIOR CHIPPEWA
INDIANS

Appendix 9

State of Wisconsin's Acceptance
of Judge Barbara Crabb's Final Judgment

Statement by Attorney General James E. Doyle, Jr.
Madison, Wisconsin
May 20, 1991, 9:30 A.M.

Sixty days ago, Judge Crabb entered a final order in the treaty rights litigation. The Federal District Court has issued a set of decisions on a variety of issues involving the treaty. Last week, lawyers for the various bands of the Chippewa tribe involved in the litigation informed us that they would not appeal any of the issues, if the State also did not appeal.

After extensive consideration and consultation, Secretary Besadny and I are announcing today that the State will not appeal to the U.S. Court of Appeals for the Seventh Circuit. This means that a long and costly legal battle has been put to rest. It allows us to open a new chapter in state, community and tribal relations.

This case has been fully litigated. Wisconsin and the tribe have been in court for nearly 17 years. Judge Crabb has heard a great deal of testimony and she has issued well-reasoned, comprehensive decisions. The matter has already been to the Seventh Circuit Court of Appeals twice.

This decision has required an extensive legal review of what the state could win or lose through a possible appeal. The D-N-R, as the client agency, in consultation with the lawyers in this office, has concluded that a further appeal of this case would serve no useful purpose, and might jeopardize the gains we have made. And, I concur.

The fundamental question of off-reservation treaty rights has already been decided by the Seventh Circuit Court of Appeals in this litigation. In 1978, my father ruled that the Chippewas' off-reservation rights set out in the treaties of 1837 and 1842 had been extinguished. On appeal, in 1983 the Seventh Circuit said my father's ruling was incorrect and declared that the off-reservation rights were valid. The State asked the U.S. Supreme Court to review that decision and the Supreme Court declined.

I know that many people in Wisconsin hold out hopes that another appeal would produce a different outcome. The general rule of law is that an issue once decided cannot be litigated again. There is no reasonable basis for a belief that the Seventh Circuit, or the Supreme Court, would deviate from this general rule and that the outcome on this basic issue would be any different today.

Our decision was reached after an exceptionally thorough legal review by many lawyers in this department over the last sixty days and extensive consultation with the D-N-R, the Department of Administration and the Governor's Office.

Wisconsin has won many significant victories in this case, all of which would be jeopardized in any appeal. These victories include:

1. The tribe cannot sue the state for past monetary damages . . . A claim the tribe has said is worth over $300 million.

2. The treaties do not extend to the commercial harvest of timber. A contrary ruling would cost the counties of this state millions of dollars annually.

3. The state has the ultimate authority to protect and manage the resources in the ceded territory.

4. Tribal members cannot enter onto privately-owned lands to exercise their rights.

5. Treaty rights do not extend to privately-owned stream beds, river bottoms and overflowed lands.

6. The tribe is not entitled to all the available resources necessary to sustain a modest standard of living. Rather, the resources must be shared on a 50-50 basis.

7. The State can impose on tribal members its boating and safety regulations, even when the Chippewa are engaging in treaty protected activity. Thus, the tribe cannot shine deer or engage in summer deer hunting.

An appeal would put all of these significant victories at risk. And, for those who doubt that, let's remember that the fundamental off-reservation rights were granted on an appeal.

This is an appropriate time to put this case to rest. The people of northern Wisconsin are tired of fighting with each other. They know that we have far more important issues facing us.

Because of outstanding community and tribal cooperation and an excellent job by law enforcement, the 1991 spearfishing season was remarkably quiet. We have had two consecutive years now of improved relations and a real understanding that both sides need to get on with their lives. Rather than spending millions of dollars on law enforcement and attorneys' fees, I think everyone in northern Wisconsin would prefer to support economic development, tourism and education.

I have been impressed with the many ways in which the citizens of northern Wisconsin . . . tribal and non-tribal . . . have been working together to bring about economic development and cultural understanding. The state has a responsibility to support those efforts through words and action.

In my short time as Attorney General, I've made seven trips to northern Wisconsin on this issue. I've seen firsthand community leaders and tribal leaders sitting down together at the same table to talk about how to improve tourism and the economy. I've seen tribal fish hatcheries that are stocking fish in off-reservation lakes for all of us to enjoy. And, I've heard the good people of northern Wisconsin talk frankly about the ugly image that some in the nation have had of our state.

I'm proud of what I've seen and the cooperation in the north convinces me even more that it is time to move on.

The long legal struggle is now over. It is time to recognize, as the Court has, that both sides have rights. The work of the Court is finished. It is now up to the State and all the people of Wisconsin to build on the relationship that we have begun.

Those of us who call Wisconsin home do so because we love the quality of life here. Our natural resources make this state special and the people here are second to none. I know that we still have a lot of work ahead of us. But, I am confident that our children will be much better off for the struggle.

End Notes

1. Chippewa mixed-blood writer William Warren refers to Chippewa lands in Wisconsin and Minnesota as "blood earned country" (1849, 20) due to their "ancient bloody feud" (1850, 95) with the Sioux. For source material on Chippewa-Sioux relations collected by an amateur historian from the Chippewa Valley, see Bartlett (1929, 1-66).

2. For information on the government trading houses, see Peake (1954); Plaisance (1954); Prucha (1984, 1: 115-34); and Viola (1974, 6-70).

3. Jefferson followed a similar approach in the South; see Satz (1981, 9-10).

4. At the Fond du Lac negotiations in 1827, for example, the treaty commissioners collected British medals and flags and gave Indian leaders and others they chose to recognize American flags and medals (Edwards 1826, 460-61, 473-74; Schoolcraft 1851, 245; Viola 1974, 145; Warren 1885, 393). Interpreter William Warren reflected on the incident years later as follows:

> At the treaty of Fond du Lac, the United States commissioners recognized the chiefs of the Ojibways, by distributing medals amongst them, the size of which were in accordance with their degree of rank. Sufficient care was not taken in this rather delicate operation, to carry out the pure civil polity of the tribe. Too much attention was paid to the recommendation of interested traders who wished their best hunters to be rewarded by being made chiefs. One young man named White Fisher, was endowed with a medal, solely for the strikingly mild and pleasant expression of his face. He is now a petty sub-chief on the Upper Mississippi.
>
> From this time may be dated the commencement of innovations which have entirely broken up the civil polity of the Ojibways. (Warren 1885, 393-94)

For a history of the use of peace medals in American Indian diplomacy, see Prucha (1962a; and 1971).

5. Lawrence Taliaferro was appointed at Fort Snelling in 1819, and Henry Rowe Schoolcraft was appointed at Sault Ste. Marie in 1822 (Hill 1974, 162, 166). As late as 1837 Governor Dodge referred to the Wisconsin Chippewas as follows: "They live remote from our military posts, and have but little intercourse with our citizens, and have had no established agent of the Government to reside with them any length of time" (Dodge 1837b, 538).

6. Grant Foreman (1946) has studied the removal of Indians from Ohio, Indiana, and Illinois. I have briefly examined the removal of Indians from the Old Northwest as part of a larger study of Jacksonian Indian policy (1975) and have reviewed the situation in the Old Northwest in more detail as a test case of Jacksonian policy (1976). Useful articles on individual Indian tribes and bands from the Saint Lawrence lowlands and the Great Lakes riverine regions appear in Trigger (1978).

Francis Paul Prucha's account of the removal of the northern Indians during the Jacksonian era unconvincingly argues that the emigration of these tribes was merely a "part of their migration history" and stresses federal paternalism in Indian affairs (Prucha 1984, 1: 243-69). Excellent maps and accompanying text dealing with the removal of the Indians from the Great Lakes region appear in Tanner (1987). For a recent analysis of the contrast between the rhetoric and reality of Jacksonian Indian policy that includes references to Wisconsin, see Satz (1991).

7. In 1911, the *Iowa Journal of History and Politics* reprinted a version of the treaty proceedings that originally appeared in volume 1, numbers 11 and 14 of the Dubuque *Iowa News* (1837, 408-28). The 1911 publication, however, is not a verbatim reproduction of the original handwritten copy (Van Antwerp 1837) on file in the National Archives and Records Service, which was utilized in this study (see Appendix 1).

8. The sutlers were civilian businessmen appointed by the War Department to sell items not furnished soldiers by the subsistence or quartermaster departments.

9. The First Infantry arrived in Florida in November of 1837 and departed on August 4, 1841. For information on the Seminole Indian War and the role of the First Infantry, see Mahon (1985).

10. For an example of one effort to open a mill along the Chippewa River in 1836, see Dousman (1836); Stambaugh (1836); Chippewa Chiefs ({1836}); Harris (1836); and Young and Robinson (1838).

11. References to documents included in the Appendices are highlighted in italics immediately after the related text. Frame numbers are provided instead of page numbers for items on microfilm.

12. Anthropologist James A. Clifton contends La Trappe's comments indicate the willingness of the Pillager and other Minnesota bands to sell the pinelands in Wisconsin, which were useless to them, while reserving from sale the deciduous forests. In addition, Clifton views later efforts of the Chippewas to clarify the meaning of La Trappe's words as evidence the Pillagers had inserted the qualification into the official record in order to be able to later "dodge undesirable ramifications of the agreement or to reopen negotiations" (Clifton 1987, 12).

13. The mixed-blood population among the Chippewas and other Wisconsin Indians never emerged as so socially cohesive a group as the Metis of central Canada. White traders not only seemed to prefer mixed-blood wives but they also took steps to educate and employ their children (Kay 1977, 329). On the significance of the mixed-bloods among the Chippewas, also see Brunson (1843a).

14. The document has recently been published with editorial notes and an historical introduction by a Canadian linguist; see Nichols (1988).

15. Governor Henry Dodge referred to William Warren as a man with "much influence" over the Chippewas who was "well qualified" to serve as an interpreter

(Dodge 1847b, 1086). A knowledgeable St. Paul trader referred to Warren as "the only correct interpreter in the Chippewa nation" (Rice 1847). For additional information on Warren, see Babcock (1946).

16. On the value of oral traditions in understanding the past, see Buffalohead (1984, xiv).

17. Strickland, Herzberg, and Owens (1990, 7 n. 13) define this term as follows: "A usufructuary right is the right of a person (or group) to enjoy, use, or harvest something to which that person does not have actual title. This principle is an established part of anglo-American law and is not limited to the treaty-rights sphere. Any person (or group) may reserve a usufructuary right in property they sell or give to another. This usufructuary right is then protected under property and contract law principles. For example, any landowner is able to convey a piece of land and lake to another, but provide in the sales contract that the seller and his heirs will be able to fish in the lake forever. If this is done, under contract and property law principles the seller may use the courts to enforce the promise made between the parties at the time of sale."

18. For information on Copway, see Smith (1988).

19. For information on the origins and use of the annuity system by federal officials as a means of social control, see Satz (1975, 104-05, 134, 143, 145, 222, 230, 246-48, 276-77, 279 n. 3, 293).

20. Historian Paul W. Gates claims that prior to the 1837 Chippewa Treaty, "the government was well ahead of the land buyers in the negotiations for Indian cessions, the surveying of the ceded lands, and the public offering of the lands" in Wisconsin. By September 30, 1836, Indian title had been surrendered to 18,512,437 acres, surveys completed on 8,679,605 acres; some 4,807,307 acres had been offered for public sale, and the government had sold 1,5051,921 acres (1969, 306 n. 1).

21. There are conflicting opinions on the extent of forest cover and deer population densities in early northern Wisconsin; compare Habeck and Curtis (1959), with Schorger (1953).

22. In 1840 Wisconsin territorial delegate John Doty informed Congress: "The Territory of Wiskonsan has as many lakes within her borders as the Empire State, and bids fair, from her fine forests, her copper, her lead, her iron, her zinc, her incomparable fish, her fertile soil, and, above all, her proverbially salubrious climate, to at least equal any other portion of the republic" (Doty 1840, 5).

23. In 1862, a committee of the U. S. Senate reported that the copper region acquired in 1842 contained "the richest and most extensive deposits of that metal yet discovered in the world." See U. S. Senate Committee on Military Affairs and the Militia (1862, 3). For an interesting account of excavations of early sites and illustrations of artifacts found, see Griffin (1961).

24. The worship of copper by the Lake Superior Chippewas attracted the notice of many white visitors from the 1600s to the 1800s. For an interesting account of religious ideas about copper held by the Chippewas and the impact of those ideas on the life of a member of the Ontonagon Band, see Peters (1989).

25. Kemble's factory, the West Point Foundry Association chartered in 1818 opposite West Point on the Hudson River, became so successful in the manufacture of military weapons that it received the special patronage of the federal government (Schulze 1933, 317).

26. The American Board of Commissioners for Foreign Missions was a Boston-centered missionary society comprised largely of Congregationalists and Presbyterians. The Board supported more Indian missionaries in the period between the War of 1812 and the Civil War than any other Protestant missionary society. For additional information, see Phillips (1954); and Berkhoffer (1965).

27. Although Armstrong's reminiscences contain some factual errors, his comments about the 1842 promise of continued usufructuary rights based on good behavior is supported by statements from contemporaries, as noted above. Also see U. S. District Court (1978, 1323 n. 1, 1327). For rebuttals of Clifton's arguments by Wisconsin Attorney General Don Hanaway and by University of Wisconsin-Stevens Point history professor David Wrone, see respectively *Eau Claire Leader-Telegram* (1988b, c).

28. In writing about what the Chippewas thought of the Treaty of 1842, historian Mark Keller erroneously claims that ''there is no mention of dissatisfaction with the terms of the eventual pact in government records. This is not unusual, for what few government records exist were made by government employees, and none mention the negotiations'' (Keller 1981, 10).

29. Anthropologist James Clifton cites Martin's letter to support a statement in his text concerning Stuart's promise that the Chippewas would not have to leave for a very long time (Clifton 1987, 36 n. 43), but he then ignores the letter when he attacks Armstrong's credibility (Clifton 1987, 36 n. 44). Armstrong's point is precisely that made by Martin in 1842, so there is indeed ''independent'' contemporaneous evidence to support Armstrong's claim. Other examples are cited in the text.

30. For information on Black Bird, see Morse (1857, 344-49).

31. In his memoirs, Brunson speaks of his ''resigning'' from office due to ''intimations'' that he refused to be a party to a ''palpable fraud'' Stuart committed by claiming Indians not party to the treaty had agreed to its terms (Brunson 1872-79, 2: 206-07).

32. In 1849, Commissioner of Indian Affairs Orlando Brown referred to the Sioux in Minnesota as ''a wild and untamable people'' who were ''the most restless, reckless, and mischievous Indians of the Northwest; their passion for war and the

chase seems unlimited and unassuageable; and so long as they remain where they are, they must be a source of constant annoyance and danger to our citizens, as well as to the Indians of our northern colony, between some of whom (the Chippewas) and themselves there exists a hereditary feud, frequently leading to collisions and bloodshed, which disturbs the peace and tranquility of the frontier, and must greatly interfere with the welfare of the Indians of that colony, and with the efforts of the government to effect their civilization'' (1849, 944).

33. See Satz (1975; 1976; 1979a; 1987; and 1989).

34. The congressional report of the Chippewa agent refers to Pahpogohmony as the seventh location. As a result of conversations with Helen Hornbeck Tanner, editor of the *Atlas of Great Lakes Indian History* (1987) and Chippewa scholar Richard St. Germaine, I have determined that Pahpogohmony is most likely a mistranslation of Pequaming.

35. There has been some confusion concerning the publication of this order. Legal scholars Rennard Strickland and Stephen J. Herzberg and law student Steven R. Owens, who mistakenly attribute the order to President Millard Fillmore, claim it was never published and that it is only available through the National Archives and Records Service in Washington (Strickland 1990, 4 n. 5). The document is available in published form (see *Fig. 18*). In 1941, attorney Charles J. Kappler included the order in his published compendium of Indian laws under a section entitled ''Executive Orders Relating to Indian Reservations,'' where it appears under the heading ''Minnesota'' (5: 663) apparently because the order was issued in response to a request from Minnesota Territorial officials as noted in Chapter 4.

36. Luke Lea (1810-1898) had no prior experience in Indian affairs. He should not be confused with his uncle, the elder Luke Lea (1783-1851), who was an Indian agent at Fort Leavenworth from August 1849 until June 1851 (Trennert 1979; Hill 1974, 67).

37. For information on Copway, see Smith (1988).

38. Reports on the mortality at Sandy Lake vary from seventy to nearly two hundred (Hall 1850b; Clifton 1987, 25). A report from the *Lake Superior News and Mining Journal* reprinted in the East asserted that ''hundreds'' died during the winter of 1850-1851 ''in the miserable region to which the Government would remove them'' (*New York Times* 1851a).

39. Watrous was eventually removed from public office for political reasons rather than for his conduct as Indian agent (Hall 1853; Clifton 1987, 38 n. 76).

40. The St. Croix and Mole Lake Bands were not provided reservations in the 1854 treaty. Not until the mid-1930s did the federal government recognize these bands and set aside land for them in northern Wisconsin (Lurie 1987, 21; Danziger 1979, 153-55).

41. Manypenny, who served as Commissioner of Indian Affairs when the 1854 treaty was negotiated, later rebuked federal removal efforts. His words, while general in nature, seem relevant to the abortive efforts to remove the Chippewa that preceded the establishment of the Chippewa reservations: "In numberless instances removals have been brought about, not because there was a necessity for them, but with a view to the plunder and profit that was expected to result from the operation" (Manypenny 1880, 134).

42. In passing the Indian Appropriations Bill for 1871-72 in March of 1871, members of the U. S. House of Representatives demonstrated their general disillusionment with the administration of Indian affairs and their jealousy of the Senate's role in ratifying treaties by attaching the following rider to a sentence providing funds for the Yankton Tribe of Sioux Indians, "*Provided,* That hereafter no Indian nation or tribe within the territory of the United States shall be acknowledged or recognized as an independent nation, tribe, or power with whom the United States may contract by treaty: *Provided, further,* That nothing herein contained shall be construed to invalidate or impair the obligation of any treaty heretofore lawfully made and ratified with any such Indian nation or tribe" (U. S. Congress 1871, 566; Priest 1942, 96-102, 244; Prucha 1984, 1: 531-33). The United States continued to deal with Indian governments through agreements (requiring House *and* Senate approval), statutes, and executive orders, which recognized rights and liabilities virtually identical to those established by treaties before 1871 (Cohen 1982, 107, 127-28). In 1924, when Congress made all Indians citizens of the United States, it again preserved their rights as tribal citizens (U. S. Congress 1924, 253).

43. The contract with William Rust of Eau Claire was renegotiated in 1873 because a counter offer had raised public questions about the terms (Kinney 1937, 255; Shifferd 1976, 22).

44. The petition was presented to Indian Commissioner William P. Dole who logged it with the notation "the same old chronic complaint" and then returned the document to the delegation (Draper {1882}). A subsequent visit by the delegation to U. S. Senator James R. Doolittle of Wisconsin also failed to bring results (Warren 1882).

45. The Wisconsin Supreme Court based its decision on evidence that President Taylor had issued a Removal Order in 1850. According to the Court:

> . . . There was offered and received in evidence that which was certified to be a copy of an executive order of removal purporting to be signed by President Taylor February 6, 1850.
> We find no grounds upon which the validity of such a document or its competency as evidence can properly be questioned. That it evidently was not presented and offered in evidence in the two {U. S. Supreme Court} cases just above quoted cannot detract from its validity now when offered and properly received. What was said by way of recital in those two cases . . . must of course extend no further than the facts presented in each. We must therefore hold that any form of title to this land then possessed by them . . . was ceded by the Indians under the treaty of 1842-43, and their right of occupancy, so far as it would interfere with the lawful occupancy of those claiming by patent from the

United States is concerned, was terminated upon said executive order of 1850. (Wisconsin Supreme Court 1927, 474)

For the details of this case involving the effort of two children and a grandson of a member of the Fond du Lac Band to recover possession of Wisconsin Point—a narrow, sandy peninsula extending northeasterly from the City of Superior in Douglas County into Lake Superior long occupied by members of the band and visited during the summer months by white campers—see Wisconsin Supreme Court (1927).

46. The actual title of the forty-eight-page Wheeler-Howard Bill was "A bill to grant to Indians living under Federal tutelage the freedom to organize for the purposes of local self-government and economic enterprise; to provide for the necessary training of Indians in administrative and economic affairs; to conserve and develop Indian lands; and to promote the more effective administration of justice in matters affecting Indian tribes and communities by establishing a federal Court of Indian Affairs" (Prucha 1984, 2: 957). Congress approved a weakened version known as the Indian Reorganization Act in 1934. Hailed by its supporters as the Indian Magna Charta, its adoption marked the climax of a bitter contest waged throughout the 1920s between what one scholar calls "Indian protectors and reformers" led by John Collier and Gertrude Bonnin and "obscurantists and exploiters" led by Albert B. Fall and Charles H. Burke (Gibson 1980, 529). For additional information, see Hertzberg (1971, 179-209); Philp (1977, 1-160); Prucha (1984, 2: 940-68). On the Indian congresses convened by Commissioner of Indian Affairs Collier and Indian opinion on the Wheeler-Howard Bill, see Philp (1977, 145-56); Prucha (1984, 2: 955-61); Deloria and Lytle (1984, 101-21).

47. On the rise of Indian activism as a social movement, see Day (1972).

48. The importance of the media during the events at Wounded Knee in 1973 was noted and criticized in *Time* (1973); D. Smith (1973); and in Schultz (1973). For an example of how the media's frame of reference sometimes impedes the recording of reality and actually helps to create events, see Landsman (1988).

49. Northern States Power (NSP) had not fulfilled the original terms of its fifty-year lease, which required the removal of Indian graves and homes when the dam was built in 1921. By 1924, NSP had flooded nearly fifteen thousand acres of federal land comprising the Chippewa Flowage, including sixteen thousand acres of Chippewa land on the Lac Courte Oreilles Reservation. Under NSP's control, the fluctuating water level of the flowage destroyed three Indian wild rice beds that had previously supplied food and significant amounts of income, and threatened the Chippewa communal economy of hunting, fishing, and wild rice gathering in other ways as well (Lurie 1987, 55-56). At the 1989 annual meeting of the Economic and Business History Society, historian James Oberly argued, "nearly seven decades . . . {after NSP received the original lease}, there is strong feeling among the LCO Chippewa that what took place in 1921 and after was truly the crime of the century" (1989a, 13).

50. The Warriors had claimed the vacant property for the Menominee tribe to use as a hospital. They apparently drew their inspiration from the take-over of the

Bureau of Indian Affairs in Washington and the Wounded Knee confrontation in South Dakota. The incident ended only after Governor Patrick J. Lucey deployed the Wisconsin National Guard (Lurie 1987, 54-55).

51. The Chippewas did not seek the broader right of engaging in usufructuary activities on privately owned land (U. S Court of Appeals 1983, 365 n. 14).

52. In numbering the Chippewa court cases, I am following Bichler (1990a).

53. At the time of the nineteenth century treaties, the Chippewas had long engaged in commercial activities and had long served, to use Judge Doyle's words, as "participants in an international market economy." As Doyle observed, "commercial activity was a major factor in Chippewa subsistence." Indeed, "the Chippewa were aware of the principles of the Euro-American market economy. They understood competition and the ramifications of the fluctuations of supply and demand, as well as the value of tangible goods and services." Although the Chippewas were "clearly engaged in commerce throughout the treaty era," they "developed an economic strategy that incorporated both their traditional economy and the market economy in such a way that they were able, on the one hand, to transact business with non-Indians who were participating in the Euro-American market economy and, on the other, to transact social and political relations with one another in the traditional manner" (U. S. District Court 1987, 1428-30).

54. After Judge Crabb's white-tailed deer ruling of May 9, 1990, there was uncertainty as to whether the Chippewas were still entitled to the entire safe harvest or whether the fifty-fifty split for deer also referred to other resources such as fish (Bichler 1990b). For Crabb's Final Judgment, see Appendix 7.

55. The Eleventh Amendment, ratified in 1798, provides that "the judicial power of the United States shall not be construed to extend to any suit in law or equity, commenced or prosecuted against one of the United States by Citizens of another State, or by Citizens or Subjects of any Foreign State."

56. The agreements have been made on the basis of biological assessments obtained from both the state and tribal biologists (Great Lakes Indian Fish and Wildlife Commission {c. 1988}, 2). Judge Barbara Crabb observed in 1989:

> The department {Department of Natural Resources} has negotiated a number of interim agreements with the tribes covering the harvesting not only of walleye and muskellunge, but other species of fish, deer, small game, migratory birds, bear, and wild rice. Its wardens, along with other state and local law enforcement officers, and GLIFWC {Great Lakes Indian Fish and Wildlife Commission} personnel, have monitored the agreements to ensure that Indian hunters and fishers have been able to implement their treaty rights. The department has done this in the face of intense opposition from individuals and groups opposed to the recognition and implementation of Indian treaty rights, with only the most modest amount of federal assistance in the form of funding for some assessment projects.
>
> It is to the tribes' credit that they have adopted an equally cooperative attitude toward the implementation of their rights. It has not been an easy time for them, either. The tribes and their members have been subjected to physical and verbal abuse over the

recognition of their treaty rights, most publicly when they have attempted to exercise their treaty rights to spearfish, but not only then. Harassment has become a way of life for them.

Tribal members have negotiated and entered into a series of interim agreements with the state that have circumscribed their rights to accommodate state concerns, despite their understandable impatience to reap the benefits of treaty rights that they have been forced to forgo for so many years.

Each tribe has joined the Great Lakes Indian Fish and Wildlife Commission; each plaintiff tribe is also a member of the Voigt Inter-Tribal Task Force. GLIFWC has hired trained fisheries biologists who participate in the State-Tribal Technical Working and Biological Issues Groups that have produced the working papers and biological issues stipulations so helpful to the court, to treaty rights negotiators, and to fisheries managers. GLIFWC wardens have participated with DNR wardens and other state and local law enforcement officers in the monitoring and enforcement of the tribal fishing efforts under the interim agreements.

Both the tribes and the officials of the State of Wisconsin responsible for implementing the tribes' treaty rights can take pride in their accomplishments over the last six years. They deserve widespread recognition and appreciation for their efforts. (U. S. District Court 1989, 1053-054)

57. For additional information, see "Fishing in Western Washington—A Treaty Right, A Clash of Cultures" in U. S. Commission on Civil Rights (1981, 61-100).

58. For evidence of the ideological connection between these organizations, see Equal Rights for Everyone (1984). In early 1991, STA attorney Fred Hatch of Sayner was retained as legal counsel by PARR as that organization began advance preparations for night protest rallies at boat landings in the spring. The official PARR newspaper recently stated, "although PARR and STA may march to a different drummer, they are still marching down the same road, at the end of which, we all hope, is equality for everyone" (*PARR Issue* 1991a, b, i).

59. Both Dane County Board Chairman Richard Wagner and Dane County Executive Richard Phelps announced they favored ending their county's membership in the Wisconsin Counties Association as a result of its handling of the Salt Lake City conference. Wagner protested, "it's inappropriate for any action to be taken to exclude Wisconsin officials whether they are Indians or not." See *Milwaukee Sentinel* (1990c).

60. For a comparison of La Follette and McCarthy, see Thompson (1988, 601). On Wisconsin's handling of the fugitive slave law issue, see Clark (1955), Campbell (1972, 53-54, 157-61, 176-77), and Current (1976, 147-48, 208-09, 219-21). Race relations in Wisconsin between 1940 and 1965 is treated in Thompson (1988, 305-400).

Bibliography and Sources Cited

Every effort has been made to provide as much information as possible for each citation listed below. References to articles from the Collection of Chippewa Hunting and Fishing Rights Newspaper Clippings in the Government Publications Department at the McIntyre Library of the University of Wisconsin-Eau Claire are cited as *UW-Eau Claire Clippings* for brevity. Page numbers from the clippings are provided when available. A plus sign (+) after a page number means that the article continues on another unnumbered page in the clippings file. (These clippings are also available at the State of Wisconsin Legislative Reference Bureau in Madison.) Also for brevity, references to documents contained in John Porter Bloom, comp. and ed., *The Territorial Papers of the United States,* Vol. 27: *The Territory of Wisconsin: Executive Journal, 1836-1848; Papers, 1836-1839* (Washington, D.C.: Government Printing Office, 1969) and Vol. 28: *The Territory of Wisconsin 1839-1848* (Washington, D.C.: National Archives and Records Service, 1975) are cited, respectively, as *Territorial Papers,* Vol. 27 and *Territorial Papers,* Vol. 28.

Ad Hoc Commission on Racism in Wisconsin.

1984 *Final Report, Wisconsin's Educational Imperative: Observations and Recommendations—Indian-White Relations.* Hayward: Lac Courte Oreilles Band of Lake Superior Chippewa Indians. (Depositories for the report include the Lac Courte Oreilles Ojibwa Community College, the Wisconsin Indian Resource Council, the Governor's Office, and the University of Wisconsin-Eau Claire School of Arts and Sciences Outreach Office. The report was reprinted in a special edition of the *Lac Courte Oreilles Journal* in January of 1985.)

Allen, Paula Gunn.

1986 *The Sacred Hoop: Recovering the Feminine in American Indian Traditions.* Boston: Beacon Press.

Anderson, Kenneth C.

1990 "The Chippewa Treaties—Federal Indian Policy," *Vilas-Forest County Landowner's Newsletter* (January-March): 2-8.

Appleton Post-Crescent.

1989 "State-Indian Resources Pact Studied." October 22. *UW-Eau Claire Clippings.*

Armstrong, Benjamin G.

1892 *Early Life Among the Indians: Reminiscences from the Life of Benj. G. Armstrong, Treaties of 1835, 1837, 1842, and 1854: Habits and Customs of the Red Men of the Forest: Incidents, Biographical Sketches, Battles, &c.* Dictated to and written by Thomas P. Wentworth. Ashland, Wis.: Press of A. W. Bowron.

{1892} "Reminiscences of Life Among the Chippewas," ed. William Converse Haygood. *Wisconsin Magazine of History,* 55 (Spring 1972): 175-96; 55 (Summer 1972): 287-309; 56 (Autumn 1972): 37-58; 56 (Winter 1972-73): 140-61.

Ashland Daily Press.

1986   "Thompson: 'Spearing is Wrong, Period.'" November 1, p. 1.

Axtell, James.

1986   *The Invasion Within: The Contest of Cultures in Colonial North America.* New
          York: Oxford University Paperbacks.

Babcock, Willoughby M., Jr.

1924   "Major Lawrence Taliafero, Indian Agent." *Mississippi Valley Historical Review*
          11 (December): 358-75.

1946   "William Warren and His Chippewa Writings," *Minnesota Archaeologist* 12
          (July): 40-42.

Bad River Tribal Council.

1959   A Declaration of War, November 10. *Department of Natural Resources Records.*
          Record Series 27, Box 419, Folder 4, Archives Division, State Historical Society
          of Wisconsin, Madison.

Bailly, Alexis.

1836   Letter to Delegate G{eorge} W. Jones, April 15. *Territorial Papers,* Vol. 27, pp.
          38-41.

Baker, Benjamin F.

1838   Letter to the Secretary of War, November 3. Office of Indian Affairs, *Letters
          Received, La Pointe Agency,* Microcopy 234, Roll 387, Record Group 75. Wash-
          ington, D.C.: National Archives and Records Service.

Bald, F. Clever.

1961   *Michigan in Four Centuries.* rev. and enlarged ed. New York: Harper & Row,
          Publishers.

Barron County Chronotype (Rice Lake, Wis.)

1878   "The Indian Scare in Wisconsin." June 27, p. 2, quoting the *St Paul Pioneer
          Press.*

Barsh, Russel Lawrence, and James Youngblood Henderson.

1980   *The Road: Indian Tribes and Political Liberty.* Berkeley: University of California
          Press.

Bartlett, William W.

1921   "Jean Brunet, Chippewa Valley Pioneer." *Wisconsin Magazine of History* 5 (1):
          33-42.

1929 *History, Tradition and Adventure in the Chippewa Valley*. Chippewa Falls: Chippewa Printery.

Berkhofer, Robert F., Jr.

1965 *Salvation and the Savage: An Analysis of Protestant Missions and American Indian Response, 1787-1862*. Lexington: University of Kentucky Press.

Besadny, C. D. "Buzz".

1989 "Excerpt from a Speech to the Wisconsin Conservation Congress." *DNR Digest* (July/August): 6-7.

Bichler, Howard J.

1990a "Three Perspectives on the Existence and Scope of the Chippewa Treaty Rights: St. Croix Chippewa Indians of Wisconsin and Lac du Flambeau Band of Chippewa." *State Bar of Wisconsin Mid-Winter Convention Program* 2 (January 17-19): 251-56.

1990b Letter to Ronald N. Satz, November 13. In possession of author.

Black Bird.

1869 Speech Made in Council at Bad River, September 12. Office of Indian Affairs, *Letters Received, La Pointe Agency*, Microcopy 234, Roll 394. Washington, D.C.: National Archives and Records Service.

Boeth, Richard, Jeff B. Copeland, Mary Hager, and Phyllis Malamud.

1978 "A Paleface Uprising," *Newsweek* (April 10): 39-40.

Boutwell, William T.

1837 Letter to Rev{erend} David Green, August 17. *American Board of Commissioners for Foreign Missions Papers*, Box 2. Minnesota Historical Society, St. Paul. Transcript of original in Houghton Library, Harvard University, Cambridge, Mass.

Bremer, Richard G.

1987 *Indian Agent and Wilderness Scholar: The Life of Henry Rowe Schoolcraft*. Mount Pleasant: Clarke Historical Library, Central Michigan University.

Bromley, Daniel W., and Basil M. H. Sharp.

1990 "Bicultural Treaties, Endowments, and de facto Property Rights: Concepts, Language, and Power." Unpublished paper. Department of Agricultural Economics, University of Wisconsin-Madison and Department of Economics, University of Auckland. September. (Photocopy courtesy of D. Bromley.)

Brophy, William A., and Sophie D. Aberle, comps.

1966   *The Indian, America's Unfinished Business: Report of the Commission on the Rights, Liberties, and Responsibilities of the American Indian.* Norman: University of Oklahoma Press.

Brown, Orlando.

1849   Annual Report of the Commissioner of Indian Affairs, November 30. U. S. Congress, *Senate Executive Document 1.* 31st Cong., 1st sess., *Serial 550,* pp. 937-58.

Brown, Ray A.

1930   "The Indian Problem and the Law." *Yale Law Journal* 39 (January): 307-31.

Brunson, Alfred.

1843a   Proceedings of a Council at La Pointe, January 5. Enclosed in letter cited below.

1843b   Letter to James D. Doty, January 6. Enclosed in Alfred Brunson to Secretary of War J{ohn} C. Spencer, January 8, 1843. Office of Indian Affairs, *Letters Received, La Pointe Agency,* Microcopy 234, Roll 388, Record Group 75. Washington: National Archives and Records Service.

1843c   Letter to Governor James D. Doty, July 19. Office of Indian Affairs, *Letters Received, La Pointe Agency,* Microcopy 234, Roll 388, Record Group 75. Washington: National Archives and Records service.

1872-79   *A Western Pioneer: Or, Incidents of the Life and Times of Rev. Alfred Brunson, A.M., D.D., Embracing a Period of Over Seventy Years, Written by Himself.* 2 vols. Cincinnati: Hitchcock and Walden.

Bryant, Ed{ward} E.

1878   Letter to Governor William E. Smith. July 10. Reprinted in *Wisconsin State Journal* (Madison), July 10, 1878, p. 1.

Buffalo, {Chief}.

1837   Speech to Subagent Daniel P. Bushnell, December 10. Enclosed in Superintendent of Indian Affairs Henry Dodge to Commissioner of Indian Affairs C{arey} A. Harris, February 19, 1838. Office of Indian Affairs, *Letters Sent, La Pointe Agency,* Microcopy 234, Roll 387, Record Group 75. Washington: National Archives and Records Service.

1842   Speech to Subagent Alfred Brunson, October 29. Enclosed in Brunson to Governor James D. Doty, January 8, 1843. Office of Indian Affairs, *Letters Received, La Pointe Agency,* Microcopy 234, Roll 388, Record Group 75. Washington: National Archives and Records Service.

Buffalo, {Chief}, Chiefs, and Head Men of the Chippeway Tribe of Indians of Lake Superior.

1851   Petition to Commissioner of Indian Affairs Luke Lea. November 6. *Indian Office Files,* 1852, No. 70, Archives Division, State Historical Society of Wisconsin,

Madison. (Reprinted in Benjamin G. Armstrong, ''Reminiscences of Life Among the Chippewa,'' ed. William Converse Haygood. *Wisconsin Magazine of History* 55 [Summer 1972]: 290-92).

Buffalo, {Chief}, Chiefs, Head Men, and Warriors of Lake Superior.

1852   Memorial to President Millard Fillmore, June 12. Office of Indian Affairs, *Letters Received, Chippewa Agency,* Microcopy 234, Roll 149, Record Group 75. Washington: National Archives and Records Service.

Buffalohead, W. Roger.

1984   ''Introduction,'' to William Warren, *History of the Ojibwa People.* St. Paul: Borealis Books, Minnesota Historical Society Press, 1984, pp. ix-xvii.

Bush, George.

1989   Inaugural Address, January 20. U. S. Congress, *Senate Document 101-10,* 101st Cong., 1 sess., *Serial 13914,* pp. 345-50.

Bushnell, Daniel P.

1839a   Letter to Governor Henry Dodge, February 13. *Territorial Papers,* Vol. 27, pp. 1196-197.

1839b   Report of Subagent at La Pointe, August 24. U. S. Congress, *Senate Document 1.* 26 Cong., 1 sess., *Serial 354,* pp. 488-89.

1840a   Letter to Governor Henry Dodge, July 15, 1840. *Territorial Papers,* Vol. 28, pp. 207-09.

{1840b}   Extract from the Report of the Sub-Agent at La Pointe, {Fall}. U. S. Congress, *Senate Document 1.* 26th Cong., 2d sess., *Serial 375,* pp. 339-40.

Busiahn, Thomas.

1989a   *Biological Impact of the Chippewa Off-Reservation Treaty Harvest, 1983-1989.* Odanah, Wis.: Great Lakes Indian Fish and Wildlife Commission.

1989b   ''Fisheries Co-Management: A Response to Legal, Social and Fiscal Imperatives.'' *Fisheries Co-Management: Symposium Sponsored by the Native Peoples' Fisheries Committee at the 117th Annual Meeting,* ed. Bruce L. Smith and Pamela Burt. Odanah, Wis.: Great Lakes Indian Fish and Wildlife Commission, pp. 1-6.

Busiahn, Thomas, Neil Kmiecik, Jim Thannum, and Jim Zorn.

1989   *1989 Chippewa Spearing Season—Separating Myth from Fact.* Odanah, Wis.: Great Lakes Indian Fish and Wildlife Commission.

Campbell, S. W.

1898   Report of La Pointe Agency, August 18. U. S. Congress, *House Document 5,* 55th Cong., 3d sess., *Serial 3757,* pp. 314-20.

Campbell, Stanley.

1972   *The Slave Catchers: Enforcement of the Fugitive Slave Law, 1850-1860.* New York: Norton Library Paperbacks.

Capital Times (Madison).

1972   "High Court Rules Indians Not Bound by Fishing Law." January 7. *UW-Eau Claire Clippings.*

1973   "State Indians, Beware!" May 17. *UW-Eau Claire Clippings.*

1974   "Indian Suit Cites Treaty in Support of Rights." September 6. *UW-Eau Claire Clippings.*

1986a   "Violence Could Arise Between Chippewas, Whites, FBI Warns." April 10. *UW-Eau Claire Clippings.*

1986b   "Spear Fishing is Symbol of Tradition—and Change." April 24, pp. 25, 30.

1989a   "If More People Knew Indians' History, Maybe They Would Understand." May 2. *UW-Eau Claire Clippings.*

1989b   "Governor Thwarted; Crabb OKs Continued Spearing; State to Appeal." May 6. *UW-Eau Claire Clippings.*

1989c   "More News on the Spearfishing Front." May 6. *UW-Eau Claire Clippings.*

1989d   "Hanaway Sets Proper Tone on Treaties." June 1. *UW-Eau Claire Clippings.*

1989e   "Spearing Effect Deflated." October 12, p. 25.

1990a   "County Reps Seek Policy on Indian Claims." January 2. *UW-Eau Claire Clippings.*

1990b   "Inouye Riding to Rescue State from its Rednecks." March 9. *UW-Eau Claire Clippings.*

{Cass, Lewis}.

1830   "Removal of the Indians: Documents and Proceedings Relating to the Formation and Progress of a Board in the City of New York, for the Emigration, Preservation, and Improvement of the Aborigines of America." *North American Review* 30 (January): 62-121.

Chicago Tribune.

1987   "It's Happy Hunting for Indians." March 1, Section 1, p. 10+, *UW-Eau Claire Clippings.*

Chippewa Chiefs.

{1836}   Petition to President {Andrew Jackson}, {May 10}. *Territorial Papers,* Vol. 27, pp. 53-55.

1843   Petition for the Restoration of the Farm & Shop to Chippewa Falls, September 12. Enclosed in Alfred Brunson to John D. Doty, September 30, 1843. Office of Indian Affairs, *Letters Received, La Pointe Agency,* Microcopy 234, Roll 388, Record Group 75. Washington, D.C.: National Archives and Records Service.

Chippewas of Lake Superior.

1864   Statement of the Treaties Between the Chippewas and the United States, from 1825 to 1864, from the Chippewa Standpoint, as Presented to the Commissioner of Indian Affairs. *Small Collections-Oversize,* File 40, Archives Division, State Historical Society of Wisconsin, Madison.

Christian Science Monitor.

1987   "Indian Treaty Rights Under Attack." September 8, pp. 1, 6.

1990   "Legal Uprising Over Indians." January 22, pp. 1, 2.

Citizens of Lake Superior.

1852   Petition to President Millard Fillmore, June 4. Office of Indian Affairs, *Letters Received, Chippewa Agency,* Microcopy 234, Roll 149, Record Group 75. Washington, D.C.: National Archives and Records Service.

Citizens of the Pineries.

{1840}   Memorial to Congress, {January 1}. *Territorial Papers,* Vol. 28, pp. 105-06.

Clark, James I.

1955   *Wisconsin Defies the Fugitive Slave Law: The Case of Sherman M. Booth.* Madison: State Historical Society of Wisconsin.

Cleland, Charles.

1985   "Testimony." *Stenographic Transcript by U. S. District Court Official Court Reporter of the Court Trial of Lac Courte Oreilles Band of Lake Superior Chippewa Indians et al. vs. State of Wisconsin.* Madison, Wis. Vol 3. Third Day, December 11. (Photocopy courtesy of attorney Howard Bichler.)

Clifton, James A.

1987   "Wisconsin Death March: Explaining the Extremes in Old Northwest Indian Removal." *Transactions of the Wisconsin Academy of Sciences, Arts and Letters* 75: 1-39.

Cohen, Felix S.

1953   "The Erosion of Indian Rights, 1950-1953: A Case Study in Bureaucracy." *Yale Law Journal* 62 (February): 348-90.

1982   *Handbook of Federal Indian Law.* Ed. Rennard Strickland *et al.* 1942; Rev. ed. Charlottesville, Va.: Michie/Bobbs-Merrill.

Continental Congress.

1787 Northwest Ordinance. July 13. Reprinted in Francis Paul Prucha, ed. *Documents of United States Indian Policy*. 2nd ed., expanded. Lincoln: University of Nebraska Press, 1990. 9-10.

Cooper, John, and Doug Stange.

1990 "Indian Rights—Indian Wrongs?" *In-Fisherman* (February): 42-54.

Copway, George.

1847 *The Life, History, and Travels of Kah-Ge-Ga-Gah-Bowh, (George Copway) . . . Written by Himself.* 6th ed. Philadelphia: James Harmstead.

1856 Letter to Editor, September 5. *New York Times,* September 8, pp. 3.

Copway's American Indian.

1851 "An Account of the Operation of the A.B.C.C.F.M. {*sic*} Among the North American Indians: Removal of the Indians." 1 (July 26): 1.

Cornell, Stephen.

1986 "The New Indian Politics." *Wilson Quarterly* (New Year's): 113-31.

Crawford, T. Hartley.

1842 Report of the Commissioner of Indian Affairs, November 16. U. S. Congress, *Senate Document 1*. 27th Cong., 3d sess., *Serial 413,* pp. 377-88.

1843 Letter to Alfred Brunson, April 3. Records of the Department of the Interior, Bureau of Indian Affairs, Part 9: *Territorial Papers of the United States, The Territory of Wisconsin, 1836-1848, Supplement.* Microcopy 236, Roll 44. Washington, D.C.: National Archives and Records Service.

Cunningham, Walter.

1844 Letter from Special Agent for Lake Superior Copper Mines to Secretary of War William Wilkins, April 11. *Territorial Papers,* Vol. 28, pp. 676-78.

Current, Richard N.

1976 *The History of Wisconsin,* Vol. 2: *The Civil War Era, 1848-1873,* ed. William F. Thompson. Madison: State Historical Society of Wisconsin.

Danziger, Edmund J., Jr.

1973 "They Would Not Be Moved: The Chippewa Treaty of 1854." *Minnesota History* 43 (Spring): 175-85.

1979 *The Chippewas of Lake Superior.* Norman: University of Oklahoma Press.

Day, David.

1873   Letter to Commissioner of Indian Affairs Edward P. Smith, March 31. Records of the Office of Indian Affairs, *Letters Received, La Pointe Agency,* Microcopy 234, Roll 395, Record Group 75. Washington, D.C.: National Archives and Records Service.

Day, Robert C.

1972   "The Emergence of Activism as a Social Movement." *Native Americans Today: Sociological Perspectives,* ed. Howard M. Bahr, Bruce A. Chadwick, and Robert C. Day. New York: Harper and Row, pp. 506-32.

Deloria, Vine, Jr., and Clifford Lytle.

1984   *The Nations Within: The Past and Future of American Indian Sovereignty.* New York: Pantheon Books.

Detroit Daily Free Press.

1848   "Important Movement Among the Chippewa Indians." November 28, p. 2, citing *St. Louis Republican.*

1849   "The Chippewa Indians and the President." February 19, p. 2.

1850   "Indians to be Removed from Lake Superior." June 1, p. 2, citing *Lake Superior Journal.*

1851   "Arrangements to Remove the Chippewa Indians." June 27, p. 2, citing *Lake Superior Journal.*

Dodge, Henry.

1836   Letter to Commissioner of Indian Affairs Carey Allen Harris, November 23. *Territorial Papers,* Vol. 27, pp. 672-74.

1837a   Letter to Commissioner of Indian Affairs Carey Allen Harris, August 7. *Documents Relating to the Negotiations of Ratified and Unratified Treaties with Various Indian Tribes, 1801-1869,* Microcopy T494, Roll 3, Record Group 75. Washington, D.C.: National Archives and Records Service.

1837b   Report to Commissioner of Indian Affairs Carey Allen Harris, {Fall}. U. S. Congress, *Senate Document 1.* 25th Cong., 2nd sess., *Serial 314,* pp. 535-38.

1838a   Letter to Commissioner of Indian Affairs Carey Allen Harris, February 17, with enclosure of Letter from a Chippewa Chief dated January 22, 1838. Office of Indian Affairs, *Letters Received, La Pointe Agency,* Microcopy 234, Roll 387. Washington, D.C.: National Archives and Records Service.

1838b   Letter to Commissioner of Indian Affairs C{arey} A. Harris, February 19, 1838. Office of Indian Affairs, *Letters Received, La Pointe Agency,* Microcopy 234, Roll 387, Record Group 75. Washington, D.C.: National Archives and Records Service.

1838c   Message to the Territorial Council and House of Representatives, June 11. *Territorial Papers,* Vol. 27, pp. 156-58.

1838d   Letter to Commissioner of Indian Affairs Carey Allen Harris, July 6. *Territorial Papers,* Vol. 27, pp. 1029-031.

1838e   Message to the Legislative Assembly, November 27. *Territorial Papers,* Vol. 27, pp. 165-77.

1839   Letter to Commissioner of Indian Affairs T. Hartley Crawford, February 8. *Territorial Papers,* Vol. 27, pp. 1185-187.

1847a   Letter to Commissioner William Medill, March 26. *Territorial Papers,* Vol. 28, pp. 1054-056.

1847b   Letter to Commissioner of Indian Affairs William Medill, July 22. *Territorial Papers,* Vol. 28, pp. 1085-086.

Doty, James D.

1840   Report of the Wiskonsan Delegate to the House of Representatives, July 1. U. S. Congress, *House Report 96,* 26th Cong., 2d sess., *Serial 388,* 1-5.

1843   Letter to Commissioner of Indian Affairs T. Hartley Crawford, March 21. Office of Indian Affairs, *Letters Received, La Pointe Agency,* Microcopy 234, Roll 388, Record Group 75. Washington, D.C.: National Archives and Records Service.

Dousman, Hercules L.

1836   Letter to Colonel Z{achary} Taylor, August 9. *Territorial Papers,* Vol. 27, pp. 645-46.

Draper, Lyman C.

{1882}   Complaints of the Chippewas: Statement about Paper Written by George P. Warren. *Small Collections-Oversize,* File 40, Archives Division, State Historical Society of Wisconsin, Madison.

Druke, Mary A.

1985   "Iroquois Treaties: Common Forms, Varying Interpretations." *The History and Culture of Iroquois Diplomacy: An Interdisciplinary Guide to the Treaties of the Six Nations and Their League,* ed. Francis Jennings *et al.* Syracuse, N. Y.: Syracuse University Press, pp. 85-98.

Eau Claire Leader-Telegram.

1984a   "Indian Rights Meeting Brings Comment." August 16, p. 7B.

1984b   "Churches Asked to Fight Indian Racism." October 30, pp. 1A, 9A.

1987a   "Speaker Calls for Annulment of Treaties." March 29, pp. 1A, 2A.

1987b   "Delegates Protest Indian Treaty Rights as Unfair." March 30, pp. 1A, 2A.

1988a   "Historian Says Facts Ignored: Indians Lost Spearing Rights Over a Century Ago, Professor Says." May 2, pp. 1A, 2A.

1988b   "Hanaway: Private Treaty Talks Not Right," May 7, p. 1A.

1988c   "Professor Denounces Treaty Myths." May 16, p. 8A.

1989   "Time Travel: Research Can Reveal History of Treaties." October 15, pp. 1A, 10A.

1990a   "Counties Association Criticized for Role on Treaty Rights." January 16, pp. 3A, 6A.

1990b   "Study: Racism Main Factor in Treaty Tension." January 18, p. 1A.

1990c   "Neighbors Practice Tolerance, Respect." January 29, pp. 1A, 2A.

1990d   "Spearfishing Important to Culture, Maulson Says." February 4, pp. 1A, 2A.

1990e   "'Simple' Treaty Solution Starts with Snacks." March 15, pp. 1B, 2B.

1990f   "Equal Rights: PARR Co-Founder Explains Stand." April 8, pp. 1A, 2A.

1990g   "Chippewa Women Face Fear at Landings." April 21, pp. 1A, 2A.

1990h   "Crabb to Hear Arguments Regarding Timber Rights." June 14, p. 1B.

1990i   "Judge: Bands Can't Sue Over Denial of Rights" October 12, pp. 1A, 2A.

1990j   "Official Says Ruling Fits into State Plan." October 12, pp. 1A, 2A.

1991   "Timber Cutting Not in the Rights." February 24, p. 3C.

Edwards, A{braham}.

1826   Copy of the Journal of Proceedings under the Treaty of Fond Du Lac, as Noted by the Secretary, August 2-7. Thomas L. McKenney, *Sketches of a Tour to the Lakes, of the Character and Customs of the Chippeway Indians, and of Incidents Connected with the Treaty of Fond Du Lac*. Baltimore: Fielding, Lucas, Jr., Appendix, pp. 457-76.

Elliott, Richard R.

1896   "The Chippewas of Lake Superior." *American Catholic Quarterly Review* 21 (82): 354-73.

Equal Rights for Everyone.

1984   Transcript of Meeting Held at Sawyer County Courthouse, Hayward, Wisconsin, February 10. (Courtesy of the Lac Courte Oreilles Ojibwa Tribal Governing Board.)

ERC Conscience (Milwaukee, Wis.)

1988   "Equal Rights Council and the Network." 1 (Summer): 1-2.

Erdman, Joyce M.

1966   *Handbook on Wisconsin Indians.* Madison: Governor's Commission on Human Rights with the Cooperation of the University of Wisconsin Extension.

Evers, Martin A., and Daniel W. Bromley.

1989   "Bicultural Negotiations over Natural Resources: The Chippewa Tribe Versus the State of Wisconsin." Unpublished paper. Department of Agricultural Economics, University of Wisconsin-Madison. October 26. (Photocopy courtesy of authors.)

Fillmore, Millard.

1852a   Endorsement on Letter of Commissioner of Indian Affairs Luke Lea to Secretary of Interior Alexander H. H. Stuart, May 6. *Indian Office Files,* No. 75, Archives Division, State Historical Society of Wisconsin, Madison.

1852b   Third Annual Message to Congress, December 6. *A Compilation of the Messages and Papers of the Presidents, 1789-1897,* comp. James D. Richardson. 10 vols. Washington, D.C.: U. S. Government Printing Office, 1900. 5: 163-82.

Fixico, Donald L.

1987   "Chippewa Fishing and Hunting Rights and the Voigt Decision." *An Anthology of Western Great Lakes Indian History,* ed. Donald L. Fixico. Milwaukee: University of Wisconsin-Milwaukee American Indian Studies Program, pp. 481-519.

Foreman, Grant.

1946   *The Last Trek of the Indians.* Chicago: University of Chicago Press.

Forsyth, George A.

1878   Letter to General P{hillip} H. Sheridan, June 23. reprinted in *Barron County Chronotype* (Rice Lake, Wis.), July 4, 1878, p. 1.

Fries, Robert F.

1951   *Empire in Pine: The Story of Lumbering in Wisconsin, 1830-1900.* Madison: State Historical Society of Wisconsin.

Gaines, Edmund P.

1843   Letter to Adjutant General Roger Jones, August 24. Office of Indian Affairs, *Letters Received, La Pointe Agency,* Microcopy 234, Roll 388, Record Group 75. Washington, D.C.: National Archives and Records Service.

Gates, Paul W.

1969   "Frontier Land Business in Wisconsin." *Wisconsin Magazine of History* 53 (Summer): 306-27.

Gedicks, Al.

1985   "Multinational Corporations and Internal Colonialism in the Advanced Capitalist Countries: The New Resource Wars." *Political Power and Social Theory: A Research Annual,* ed. Maurice Zeitlin. Vol. 5. Greenwich, Conn.: JAI Press, Inc., 1985, pp. 169-205.

1989   "Chippewa Treaties Could Prevent Ecological Disaster." *Green Net* 2 (October): 1, 8.

Ghent, W. J.

1936   "Robert Stuart." *Dictionary of American Biography,* ed. Dumas Malone. Vol. 18. New York: Charles Scribner's Sons, pp. 175-76.

Gibson, Arrell Morgan.

1980   *The American Indian: Prehistory to the Present.* Lexington, Mass.: D. C. Heath and Company.

Giddings, Joshua R.

1850   Letter to President Zachary Taylor, July 30, 1850, forwarding Petition of Citizens of the United States on the South Coast of Lake Superior and bearing an Endorsement by the Secretary of Interior Ad Interim, August 3, 1850. Office of Indian Affairs, *Letters Received, La Pointe Agency,* Microcopy 234, Roll 390, Record Group 75. Washington, D.C.: National Archives and Records Service.

Gilbert, Henry C.

1854   Letter to Commissioner of Indian Affairs Geo{rge} W. Manypenny, October 17. *Documents Relating to the Negotiation of Ratified and Unratified Treaties with Various Indian Tribes, 1801-1869,* Microcopy T494, Roll 5, Record Group 75. Washington, D.C.: National Archives and Records Service.

Glad, Paul W.

1990   *The History of Wisconsin,* Vol. 5: *War, A New Era, and Depression, 1914-1940,* ed. William F. Thompson. Madison: State Historical Society of Wisconsin.

Great Lakes Indian Fish and Wildlife Commission.

{c.1988}   *Chippewa Treaty Rights: Hunting . . . Fishing . . . Gathering on Ceded Territory.* Odanah, Wis.: The Commission.

{c.1989}   *Chippewa Treaty Rights: A Guide to Understanding Treaty Rights, Hunting . . . Fishing . . . Gathering . . ., A Chippewa Tradition.* Odanah, Wis.: The Commission.

Green Bay Advocate.

1849a   "The Chippewa Indians at Washington," March 22, p. 2.

1849b   "The Chippewa Delegation," April 5, p. 2.

Green Bay Press Gazette.

1987a   "Kasten Links Support of Aid to Chippewa Fishing Pact." July 15. *UW-Eau Claire Clippings.*

1987b   "Indians Agree to Treaty Talks." August 11. *UW-Eau Claire Clippings.*

1989   "Tribal Official Hails Treaty Deal." September 27, pp. 1A, 2A. *UW-Eau Claire Clippings.*

1990   "Trial to Decide if Indians Have Special Rights to State Timber." February 5. *UW-Eau Claire Clippings.*

Greschner, Larry.

1987   Statement of Protect Americans' Rights and Resources, PARR National Convention, March 22-29, Wausau, Wisconsin. Reprinted in Great Lakes Indian Fish and Wildlife Commission, *A Look at Racism in Wisconsin*. Odanah, Wis.: The Commission, 1987, (unpaginated).

Griffin, James B., ed.

1961   *Lake Superior Copper and the Indians: Miscellaneous Studies of Great Lakes Prehistory*. Anthropological Papers, Museum of Anthropology, University of Michigan, no. 17. Ann Arbor: University of Michigan.

Habeck, J. R., and J. T. Curtis.

1959   "Forest Cover and Deer Population Density in Early Northern Wisconsin." *Transactions of the Wisconsin Academy of Sciences, Arts and Letters* 48: 49-56.

Hall, S.

1850a   Letter to Rev{erend} S. B. Treat, March 28.

1850b   Letter to Rev{erend} S. B. Treat, December 30.

1852a   Letter to Rev{erend} S. B. Treat, October 7.

1852b   Letter to Major J{ohn} S. Watrous, September 10. Commissioner of Indian Affairs, *Annual Report for 1852*. Washington, D.C.: Robert Armstrong, Printer, pp. 48-50.

1853   Letter to Rev{erend} S. B. Treat, May 17.

All of the above Hall letters except the one dated 1852b are from *American*

Board of Commissioners for Foreign Missions Papers, Boxes 5-6, Minnesota Historical Society, St. Paul. Typescripts of originals from Harvard University, Houghton Library, Cambridge, Mass.

Hamilton, Holman.

1951   *Zachary Taylor: Soldier in the White House.* Indianapolis: Bobbs-Merrill Co., Inc.

Hanaway, Donald J.

1989   "History of the Chippewa Treaty Rights Controversy." Unpublished paper, State of Wisconsin, Department of Justice, March.

1990   "History of the Chippewa Treaty Rights Controversy." Unpublished paper, State of Wisconsin, Department of Justice. Updated edition, March.

    (A copy of each of the above documents is on file in the Government Publications Department, McIntyre Library, University of Wisconsin-Eau Claire.)

Harris, Carey Allen.

1836   Letter to Thomas P. Street, August 10.

1837a   Letter to Joseph Pitt, January 3.

    Both of the above letters are from Records of the Department of the Interior, Bureau of Indian Affairs, Part 9: *Territorial Papers of the United States, The Territory of Wisconsin, 1836-1838, Supplement,* Microcopy 236, Roll 43. Washington, D.C.: National Archives and Records Service.

1837b   Letter to Secretary of War Ad Interim Benjamin F. Butler, January 9. U. S. Congress, *House Document 82,* 24th Cong., 2d sess., *Serial 303,* pp. 1-9.

1837c   Annual Report, December 1. U. S. Congress, *Senate Document 1,* 25th Cong., 2d sess., *Serial 314,* pp. 525-672.

Haskins, Stanley G.

1909   "An Account of the Chippewa." Indians of North America Papers, Box 1, Folder 2, Wisconsin Indians, Archives Division, State Historical Society of Wisconsin, Madison.

Hays, James P.

1847   Report of the La Pointe Subagent to Superintendent of Indian Affairs Henry Dodge, September 15. U. S. Congress, *Senate Executive Document 1,* 30th Cong., 1st sess., *Serial 503,* pp. 824-28.

Hazelbaker, Mark.

1984   "Indian Treaties and Hunting Rights on Public Lands." *Wisconsin Counties* (March): 5-6.

Head Chiefs of the Chippewa Indians on Lake Superior.

1849   Petition . . . For a Grant of Lands, &c., February 7. U. S. Congress, *House Miscellaneous Document 36*, 30th Congress, 2d sess., *Serial 544*, pp. 1-2.

Herring, Elbert.

1835   Letter to Governor Henry Dodge, June 22. *Territorial Papers*, Vol. 27, pp. 63-67.

Hertzberg, Hazel W.

1971   *The Search for an American Indian Identity: Modern Pan-Indian Movements*. Syracuse, N. Y.: Syracuse University Press.

Hickerson, Harold.

1962   *The Southwestern Chippewa: An Ethnohistorical Study*. Memoirs of the American Anthropological Association, No. 92. Menasha, Wis.: George Banta Co., Inc.

1973   "Fur Trade Colonialism and the North American Indians." *Journal of Ethnic Studies* 1 (Summer): 15-44.

1988   *The Chippewa and Their Neighbors*. Revised and expanded ed. Prospect Heights, Ill.: Waveland Press.

Hill, Edward E.

1974   *The Office of Indian Affairs, 1824-1880: Historical Sketches*. New York: Clearwater Publishing Co., Inc.

Hill, Edward E., comp.

1981   *Guide to Records in the National Archives of the United States Relating to American Indians*. Washington, D.C.: National Archives and Records Service.

Hole in the Day.

1839   Letter to Maj{or} L{awrence} Toliffero {*sic*}, June 14. Enclosed in Superintendent of Indian Affairs Henry Dodge to Commissioner of Indian Affairs T. Hartley Crawford, June 20. Office of Indian Affairs, *Letters Received, La Pointe Agency*, Microcopy 234, Roll 387, Record Group 75. Washington, D.C.: National Archives and Records Service.

Holzhueter, John O.

1980   "Wisconsin's Flag." *Wisconsin Magazine of History* 63 (Winter 1979-80): 91-121.

HONOR.

{1989}   *History of Honor Our Neighbors Origins and Rights*. Milwaukee: HONOR.

Horsman, Reginald.

1970   *The Frontier in the Formative Years, 1783-1815.* New York: Holt, Rinehart and Winston.

Iowa News (Dubuque).

1837   "Proceedings of a Council with the Chippewa Indians." Reprinted in *Iowa Journal of History and Politics* 5 (1911): 408-28.

Isthmus (Madison).

1987   "Pandering to Prejudices." September 4, p. 7.

1990   " 'We'll Be There': Treaty-Rights Foes Pledge Resistance to the 'Injustice' of Chippewa Spearfishing." March 30, pp. 1, 9.

James, Bernard J.

1954   "An Analysis of an American Indian Village: A Situational Approach to Community Study." Ph.D. dissertation, University of Wisconsin-Madison.

Jefferson, Thomas.

1803   Letter to Indiana Territorial Governor William H{enry} Harrison, February 27. *The Writings of Thomas Jefferson*, ed. Andrew A. Lipscomb. 20 vols. Washington, D.C.: Thomas Jefferson Memorial Association, 1903-05, 10: 368-73.

Johnson, Daniel H.

1858   Letter to Senate and House of Representatives of the United States in Congress Assembled, March 1, with Accompanying Affidavits. U. S. Congress, *House Report 76*. 35th Cong., 2d sess., *Serial 1018*, pp. 1-3.

Johnston, Basil.

1990   *Ojibwe Heritage.* 1976; repr. ed. Lincoln: University of Nebraska Press.

Jones, De Garmo.

1841   Letter to Secretary of War {John C. Spencer}, December 17, 1841. *Territorial Papers*, Vol. 28, p. 378.

Jones, Dorothy V.

1982   *License for Empire: Colonialism by Treaty in Early America.* Chicago: University of Chicago Press.

Jones, Geo{rge} W.

1836   Letter to Senator Robert J. Walker, December 23. *Territorial Papers*, Vol. 27, p. 694.

1838   Letter to Commissioner of Indian Affairs Carey Allen Harris, January 2. *Territorial Papers*, Vol. 27, p. 897.

Kappler, Charles J., comp. and ed.

1904-41   *Indian Affairs: Laws and Treaties*. 5 vols. Washington, D.C.: Government Printing Office.

Kay, Jeanne.

1977   ''The Land of La Baye: The Ecological Impact of the Green Bay Fur Trade, 1634-1836.'' Ph.D. dissertation, University of Wisconsin-Madison.

Keller, Mark.

1981   *The Chippewa Land of Keweenaw Bay: An Allotment History*. Baraga, Mich.: Keweenaw Bay Indian Community for Inter-Tribal Council of Michigan, Inc.

Keller, Robert H.

1978   ''An Economic History of Indian Treaties in the Great Lakes Region.'' *American Indian Journal* 4 (February): 2-20.

1989   ''America's Native Sweet: Chippewa Treaties and the Right to Harvest Maple Sugar.'' *American Indian Quarterly* 13 (Spring): 117-35.

Kellogg, Louise Phelps.

1933   ''Increase Allen Lapham.'' *Dictionary of American Biography*, ed. Dumas Malone. Vol. 5. New York: Charles Scribner's Sons, pp. 611-12.

Kenyon, Richard L.

1989   ''Life Among the Chippewa: 'If We Give Up Our Ways, We Die'.'' *Wisconsin: The Milwaukee Journal Magazine*. July 23, pp. 18-30.

Kerr, Scott.

1990a   ''Chippewa Treaty Rights: Wisconsin Must Choose Between Confrontation and Cooperation.'' *Wisconsin West* (March/April): 10-14.

1990b   ''The Greater Hayward-LCO Progress, Inc.: One Example of Cooperation at Work.'' *Wisconsin West* (March/April): 14.

Kickingbird, Kirke, Lynn Kickingbird, Alexander Tallchief Skibine, and Charles Chibilty.

1980   *Indian Treaties*. Washington, D.C.: Institute for the Development of Indian Law.

Kinney, J. P.

1937   *A Continent Lost—A Civilization Won: Indian Land Tenure in America*. Baltimore: Johns Hopkins Press.

Knobel, Dale T.

1984   ''Know-Nothings and Indians: Strange Bedfellows?'' *Western Historical Quarterly* 15 (April): 175-98.

Knox, H{enry}.

1789a   Letter to President {George Washington}, May 23.

1789b   Report Relative to Northwestern Indians, June 15.

         Both letters may be found in United States Congress, *American State Papers, Class II: Indian Affairs*. Vol. 1. Washington, D.C.: Gales & Seaton, 1832. pp. 7-8 and 12-14, respectively.

Kohl, Johann G.

1860   *Kitchi-Gami: Wanderings Around Lake Superior*. London: Chapman and Hall.

La Crosse Tribune (Wis.).

1990   ''Spearing Opponent Denies Racial Motives.'' April 8, 1990, p. 1 + , *UW-Eau Claire Clippings*.

Lac du Flambeau Band and State of Wisconsin.

1989   *Lac du Flambeau Band/State of Wisconsin Agreement*. (A certified copy is on file in the Government Publications Department, McIntyre Library, University of Wisconsin-Eau Claire.)

Lake Superior News and Mining Journal (Sault Ste. Marie, Mich.).

1850a   ''Removal of the Indians.'' June 5, p. 2.

1850b   ''Chippewas of L'Anse.'' June 12, p. 2.

Landsman, Gail H.

1988   *Sovereignty and Symbol: Indian-White Conflict at Ganienkeh*. Albuquerque: University of New Mexico Press.

Lapham, I. A., Levi Blossom, and George G. Dousman.

1870   *A Paper on the Number, Locality and Times of Removal of the Indians of Wisconsin; An Appendix Containing A Complete Chronology of Wisconsin, from the Earliest Times Down to the Adoption of the State Constitution in 1848*. Milwaukee: Starr's Book and Job Printing House.

Lea, Luke.

1850   *Annual Report for 1850*. Washington, D.C.: Office of the Commissioner of Indian Affairs.

1851a   Letter to Secretary of the Interior A. H. H. Stuart, June 3. *Report Books of the Office of Indian Affairs*, Microcopy 348, Roll 6. Washington, D.C.: National Archives and Records Service.

1851b   *Annual Report for 1851*. Washington, D.C.: Gideon & Co., Printers.

Leahy, M. A.

1891   Report of La Pointe Agency, September 10. U. S. Commissioner of Indian Affairs, *Annual Report for 1891*. Washington, D.C.: Government Printing Office, 1891, pp. 465-75.

Levi, Sister M. Carolissa.

1956   *Chippewa Indians of Yesterday and Today*. New York: Pageant Press, Inc.

Lewis, Mark D.

1987   Letter to Governor Tommy Thompson, September 30. Reprinted in *News from Indian Country* (November 1987): 6.

Lurie, Nancy Oestreich.

1985   "Epilogue: Non-Claims Commission Cases." *Irredeemable America: The Indians' Estate and Land Claims*, ed. Imre Sutton. Albuquerque: University of New Mexico Press, pp. 378-82.

1987   *Wisconsin Indians*. Madison: State Historical Society of Wisconsin.

Lyon, Lucius.

1839a   Letter to Commissioner of Indian Affairs T. Hartley Crawford, July 15. Office of Indian Affairs, *Letters Received, La Pointe Agency*, Microcopy 234, Roll 387, Record Group 75. Washington, D.C.: National Archives and Records Service.

1839b   Letter to Commissioner of Indian Affairs T. Hartley Crawford, December 16. *Territorial Papers*, Vol. 28, pp. 91-98.

Madison Weekly Democrat (Wis.).

1878a   "The Wisconsin Indian Lands." June 18, p. 2.

1878b   "The Indian Insurrection." June 25, p. 4.

Mahan, I{saac} L.

1878   Annual Report to Commissioner of Indian Affairs E{zra} A. Hayt, September 1. U. S. Commissioner of Indian Affairs. *Annual Report for 1878*. Washington, D. C.: Government Printing Office, 1878, pp. 144-48.

Mahon, John K.

1985   *History of the Second Seminole War*. Rev. ed. Gainesville: University Presses of Florida.

Manypenny, George W.

1853   Annual Report, November 26. U. S. Congress, *Senate Executive Document 1,*
        33d Cong., 1st sess., *Serial 690,* pp. 243-64.

1854   Annual Report, November 25. U. S. Congress, *Senate Executive Document 1,*
        33d Cong., 2d sess., *Serial 764,* pp. 211-31.

1855   Annual Report, November 26. U. S. Congress, *Senate Executive Document 1,*
        34th Cong., 1st sess., *Serial 810,* pp. 321-41.

1856   Annual Report, November 22. U. S. Congress, *Senate Executive Document 1,*
        34th Cong., 2d sess., *Serial 875,* pp. 554-75.

1880   *Our Indian Wards.* Cincinnati: Robert Clarke & Co., 1880.

Mardock, Robert W.

1971   *The Reformers and the American Indian.* Columbia: University of Missouri Press.

Martin, {Chief}.

{1842} Talk to Subagent Alfred Brunson, {undated but before January 8, 1843}. Enclosed
        in Brunson to Governor James D. Doty, January 8, 1843. Office of Indian Affairs,
        Letters Received, La Pointe Agency, Microcopy 234, Roll 388, Record Group
        75. Washington, D.C.: National Archives and Records Service.

Masinaigan. (*Masinaigan* {Talking Paper} is a bi-monthly publication of the Great Lakes
Indian Fish and Wildlife Commission, P.O Box 9, Odanah, Wisconsin, 54861).

1985   "The St. Croix Band of Chippewa: A Brief History," (March). *UW-Eau Claire
        Clippings.*

1990a   "Chippewa Treaty Rights: An Overview." (January/February): 7.

1990b   "Impact of Chippewa Treaty Rights: Biological Impact." (January/February):
        4, 15.

1990c   "Impact of Chippewa Treaty Rights: Economic Impact." (January/February): 4-5.

1990d   "Impact of Chippewa Treaty Rights: Political Impact." (January/February): 5.

1990e   "Impact of Chippewa Treaty Rights: Tribal Impact." (January/February): 5.

1990f   "Treaty Rights and Racism." (January/February): 7-9.

1990g   "Bad River Renovates Hatchery." (March/April): 3.

1990h   "Does the Treaty Harvest Ruin Tourism?" (November/December): 7, 11.

1991a   "Tribes Declare '91 Quotas for Walleye/Musky." (February/March): 2.

1991b   "*Voigt* Timber Decision Issued." (February/March): 2.

1991c   "Profile: Anti-Indian Organizations in Wisconsin." (February/March): 7-8.

Mason, Carol I.

1988   *Introduction to Wisconsin Indians: Prehistory to Statehood.* Salem, Wis.: Sheffield Publishing Co.

McKenney, Thomas L., and James Hall.

{1838} *Biographical Sketches and Anecdotes of Ninety-Five of 120 Principal Chiefs from the Indian Tribes of North America.* 1967, repr. ed., Washington, D.C.: U. S. Department of the Interior, Bureau of Indian Affairs.

Medill, William.

1846a   Letter to Henry M. Rice, October 31. *Territorial Papers,* Vol. 28, pp. 1015-016.

1846b   Annual Report of the Commissioner of Indian Affairs, November 30. U. S. Congress, *House Document 4.* 29th Cong., 2d sess., *Serial 497,* pp. 214-28.

1847   Letter to J. A. Verplanck and Charles E. Mix, June 4. Records of the Department of the Interior, Bureau of Indian Affairs. Part 9: *The Territorial Papers of the United States, The Territory of Wisconsin, 1836-1848, Supplement,* Microcopy 236, Roll 46, Record Group 75. Washington D.C.: National Archives and Records Service.

1848   Annual Report of the Commissioner of Indian Affairs, November 30. U. S. Congress, *House Executive Document 1.* 30th Cong., 2d sess., *Serial 537,* pp. 385-408.

Message Carrier: Wisconsin Indian Resource Council News Digest (Stevens Point, Wis.)

1986   "Treaty Opponents 'Blowing Smoke' Says Earl." October, p. 4.

Michetti, Susan.

1991   "Indian Treaty Rights Have Environmental Implications." *Muir View: News of the Sierra Club* 29 (January/February): 6-7.

Midwest Treaty Network.

{1990} *Justice, Reconciliation, Respect for Diversity, Protection of All Resources Through Treaties: Witness for Nonviolence.* {Milwaukee: Southeast Wisconsin Witness for Nonviolence}.

Milwaukee Journal.

1972a   "Fishermen Argue Over Indian Rights." April 20. *UW-Eau Claire Clippings.*

1972b   "Lake Superior is Turf in Heated Squabble on Indian Fishing." July 9. *UW-Eau Claire Clippings.*

1984a   "State Tribes Form Wildlife Panel." April 8, pt. 2, p. 7.

1984b   "Counties Want U. S. to Limit Indians' Hunting, Fishing." September 26. *UW-Eau Claire Clippings*.

1984c   *Treaty Rights*. (Special reprint edition featuring articles by Dennis McCann and Don Boehm that originally appeared in the *Journal* between October 14-17; unpaginated.)

1985   Letter to the Editor from Paul A. Mullaly. May 17. *UW-Eau Claire Clippings*.

1986a   "Thompson, Watts Hit Indian Treaty Rights." June 20, pt. 2, p. 3.

1986b   "Earl Names Indian Relations Panel." June 26, pt. 1, p. 19.

1986c   "Indian-Treaty Panel Criticized." July 11, p. 3B.

1987a   "State to Appeal Ruling on Chippewa Treaties." February 19, pp. 1A, 22A.

1987b   "Hanaway Invites Indians to Treaty Talks." April 29. *UW-Eau Claire Clippings*.

1989a   "Time to Call Out the Guard." May 4, 1989. *UW-Eau Claire Clippings*.

1989b   "As Spears of Racism Pierce the North." May 14. *UW-Eau Claire Clippings*.

1989c   "Tribes Urged to Keep Treaty Rights." July 25. *UW-Eau Claire Clippings*.

1989d   "Forest Group Asks to Join Treaty Case." August 16. *UW-Eau Claire Clippings*.

1989e   "Call Prompts New Class on Treaty Rights: Eau Claire Professor Aims to Provide the Facts." September 19, pp. 1B, 7B.

1989f   "Politicians Exasperated by Treaty Failure." November 5, 1989. *UW-Eau Claire Clippings*.

Milwaukee Sentinel.

1983   "Indian Hunting, Fishing Rights Upheld by U. S. Supreme Court." October 4. *UW-Eau Claire Clippings*.

1987   "Bill Would Repeal Treaty Rights." July 29, pp. 1, 11.

1989a   "U.S. Official 'Appalled' by Tapes of Protests During Spearfishing." June 2. *UW-Eau Claire Clippings*.

1989b   "Treaty Protests are Likened to Selma in '60s." September 16. *UW-Eau Claire Clippings*.

1989c   "Treaty Pact May Cost $35 Million." September 29, pp. 1, 7.

1989d   "Treaty Pact May Spark Legal Battle Between Chippewa Bands." October 16. *UW-Eau Claire Clippings*.

1989e   "2 Lac du Flambeau Officials Ousted from Posts." October 17, p. 5.

1989f   "County Foresters Fear Timber Treaty Issues." November 20, p. 5.

1990a   "Indian Groups Disrupt Treaty Meeting, Conferees are Called Cockroaches." January 19. *UW-Eau Claire Clippings.*

1990b   "Treaty Rights Called State, Tribal Matter." January 19, pp. 1, 12.

1990c   "Dane County Officials Quitting Association." January 31, 1990. *UW-Eau Claire Clippings.*

1990d   "Crackdown Sought at Landings, Arrests Are Urged for Abusive Language." February 3. *UW-Eau Claire Clippings.*

1990e   "Counties Ask Court for Power to Limit Chippewa Timber Use." February 6. *UW-Eau Claire Clippings.*

1990f   "Governor Fears a 'Media Event' at Boat Landings." March 31. *UW-Eau Claire Clippings.*

Mix, Charles E.

1867   Letter to La Pointe Agent Luther. E. Webb, November 13. Office of Indian Affairs, *Letters Received, La Pointe Agency,* Microcopy 234, Roll 394, Record Group 75. Washington, D.C.: National Archives and Records Service.

Monette, Richard.

1990   "Indian Country Jurisdiction and the Assimilative Crimes Act." *Oregon Law Review* 69 (2): 269-94.

Morse, Richard F.

1857   "The Chippewas of Lake Superior." *Collections of the State Historical Society of Wisconsin* 3: 338-69.

Mulcahy, Robert W., and Brian M. T. Selby.

1989   "Indian Treaty Rights and Wisconsin's County Forests." *Wisconsin Counties* (December): 23-24.

Museum Memo (State Historical Museum of Wisconsin).

1990   "Indian Fishing." (December/January 1990): 1.

Neill, Edward D.

1885   "History of the Ojibways, and Their Connection with Fur Traders, Based Upon Official and Other Records." *Collections of the Minnesota Historical Society* 5: 395-510.

Nesbit, Robert C.

1985   *Urbanization and Industrialization, 1873-1893,* Vol. 3: *The History of Wisconsin,* ed. William F. Thompson. Madison: State Historical Society of Wisconsin.

Nesbit, Robert C., and William F. Thompson.

1989   *Wisconsin: A History*. 2nd revised ed. Madison: University of Wisconsin Press.

New York Times.

1851a   "Removal of the Indians." September 29, p. 4, quoting the *Lake Superior News and Mining Journal*.

1851b   "Indian Moneys." September 29, p. 4, quoting the *Cleveland Herald*.

1871   "Another Swindle Exposed: Government and Indians Defrauded by a Set of Sharpers." October 7, p. 4.

1888a   "Another Indian Claim." February 12, p. 16.

1888b   "Indian Timber Contracts: Irregularities Discovered by the Senate Committee." March 14, p. 3.

1888c   "Investigation of Affairs at the Chippewa Agency." April 24, p. 4.

1889   "The Chippewa Troubles." June 17, p. 4.

News from Indian Country: The Journal (Hayward, Wis.).

1988   "HONOR Adopts Constitution." July, p. 6.

1989a   "Co-Management, Recognition and Respect Corner-Stone of Better Relations with Resource Owners," November, p. 7.

1989b   "History of HONOR." November, p. 21.

1990a   "Co-Management: The Possibilities in Power-Sharing." January 19, p. 19.

1990b   "Inouye Seeks Permanent Settlement in Wisconsin Treaty Dispute, " April 11, p. 13.

1990c   "Federal Judge Rules Resources to be Split Between State and Ojibway." Early June, p. 5.

1990d   "Some See Ruling as New Beginning." Early June, p. 5.

1990e   "Chippewa Tribal Status as Resource Managers Disputed." Early July, p. 5.

1990f   "Attorney General Candidate Doyle Says He Would Seek to Reopen Negotiations with Chippewa," Early October, p. 7.

1990g   "Group Has 150 Reports of Spearfishing Problems," Early October, p. 7.

1990h   "Wisconsin State, Tribal Wardens to Team Up." Mid-November, p. 7.

Nichols, John D., ed.

1988   *''Statement Made By the Indians'': A Bilingual Petition of the Chippewas of Lake Superior, 1864*. London, Ontario: University of Western Ontario Centre for Research and Training of Canadian Native Languages, TEXT+ Series, no. 1, *Studies in the Interpretation of Canadian Native Languages and Cultures*.

Nute, Grace Lee.

1926   ''The American Fur Company's Fishing Enterprises on Lake Superior.'' *Mississippi Valley Historical Review* 12 (March): 483-502.

1944   *Lake Superior*. Indianapolis: Bobbs-Merrill Company.

Oberly, James.

1989a   ''Communalism, Individualism and Corporate Capitalism: The Lac Courte Oreilles Indians, Northern States Power Company and the 1921 Chippewa Flowage Dam.'' Unpublished paper presented at the Annual Meeting of the Economic and Business History Society. (Photocopy courtesy of the author.)

1989b   ''Race and Class Warfare: Spearing Fish, Playing 'Chicken.' '' *The Nation* 248 (June 19): 844-45, 848.

O'Connor, Colleen, and Shawn Doherty.

1985 '' 'Open Season' on Indians,'' *Newsweek* 106 (September 30): 35.

Olson, Mary B.

1984   ''Social Reform and the Use of the Law as an Instrument of Social Change: Native Americans' Struggle for Treaty Fishing Rights.'' Ph.D. dissertation, University of Wisconsin-Madison.

Otis, D. S.

1973   *The Dawes Act and the Allotment of Indian Lands,* ed. Francis Paul Prucha, 1934; Reprint ed. Norman: University of Oklahoma Press.

Ourada, Patricia K.

1979   *The Menomonie Indians: A History*. Norman: University of Oklahoma Press.

Paredes, J. Anthony.

1980   ''Anishinabe, a People.'' *Anishinabe, 6 Studies of Modern Chippewa*, ed. J. Anthony Paredes *et al*. Tallahassee: University Presses of Florida, pp. 397-410.

Park Falls Herald.

1989   ''PARR Chairman Plans to Take Course on Treaty Rights; Group Satisfied with Recent Meeting with Gov{ernor} Thompson.'' August 24, p. 3.

PARR Issue.

1987   "PARR Hires Executive Director" (June). Reprinted in *A Look at Racism in Wisconsin*, comp. Great Lakes Indian Fish and Wildlife Commission. Odanah, Wis.: The Commission, 1987, (unpaginated).

1991a   "Attorney Hatch Retained by PARR." (Winter/Spring): 1.

1991b   "Boat Landings . . . See You There." (Winter/Spring): 1, 4.

1991c   "Chairman's Report." (Winter/Spring): 4.

1991d   "In Search of the Whole Truth." (Winter/Spring): 3.

1991e   "Issue Item." (Winter/Spring): 3.

1991f   "Issue Items." (Winter/Spring): 6.

1991g   "Issue Items." (Winter/Spring): 9.

1991h   "Issue Items." (Winter/Spring): 12.

1991i   "Issue Items." (Winter/Spring): 13.

1991j   "Issue Items." (Winter/Spring): 14.

1991k   "Issue Items." (Winter/Spring): 15.

1991l   "Issue Items." (Winter/Spring): 16.

1991m   "Is Wisconsin Becoming the Home of the Dead Seas?" (Winter/Spring): 12.

1991n   "Judicial Wisdom or Blatant Bias?" (Winter/Spring): 10.

1991o   "Letter from the Editor." (Winter/Spring): 3.

1991p   "Schumacher 'Agrees' with 'Mother Jones'; Maulson." (Winter/Spring): 11.

1991q   "PARR's Parade of Activities—1990." (Winter/Spring): 8-9.

1991r   "PARR's 'Traitor's to the Constitution' Awards." (Winter/Spring): 6.

1991s   "Senator Daniel Inouye—Friend or Foe?" (Winter/Spring): 1, 2.

1991t   "Treaties with the Chippewa." (Winter/Spring): 7, 10.

1991u   "Tribal Wardens Won't Work." (Winter/Spring): 5.

1991v   "What Does PARR Want?" (Winter/Spring): 2.

Peake, Ora Brooks.

1954   *A History of the United States Indian Factory System, 1795-1822*. Denver: Sage Books.

Peters, Bernard C.

1989   ''Wa-Bish-Kee-Pe-Nas and the Chippewa Reverence for Copper.'' *Michigan Historical Review* 15 (Fall): 47-60.

Phillips, Clifford J.

1954   ''Protestant America and the Pagan World: The First Half Century of the American Board of Commissioners for Foreign Missions, 1810-1860.'' Ph.D. dissertation, Harvard University.

Philp, Kenneth R.

1977   *John Collier's Crusade for Indian Reform, 1920-1954.* Tucson: University of Arizona Press.

Pitezel, John H.

1859   *Lights and Shades of Missionary Life: Containing Travels, Sketches, Incidents, and Missionary Efforts, During Nine Years Spent in the Region of Lake Superior By Rev. John H. Pitezel, Alias, Wa-Zah-Wa-Wa-Doong, or ''The Yellow Beard.''* Cincinnati: Western Book Concern, R. P. Thompson, Printer, 1859.

Plaisance, Aloysius.

1954   ''The United States Government Factory System, 1796-1822.'' Ph.D. dissertation. St. Louis University.

Poinsett, Joel R.

1837   Letter to Governor Henry Dodge, March 25. Records of the Department of the Interior, Bureau of Indian Affairs, Part 9: *Territorial Papers of the United States, The Territory of Wisconsin, 1836-1838, Supplement,* Microcopy 236, Roll 46, Record Group 75. Washington, D.C.: National Archives and Records Service.

Porter, James M.

1843   Endorsement, October 20. Enclosed in Letter of Commissioner T. Hartley Crawford to Secretary of War James M. Porter, October 20. *Territorial Papers,* Vol. 28, p. 601.

Priest, Loring Benson.

1942   *Uncle Sam's Step Children: The Reformation of the United States Indian Policy, 1865-1887.* Rutgers, N.J.: Rutgers College University Press.

Prucha, Francis Paul.

1953   *Broadax and Bayonet: The Role of the United States Army in the Development of the Northwest, 1815-1860.* Madison: State Historical Society of Wisconsin.

1962a   *American Indian Policy in the Formative Years: The Indian Trade and Intercourse Acts, 1790-1834.* Cambridge, Mass.: Harvard University Press.

1962b   "Early Indian Peace Medals." *Wisconsin Magazine of History* 45 (Spring): 279-89.

1966   "Army Sutlers and the American Fur Company." *Minnesota History* 40 (Spring): 22-31.

1969   *The Sword of the Republic: The United States Army on the Frontier, 1783-1846.* New York: Macmillan Co.

1971   *Indian Peace Medals in American History.* Madison: State Historical Society of Wisconsin.

1984   *The Great Father: The United States Government and the American Indians.* 2 vols. Lincoln and London: University of Nebraska Press.

1990   *Atlas of American Indian Affairs.* Lincoln: University of Nebraska Press.

Quaife, Milo M.

1917   "Increase Allen Lapham, First Scholar of Wisconsin." *Wisconsin Magazine of History* 1 (September): 3-15.

Racine Journal Times.

1988   "Treaty Foes Form New Organization." March 21, pp. 1A, 2A.

Ramsey, Alexander.

1850   Annual Report to Commissioner of Indian Affairs Luke Lea, October 21. Commissioner of Indian Affairs, *Annual Report for 1850.* Washington, D.C.: Office of the Commissioner of Indian Affairs, pp. 43-64.

1851   Annual Report to Commissioner of Indian Affairs Luke Lea, November 3. Commissioner of Indian Affairs, *Annual Report for 1851.* Washington, D.C.: Gideon & Co., Printer, 1851, pp. 149-64.

1852   Annual Report to Commissioner of Indian Affairs Luke Lea, October 26. Commissioner of Indian Affairs, *Annual Report for 1852.* Washington, D.C.: Robert Armstrong, Printer, 1852, pp. 37-47.

Residents Near Lake Superior.

1847   Petition to Secretary of War William L. Marcy, February 18. *Territorial Papers,* Vol. 28, pp. 1043-044.

Rice, Henry M.

1847   Letter to Commissioner of Indian Affairs William Medill, June 30. *Territorial Papers,* Vol. 28, p. 1076.

Richardson, James D., comp. and ed.

1896-99 *A Compilation of the Messages and Papers of the Presidents.* 10 vols. Washington, D.C.: Government Printing Office.

Richmond, William A.

1846   Letter to Commissioner of Indian Affairs William Medill, August 24. *Territorial Papers,* Vol. 28, pp. 989-90.

Ritzenthaler, Robert E.

1978   "Southwestern Chippewa." *Northeast,* ed. Bruce G. Trigger. Vol. 15: *Handbook of North American Indians,* ed. William C. Sturtevant. Washington: Smithsonian Institution, pp. 743-59.

Robbins, Roy M.

1960   *Our Landed Heritage: The Public Domain, 1776-1936.* 1942; Repr. ed. Gloucester, Mass.: Peter Smith.

Ross, John.

1831   Annual Message, October 24. *The Papers of Chief John Ross,* Vol. 1: *1807-1839,* ed. Gary E. Moulton. Norman: University of Oklahoma Press, 1985, p. 224-31.

Royce, Charles C., comp.

1899   *Indian Land Cessions in the United States.* Vol. 2: *Eighteenth Annual Report of the Bureau of American Ethnology to the Secretary of the Smithsonian Institution, 1896-97.* Washington, D.C.: Government Printing Office.

St. Paul Pioneer Press (Minn.)

1878   "Indian Scare in Wisconsin." Reprinted in *Barron County Chronotype* (Rice Lake, Wis.) June 27, p. 3.

Satz, Ronald N.

1975   *American Indian Policy in the Jacksonian Era.* Lincoln: University of Nebraska Press.

1976   "Indian Policy in the Jacksonian Era: The Old Northwest as a Test Case." *Michigan History* 60 (Spring): 71-93.

1979a   *Tennessee's Indian Peoples: From White Contact to Removal.* Knoxville: University of Tennessee Press.

1979b   "Thomas Hartley Crawford (1838-45)." *The Commissioners of Indian Affairs, 1824-1977,* ed. Robert M. Kvasnicka and Herman J. Viola. Lincoln: University of Nebraska Press, pp. 23-27.

1981   "The Jackson Purchase Treaty of 1818 in Historical Perspective." *Journal of the Jackson Purchase Historical Society* 9 (June): 9-16.

1985   "Cherokee Traditionalism, Protestant Evangelism, and the Trail of Tears." *Tennessee Historical Quarterly* 44 (Fall): 285-301, 44 (Winter): 380-401.

1987   "The United States Constitution and the Cherokees." *Kennesaw Review* 1 (Fall): 34-49.

1988   "William Medill." *History of Indian-White Relations*, ed. Wilcomb E. Washburn. Vol. 4: *Handbook of North American Indians*, ed. William C. Sturtevant. Washington: Smithsonian Institution, pp. 666-67.

1989   "The Cherokee Trail of Tears: A Sesquicentennial Perspective." *Georgia Historical Quarterly* 73 (Fall): 431-66.

1990   "Treaty Rights History Readings." *Wisconsin West* (March/April): 17.

1991   "Rhetoric Versus Reality: The Indian Policy of Andrew Jackson." *Cherokee Removal: Before and After*, ed. William L. Anderson. Athens: University of Georgia Press, pp. 29-54.

Schoolcraft, Henry R.

1828   "Travels Among the Aborigines: The Chippewa Indians." *North American Review* 27 (July): 89-114.

1851   *Personal Memoirs of a Residence of Thirty Years with the Indian Tribes on the American Frontiers: With Brief Notices of Passing Events, Facts, and Opinions, A.D. 1812 to A.D. 1842*. Philadelphia: Lippincott, Grambo and Co.

Schorger, A. W.

1953   "The White-Tailed Deer in Early Wisconsin." *Transactions of the Wisconsin Academy of Sciences, Arts and Letters* 42: 197-247.

Schultz, Terri.

1973   "Bamboozle Me Not at Wounded Knee." *Harper's Magazine* 246 (June): 46-48, 53-56.

Schulze, Eldor P.

1933   "Gouverneur Kemble." *Dictionary of American Biography*, ed. Dumas Malone. Vol. 5. New York: Charles Scribner's Sons, pp. 316-17.

Sherman, Samuel S.

1876   *Increase Allen Lapham, LL.D., A Biographical Sketch Read Before the Old Settlers' Club, Milwaukee, Wis., December 11, 1875*. Milwaukee: Milwaukee News Company, Printer.

Shifferd, Patricia A.

1976   "A Study in Economic Change, The Chippewa of Northern Wisconsin: 1854-1900." *Western Canadian Journal of Anthropology* 6 (4): 16-41.

Smith, Alice E.

1954   *James Duane Doty: Frontier Promoter*. Madison: State Historical Society of Wisconsin.

1973   *The History of Wisconsin*, Vol. 1: *From Exploration to Statehood*, ed. William F. Thompson. Madison: State Historical Society of Wisconsin.

Smith, Desmond.

1973   "Wounded Knee: The Media Coup d'Etat." *Nation* 216 (June 25): 806-09.

Smith, Donald.

1988   "The Life of George Copway or Kah-ge-ga-gah-bowh (1818-1869)—and a Review of His Writings." *Journal of Canadian Studies* 23 (Fall): 5-38.

Solterman, Susan.

1991   "Learning and Unlearning Hatred: Treaty Rights and the Wisconsin Curriculum." *Rethinking Schools: An Urban Educational Journal* 5 (January/February): 19.

Stambaugh, Samuel C.

1836   Letter to President Andrew Jackson, September 6, enclosing application from Hercules L. Dousman with endorsements from Chippewa Chiefs and Head Men. Office of Indian Affairs, *Letters Received, La Pointe Agency*, Microcopy 234, Roll 387, Record Group 75. Washington, D.C.: National Archives and Records Service.

State Historical Museum of Wisconsin.

1990-91 "Indian Fishing." *Museum Memo* (December/January): 1, 3.

State Historical Society of Wisconsin.

1960   *Dictionary of Wisconsin Biography*. Madison: State Historical Society of Wisconsin.

State of Wisconsin *et al.*

1990   *Defendants' Proposed Post-Trial Findings of Fact and Conclusions of Law, Submitted to the U. S. District Court, Western District, Wisconsin*. June 15. (Courtesy of Howard Bichler.)

State of Wisconsin Executive Department.

1983   *Executive Order No. 31*. October 13. Wisconsin Governor, Executive Orders, 1983-1986, microfilm, State Historical Society of Wisconsin Library, Madison, Wis. (Reprinted in *Masinaigan* [January 1985]: 8.)

Sterling, Levi.

1840   Letter to Delegate John D. Doty, March 22. *Territorial Papers*, Vol. 28, pp. 168-69.

Strickland, Rennard, Stephen J. Herzberg, and Steven R. Owens.

1990 ''Keeping Our Word: Indian Treaty Rights and Public Responsibilities—A Report on a Recommended Federal Role Following Wisconsin's Request for Federal Assistance.'' Unpublished manuscript, University of Wisconsin-Madison School of Law, 1990. (The News and Information Service of the University of Wisconsin-Madison provided a copy of this report, which was submitted to the staff of the U. S. Senate Select Committee on Indian Affairs on April 16, 1990.)

Stuart, Robert.

1842a Annual Report of the Acting Superintendent of the Michigan Superintendency, October 28. Office of Indian Affairs, Letters Received, *Michigan Superintendency,* Microcopy 234, Roll 425, Record Group 75. Washington, D.C.: National Archives and Records Service.

1842b Letter to Commissioner of Indian Affairs T. Hartley Crawford, November 19. Records of the Department of the Interior, Bureau of Indian Affairs, Part 9: *Territorial Papers of the United States, The Territory of Wisconsin, 1836-1848, Supplement,* Microcopy 236, Roll 46, Record Group 75. Washington, D.C.: National Archives and Records Service.

1842c Letter to Rev. David Greene, December 8, *American Board of Commissioners for Foreign Missions Correspondence,* Box 3, Minnesota Historical Society, St. Paul. Transcript of original in Houghton Library, Harvard University.

1843a Letter to Commissioner of Indian Affairs T. Hartley Crawford, March 15, enclosing Extract of a Letter from R{obert} Stuart to Alfred Brunson, March 10, 1843. Office of Indian Affairs, *Letters Received, La Pointe Agency,* Microcopy 234, Roll 388, Record Group 75. Washington, D.C.: National Archives and Records Service.

1843b Extract from a Letter to Commissioner of Indian Affairs T. Hartley Crawford, June 2. *Senate Document 403.* 29th Cong. 1st sess., *Serial 477,* p. 3.

1844 Letter to Commissioner of Indian Affairs T. Hartley Crawford, March 29, enclosing Substance of a Talk to the Chippewa, September 29, 1842. Office of Indian Affairs, *Letters Received, La Pointe Agency,* Microcopy 234, Roll 389, Record Group 75. Washington, D.C.: National Archives and Records Service.

Talcott, Lt. Col. G.

1845 Letter to Secretary of War W{illiam} L. Marcy, March 17. *Territorial Papers,* Vol. 28, pp. 811-13.

Tanner, Helen Hornbeck.

1976 *The Ojibwas: A Critical Bibliography.* Bloomington: Indiana University Press for the Newberry Library.

Tanner, Helen Hornbeck, ed.

1987   *Atlas of Great Lakes Indian History*. Norman: University of Oklahoma Press for the Newberry Library.

Thannum, Jim.

{1990}   *1990 Chippewa Spearing Season—Conflict and Cooperation: The Two States of Wisconsin*. Odanah, Wis.: Great Lakes Indian Fish and Wildlife Commission.

Thomas, Gale E., ed.

1990   *U. S. Race Relations in the 1980s: Challenges and Alternatives*. New York: Hemisphere Publishing Corporation.

Thompson, William F.

1988   *Continuity and Change, 1940-1965*. Vol. 6: *The History of Wisconsin,* series ed. William F. Thompson. Madison: State Historical Society of Wisconsin.

Time.

1973   "Trap at Wounded Knee." (March 26): 67.

Tocqueville, Alexis de.

1831-32   *Journey to America*, rev. ed., trans. George Lawrence, ed. J. P. Mayer. New York: Anchor Books, 1971.

1848   *Democracy in America*, 12th ed., trans George Lawrence, ed. J. P. Mayer. New York: Anchor Books, 1969.

Treat, S. B.

1851   Letter to S. Hall, September 24. *American Board of Commissioners for Foreign Missions Papers,* Box 5, Minnesota Historical Society, St. Paul. Typescripts of originals from Harvard University, Houghton Library, Cambridge, Mass.

1852   Letter to Commissioner of Indian Affairs L{uke} Lea, May 12. *Indian Office Files,* 1852, No. 102, Archives Division, State Historical Society of Wisconsin, Madison.

Trennert, Robert A.

1975   *Alternative to Extinction: Federal Indian Policy and the Beginnings of the Reservation System, 1846-51*. Philadelphia: Temple University Press.

1979a   "Orlando Brown, 1849-50."

1979b   "Luke Lea, 1850-53."

1979c   "William Medill, 1845-49."

        All (1979a-c) of the above are in *The Commissioners of Indian Affairs, 1824-1977,* ed. Robert M. Kvasnicka and Herman J. Viola. Lincoln and London: University of Nebraska Press, see respectively pp. 41-56, 49-56, and 29-39.

Trigger, Bruce G., ed.

1978   *Northeast*. Vol. 15: *Handbook of North American Indians*, ed. William C. Sturtevant. Washington, D.C: Smithsonian Institution.

U. S. Bureau of Indian Affairs.

1934   *Testimony Taken at Hayward, Wisconsin, April 23 and 24, Where Indians of Wisconsin, Minnesota and Michigan Gathered for a Two Day Conference to Discuss The Wheeler-Howard Bill of Indian Rights*. Mimeographed minutes. Washington, D.C.: U. S. Department of Interior Library. (Photocopy courtesy of Vine Deloria, Jr.).

U. S. Commission on Civil Rights.

1981   *Indian Tribes: A Continuing Quest for Survival*. Washington, D.C.: U. S. Government Printing Office.

U. S. Congress.

1830   Act of May 28. *Statutes at Large*. Vol. 4, p. 411-12.

1849   Delegation of Chippewa Indians, February 15. *Congressional Globe*. 30th Cong., 2d session, p. 535-37.

1871   Act of March 3. *Statutes at Large*. Vol. 16, p. 566.

1885   Act of March 3. *Statutes at Large*. Vol. 23, p. 385.

1919   Act of November 6. *Statutes at Large*. Vol. 41, p. 350.

1924   Act of June 2. *Statutes at Large*. Vol. 43, p. 253.

1934   Act of June 18. *Statutes at Large*. Vol. 48, pp. 984-88.

1953   Act of August 15. *Statutes at Large*. Vol. 67, p. 588-90.

1987a   *Congressional Record*. 100th Cong., 1st sess., Vol. 133, no. 125, (July 28): 1845.

1987b   House of Representatives. Bill No. 3034: *A Bill to Abrogate Off-Reservation, Usufructuary Rights of Indian Tribes to Hunt, Fish, and Gather in the State of Wisconsin*. 100th Cong., 1st sess., July 28.

1989a   *Congressional Record*. 101st Cong., 1st sess., Vol. 135, no. 46, (April 18): 1328.

1989b   House of Representatives. Bill No. 2058: *A Bill to Abrogate Off-Reservation, Usufructuary Rights of Indian Tribes to Hunt, Fish, and Gather in the State of Wisconsin*. 101st Cong., 1st sess., April 18.

U. S. Court of Appeals, Seventh Circuit.

1983   *Lac Courte Oreilles Band of Lake Superior Chippewa Indians et al.* v. *Voigt et al.* 700 *Federal Reporter* 2d 341-65.

1985   *Lac Courte Oreilles Band of Lake Superior Chippewa Indians et al.* v. *State of Wisconsin et al.* 760 *Federal Reporter* 2d 177-83.

1987   *Lac Courte Oreilles Band of Lake Superior Chippewa Indians et al.* v. *State of Wisconsin et al.* 829 *Federal Reporter* 2d 601-03.

U. S. Court of Appeals, Ninth Circuit.

1975   *United States* v. *State of Washington* 520 *Federal Reporter* 2d, 676-693.

U. S. Court of Claims.

1967   *Menominee Tribe of Indians* v. *United States* 388 *Federal Reporter* 2d, 998-1012.

U. S. Department of the Interior

1991   *Casting Light Upon the Waters: A Joint Fishery Assessment of the Wisconsin Ceded Territory.* Minneapolis, Minn.: Bureau of Indian Affairs.

U. S. District Court, Western District, Washington.

1974   *United States* v. *State of Washington* 384 *Federal Supplement* 312-420.

U. S. District Court, Western District, Wisconsin.

1901   *In Re Blackbird* 109 *Federal Reporter* 139-45.

1978   *Lac Courte Oreilles Band of Lake Superior Chippewa Indians et al.* v. *Voigt et al.,* reported sub. nom. *U. S.* v. *Ben Ruby* 464 *Federal Supplement* 1316-376.

1987a   *Lac Courte Oreilles Band of Lake Superior Chippewa Indians et al.* v. *State of Wisconsin et al.* 653 *Federal Supplement* 1420-435.

1987b   *Lac Courte Oreilles Band of Lake Superior Chippewa Indians et al.* v. *State of Wisconsin et al.* 668 *Federal Supplement* 1233-242.

1988   *Lac Courte Oreilles Band of Lake Superior Chippewa Indians et al.* v. *State of Wisconsin et al.* 686 *Federal Supplement* 226-33.

1989   *Lac Courte Oreilles Band of Lake Superior Chippewa Indians et al.* v. *State of Wisconsin* 707 *Federal Supplement* 1034-062.

1990a   *Lac Courte Oreilles Band of Lake Superior Chippewa Indians et al.* v. *State of Wisconsin* 740 *Federal Supplement* 1400-27.

1990b   *Lac Courte Oreilles Band of Lake Superior Chippewa Indians et al.* v. *State of Wisconsin et al.* 749 *Federal Supplement* 913-23.

1991a   *Lac Courte Oreilles Band of Lake Superior Chippewa Indians et al.* v. *State of Wisconsin et al.* Photocopy of unpublished opinion and order, 74-C-313-C, pp. 1-39. (Courtesy of Howard Bichler.)

1991b   *Lac Courte Oreilles Band of Lake Superior Chippewa Indians et al.* v. *State of Wisconsin et al.* Photocopy of unpublished opinion and order, 74-C-313-C, no. 2, pp. 1-6. (Courtesy of Howard Bichler.)

1991c   *Lac Courte Oreilles Band of Lake Superior Chippewa Indians et al.* v. *State of Wisconsin et al.* Photocopy of unpublished opinion and order, 74-C-313-C, no. 3, pp. 1-2. (Courtesy of Howard Bichler.)

1991d   *Lac du Flambeau Band of Lake Superior Chippewa Indians et al.* v. *Stop Treaty Abuse-Wisconsin, Inc. et al.* Photocopy of unpublished opinion and order, 91-C-117-C, pp. 1-39. (Courtesy of Howard Bichler.)

1991e   *Lac Courte Oreilles Band of Lake Superior Chippewa Indians et al.* v. *State of Wisconsin et al.* Photocopy of unpublished Final Judgment, 74-C-313-C, pp. 1-9. (Courtesy of Howard Bichler.)

U. S. Secretary of the Interior.

1889   Correspondence Relative to Timber-Cutting on the Chippewa Reservation, February 19. U. S. Congress, *Senate Executive Document 128.* 50th Cong., 2d sess., *Serial 2612,* pp. 1-20.

U. S. Senate Committee on Indian Affairs.

1892   Report on Fulfillment of the Treaties of 1837, 1842, and 1854, April 3. U. S. Congress, *Senate Report 571.* 52d Cong., 1st sess., *Serial 2913,* pp. 1-7.

U. S. Senate Committee on Military Affairs and the Militia.

1862   Report on a Road in Wisconsin and Michigan, April 30. U. S. Congress, *Senate Report 40,* 37th Cong., 2d sess., *Serial 1125,* pp. 1-9.

U. S. Supreme Court.

1831   *Cherokee Nation* v. *State of Georgia* 30 *U. S.* (5 Peters): 1-20.

1832   *Samuel A. Worcester* v. *State of Georgia* 31 *U. S.* (6 Peters) 515-63.

1894   *U. S.* v. *Thomas* 151 *U. S.* 577-584, 14 *Supreme Court* 426-29.

1918   *U. S.* v. *J. S. Stearns Lumber Company* 245 *U. S.* 436-37, 38 *Supreme Court* 137-38.

1968   *Menominee Tribe of Indians* v. *United States* 391 *U. S.* 404-17.

1976   Appeal No. 75-588 from Ninth Circuit Court Decision in *United States* v. *State of Washington* 423 *U. S.* 1086.

1983   Appeal No. 83-6 from Seventh Circuit Court of Decision in *Lac Courte Oreilles Band of Lake Superior Chippewa Indians et al.* v. *Voigt* 464 *U. S.* 805.

USA Today.

1990   "Battle Builds Over Indians' Fishing Rights." March 21, pp. 1A, 2A.

Van Antwerp, Verplanck.

1837   Proceedings of a Council Held by Governor Henry Dodge, with the Chiefs and Principal Men, of the Chippewa Nation of Indians, July 20-29. *Documents Relating to the Negotiations of Ratified and Unratified Treaties with Various Indian Tribes, 1801-1869.* Microcopy T494, Roll 3, Record Group 75. Washington, D.C.: National Archives and Records Service.

Van Buren, Martin

1838   Message Upon the Subject of the Disturbance on the Northern Frontier of the United States, January 8. *House Executive Document 73.* U. S. Congress, 25th Cong., 2nd sess., *Serial 323,* 1-6.

Vanguard (Milwaukee).

1988   "It's a Matter of Honor." 35 (May/June): 3.

Vecsey, Christopher.

1983   *Traditional Ojibwa Religion and its Historical Changes.* Memoirs of the American Philosophical Society, Vol 152. Philadelphia: American Philosophical Society.

Vennum, Thomas, Jr.

1988   *Wild Rice and the Ojibway People.* St. Paul: Minnesota Historical Society Press.

Verplanck, J. A.

1847   Letter to Commissioner of Indian Affairs William Medill, August 2. Records of the Department of Interior, Bureau of Indian Affairs, Part 9: *The Territorial Papers of the United States, The Territory of Wisconsin, 1836-1848, Supplement,* Microcopy 236, Roll 46, Record Group 75. Washington, D.C.: National Archives and Records Service.

Vineyard, Miles M.

1838   Report of Crow Wing Subagent, {March 31}. *Territorial Papers,* Vol. 27, pp. 960-62.

Viola, Herman J.

1974   *Thomas L. McKenney, Architect of America's Early Indian Policy: 1816-1830.* Chicago: Swallow Press, Inc.

Vizenor, Gerald.

1984   *The People Named the Chippewa: Narrative Histories*. Minneapolis: University of Minnesota Press.

Warren, George P.

1882   Letter to Lyman C. Draper, November 9. *Small Collections-Oversize,* File 40, Archives Division, State Historical Society of Wisconsin, Madison.

Warren, Lyman M.

1841   Letter to Governor James D. Doty, October 2. Office of Indian Affairs, *Letters Received, La Pointe Agency,* Microcopy 234, Roll 388, Record Group 75. Washington, D.C.: National Archives and Records Service.

Warren, William W.

1849   "Answers to Inquiries Regarding Chippewas." *Minnesota Pioneer,* December 5, 12, 19, 26. Reprinted in *Minnesota Archaeologist* 13 (January 1947): 5-21.

1850   "Sioux and Chippewa Wars." *Minnesota Chronicle & Register,* June 3 and 10. Reprinted in *Minnesota Archaeologist* 12 (October 1946): 95-107.

1851   "A Brief History of the Ojibwas," *Minnesota Democrat,* February 11, 18, 25, March 4, 11, 25, and April 1. Reprinted in *Minnesota Archaeologist* 12 (July 1947): 45-91.

1852   Sworn Affadavit Before a Justice of the Peace Regarding U. S. Indian Agent Watrous, January 21. *Indian Office Files,* 1852, No. 73, Archives Division, State Historical Society of Wisconsin, Madison.

1885   "History of the Ojibways, Based Upon Traditions and Oral Statements." *Collections of the Minnesota Historical Society* 5: 21-394.

Washburn, Wilcomb E.

1959   "The Moral and Legal Justifications for Dispossessing the Indians." *Seventeenth-Century America: Essays in Colonial History,* ed. James Morton Smith. Chapel Hill: University of North Carolina Press for Institute of Early American History and Culture at Williamsburg, Virginia, pp. 15-32.

1964   "Introduction." *The Indian and the White Man,* ed. Wilcomb E. Washburn. *Documents in American Civilization Series.* Garden City, N.Y.: Anchor Books, pp. xi-xv.

1975   *The Indian in America.* New York: Harper & Row.

Watrous, John S.

1850   Letter to Superintendent of Indian Affairs and Governor of Minnesota Territory Alexander Ramsey, October 14. Commissioner of Indian Affairs, *Annual Report for 1850*. Washington, D.C.: Office of the Commissioner of Indian Affairs, pp. 88-90.

1851   Letter to Commissioner of Indian Affairs Luke Lea, July 1. Office of Indian Affairs, *Letters Received, Chippewa Agency*, Microcopy 234, Roll 149, Record Group 75. Washington, D.C.: National Archives and Records Service.

1852a   Letter to Commissioner of Indian Affairs Luke Lea, June 7. Office of Indian Affairs, *Letters Received, Chippewa Agency*, Microcopy 234, Roll 149, Record Group 75. Washington, D.C.: National Archives and Records Service.

1852b   Letter to Superintendent of Indian Affairs Governor Alexander Ramsey, September 15. Commissioner of Indian Affairs. *Annual Report for 1852*. Washington, D.C.: Robert Armstrong, Printer, pp. 47-48.

Wax, Rosalie H., and Robert K. Thomas.

1961   "American Indians and White People." *Phylon* 22 (Winter): 305-17.

Webb, L. E.

1861   Annual Report to Superintendent Clark W. Thompson, October 28. U. S. Commissioner of Indian Affairs, *Annual Report for 1861*. Washington, D.C.: Government Printing Office, 1861, pp. 74-76.

Wheeler, Leonard H.

1843   Letter to Rev{erend} David Greene, May 3. *American Board of Commissioners of Foreign Missions Papers*, Box 3, Minnesota Historical Society, St. Paul. Typescript of original from Harvard University, Houghton Library, Cambridge, Mass.

White, Leonard D.

1954   *The Jacksonians: A Study in Administrative History, 1829-1861*. New York: Macmillan Co.

White Crow, {Chief}.

1842   Talk to Subagent Alfred Brunson, December 18. Enclosed in Letter of Brunson to Governor James D. Doty, January 8, 1843. Office of Indian Affairs, *Letters Received, La Pointe Agency*, Microcopy 234, Roll 388, Record Group 75. Washington, D.C.: National Archives and Records Service.

Wilkinson, Charles F.

1987   *American Indians, Time, and the Law: Native Societies in a Modern Constitutional Democracy*. New Haven: Yale University Press.

1990   *To Feel the Summer in the Spring: The Treaty Fishing Rights of the Wisconsin Chippewa*. Occasional Papers: Oliver Rundell Lecture, April 19. Madison: University of Wisconsin-Madison Law School. (Available through the Continuing

Education and Outreach Office of the University of Wisconsin-Madison Law School.)

Williams, C. Herb, and Walt Neubrech.

1976   *Indian Treaties: American Nightmare*. Seattle, Wash.: Outdoor Empire Publishing, Inc.

Williams, J. Fletcher.

1885   "Memoir of William W. Warren." *Collections of the Minnesota Historical Society*, 5: 9-20.

Wind, The.

1837   Speech of The Wind {c. September 1837}. Enclosed in Frederick Ayer to President Martin Van Buren, September 30, 1837. Office of Indian Affairs, *Letters Received, La Pointe Agency*, Microcopy 234, Roll 387, Record Group 75. Washington, D.C.: National Archives and Records Service.

Wisconsin Advisory Committee to the U. S. Commission on Civil Rights.

1989   *Discrimination Against Chippewa Indians in Northern Wisconsin: A Summary Report*. Madison: The Committee.

Wisconsin Counties.

1985   "Tribal/County Issues—WCA Resolution 59." (March): 6, quoting *ERFE News*.

Wisconsin County Forests Association *et al*.

1990   *Intervening Defendants{'} Proposed Post-Trial Findings of Fact and Conclusions of Law, Submitted to the U. S. District Court, Western District, Wisconsin*. June 15. (Courtesy of Howard Bichler.)

Wisconsin Education Association Council.

1989   "Understanding Indians." *News & Views* (September): 1-2.

Wisconsin Legislature.

1854   Memorial to the President and Congress of the United States, Relative to the Chippewa Indians of Lake Superior, February 27. *Laws of 1854*, Memorial 8, pp. 156-57, quoted in *State* v. *Gurnoe* 53 *Wisconsin Reports 2d* (1971) 397.

Wisconsin Sportsman.

1985   "A Matter of Interpretation: Dealing with the Voigt Decision." 14 (March): 35-43.

Wisconsin State Journal (Madison).

1987   "It's Far Too Early to Scrap Treaties." August 7. *UW-Eau Claire Clippings*.

1989a   " '86 Thompson Speech Opposed Spearfishing.'' May 5, 1B.

1989b   ''Judge Compares Case to '60s Rights Battles.'' May 7. *UW-Eau Claire Clippings*.

1989c   ''Protect Indians Because It's Right: Guest Column.'' By Joe DeCecco. May 12. *UW-Eau Claire Clippings*.

1989d   ''No Deal, Indians Say.'' October 26, 1A, 2A.

1989e   ''Culture, Politics Played Vital Roles.'' October 27, p. 2B.

1989f   ''Treaty Answers: Few Have Them.'' October 30, pp. 1D, 2D.

1990a   ''Minocqua, not Managua.'' March 18, pp. 1A, 17A.

1990b   ''Bush Asked to Appoint Treaty Aide.'' March 28. *UW-Eau Claire Clippings*.

1990c   *Treaty Crisis: Cultures in Conflict,* pp. 1-56. (Special edition featuring a reprinting of articles published between December 10, 1989, and April 8, 1990.)

Wisconsin Supreme Court.

1879a   *State* v. *Doxtater* 47 *Wisconsin Reports* 278-97.

1879b   *State* v. *Harris* 47 *Wisconsin Reports* 298.

1908   *State* v. *Morrin* 136 *Wisconsin Reports* 552-57.

1916   *Dagan* v. *The State* 162 *Wisconsin Reports* 353-55.

1927   *Lemieux* v. *Agate Land Company* 193 *Wisconsin Reports* 462-76.

1931   *State* v. *Rufus* 205 *Wisconsin Reports* 317-39.

1933   *State* v. *Johnson* 212 *Wisconsin Reports* 301-13.

1940   *State* v. *La Barge* 234 *Wisconsin Reports* 449-51.

1971   *State* v. *Gurnoe et al.* and *State* v. *Connors et al.* 53 *Wisconsin Reports 2d* 390-412.

Woodbridge, William.

1843   Confidential Letter to Ramsey Crooks, January 5. *Calendar of the American Fur Company's Papers, Part 2: 1841-1849,* ed. Grace Lee Nute. *Annual Report of the American Historical Association for the Year 1944.* Vol. 3. Washington, D.C.: United States Government Printing Office, 1945, p. 1291, entry 13,433.

Wrone, David R.

1986-87   ''Indian Treaties and the Democratic Idea.'' *Wisconsin Magazine of History* 70 (Winter): 83-106.

1989   "Economic Impact of the 1837 and 1842 Chippewa Treaties." Unpublished paper, History Department, University of Wisconsin-Stevens Point. July 20. (A copy of this paper is on file in the State of Wisconsin Legislative Reference Bureau in Madison.)

Young, Richard M., and John M. Robinson.

1838   Letter to Quartermaster General T{homas} S. Jesup, December 18. *Territorial Papers*, Vol. 27, pp. 1109-111.

CPSIA information can be obtained
at www.ICGtesting.com
Printed in the USA
LVHW020129060121
675793LV00010B/674

9 780299 930226